# AS Drama and Theatre Studies

John Davey        Steve Lewis        Consultant: Ginny Spooner

**STUDENT BOOK**

A PEARSON COMPANY

# Contents

Introduction 3

AS Drama and Theatre Studies 5

Developing drama skills 6

Imagination and research 6

Voice 12

Movement 14

Communicating with the audience 16

Unit 1: Exploration of Drama and Theatre 17

Practical exploration and Exploration Notes 20

What does 'exploring a text' mean? 20

Assessment requirements 22

What goes in the Exploration Notes? 24

Building your Exploration Notes: the sequence 25

Exploration Notes: the final version 29

Language 31

Non-verbal communication 39

Vocal awareness 43

Characterisation 49

Social, historical, cultural and political context 53

Visual, aural and spatial elements 57

Interpretation 62

Working with a practitioner 66

Evaluation of a live theatre performance 67

What are the functions of a review? 68

Approaching the evaluation of live performance 69

Structuring your evaluation 77

Unit 2: Theatre Text in Performance 80

Section A 81

Being a performer in Unit 2 Section A 85

Assessment requirements 85

Selecting the play for Section A (performers) 86

The acting process 90

Approaches to performing a monologue 93

Approaches to performing a duologue 109

Written performance concept 116

Being a designer in Unit 2 Section A 117

Assessment requirements 118

Written design concept 119

Costume design 120

Set and props design 123

Masks and makeup design 126

Lighting design 129

Sound design 131

Section B 134

Working with a director 135

Performing for Unit 2, Section B 137

Assessment requirements: performers 138

The production process for performers 138

Designing for Unit 2, Section B 142

Assessment requirements: designers 143

The production process for designers 144

Written design concept 146

Reference guide 147

Glossary 156

# Introduction

Welcome to Drama and Theatre Studies at advanced level. You will have chosen to take Drama and Theatre Studies because you have an interest in how play texts are brought to life in performance. You may have gained this from being involved in productions or from seeing live theatre. Although in the 21st century we get much of our engagement with drama through other media, including television and films, there is something very special about live performance to an audience. This form of communication has been part of human life for thousands of years and is still very much alive today.

In following this course you will gain a deeper understanding of how theatre works and you will have opportunities to be a performer, a designer and an active audience member. In all these areas you will gain skills and understanding that will prove to be valuable and rewarding into the future.

## What plays will you explore?

For the AS year, there are no set, approved or recommended play texts. The texts you explore will be chosen by your teacher(s) from the many thousands available as the ones that they believe will engage your interest and enthusiasm.

## How can you make Drama and Theatre Studies rewarding?

Whatever your previous experience, being an AS Drama and Theatre Studies student will be thought-provoking, challenging and exciting.

- Much of your time will be spent working practically with others. A lot of your enjoyment and achievement depends on your commitment to working as a member of a team. Regular attendance and punctuality is important.

- There are no 'right answers': you have only to read a selection of theatre reviews to realise that people have very different individual views on plays and performances. You will need to listen to and respect the views of others.

- You will also need to work as an individual in researching material and putting your knowledge and understanding down on paper. You must be prepared to put in your own time, whether for seeing theatre performances, carrying out research, learning lines, acquiring props, or rehearsing for performance.

## How are you assessed?

There are two units in this AS course.

- In Unit 1: Exploration of Drama and Theatre, you work practically on two plays chosen by your teacher and complete a set of notes covering both texts. You must also see at least one live theatre performance and complete a written evaluation of it. Your work is marked by your teacher.

- In Unit 2: Theatre Text in Performance, there are two sections. The first section requires you to offer either a monologue or duologue, or a design skill in support of performer(s). The second section requires you to contribute to a performance of a professionally published play, either as a performer or designer. Your work is marked by an external examiner.

## The Assessment objectives

There are four Assessment objectives that will be used to assess your work. These are explained in the table below, along with a guide to which parts of the course each objective relates to. In the units you'll find more detailed guidance on what is required for each element of assessment.

| Assessment objective | | What do you have to do? |
|---|---|---|
| AO1 (30%) | Demonstrate the application of performance and/or production skills through the realisation of drama and theatre | This objective is assessed in Unit 2. For performers, it refers to your vocal and movement skills in performance. For designers it refers to the way you use materials and equipment, and how you realise your design in performance. |
| AO2 (30%) | Demonstrate knowledge and understanding of practical and theoretical aspects of drama and theatre using appropriate terminology | This objective is assessed in Unit 1 in the practical activities and through the Exploration Notes. |
| AO3 (30%) | Interpret plays from different periods and genres | This objective is assessed in Unit 2. For performers it relates to characterisation, the written performance concept (Section A), and communication (Section B). For designers it relates to the written design concept, design documentation (Section A), and interpretation of the director's concept (Section B). |
| AO4 (10%) | Make critical and evaluative judgements of live theatre | This objective in assessed in Unit 1 through the live theatre evaluation. |

## How to use this book

This book is designed to support you with the range of activities you will undertake in your AS year of Drama and Theatre Studies. A Planning, Teaching and Assessment Guide is available to support the Student Book.

The Student Book supports the two units of the course and provides:

- clear explanations of what is required of you, what you need to do, and how you will be assessed, along with examiner tips

- a practical approach to each of the units with activities that develop the skills you need, using a wide range of plays as examples and building a process that can be applied to your own plays

- information and knowledge to deepen your understanding of key aspects such as practitioners and contexts

- structured support in developing your analysis and evaluation skills, and putting your knowledge and understanding down on paper.

In addition, a section at the beginning of the book equips you with essential drama skills and a reference section at the end supports you with information on staging forms, practitioners and a clear glossary of dramatic terms.

We hope that you will enjoy studying drama and theatre and wish you much success with the course.

Ginny Spooner,

Edexcel

# AS Drama and Theatre Studies

At the beginning of your AS year, it's worth getting into good working practices that will help you be successful on the course. In this section, we look at some of the practical issues that you should consider before embarking on the course.

## Working methods

In lessons, you'll be working as you often have before: recording information, notes and thoughts, or responding to worksheets, whiteboard prompts, and so on. The organisation and filing of these notes are important and you should try to do them promptly. It's a good idea to use ringbinders (with dividers), keeping a different file for each unit (and sections within units).

When researching, you'll need to record details of your sources. This includes:

- titles, authors and page references (books/journals/magazines)

- website addresses (as well as titles/authors where relevant)

- quotations that you have copied down from sources (highlighting can be a useful method).

For practical sessions, you may well need to make preparatory notes or plans and make sure that you have these with you. During the session, you may need to make brief notes to capture information or to remind yourself of points/ideas, and you'll have to get used to making notes while being active. You may also find yourself writing down moves in your text. Near the end, or possibly just after the session, you will need an opportunity to make fuller notes so that no information is lost, or to remind yourself about what you have agreed to organise, prepare or think about for the following session. You may follow this up at home by expanding these notes or grouping them.

> **Tip**
>
> Take pencils, a sharpener and eraser to all your sessions. Pencils are preferable to pens when you're working on texts and changing ideas, moves, and so on. Ideas are provisional and experimental, and will be changed or overwritten. Highlighters are also useful for highlighting words in a text, for example using a different colour for relevant stage directions. You can use them too for marking key words in your notes.

## Resources: thinking ahead

As well as your own resources, you'll be using the resources of your school or college and possibly some other resources as well. This needs a bit of thought on occasions, and a small amount of planning can save you a good deal of time.

- **Space**: for your lessons, you'll be allocated working space. If you want to use space outside your normal classes to rehearse a scene or to develop an improvisation, you will probably need to make special arrangements to book it. There may be health and safety issues involved which need to be considered.

- **Props and costumes**: these are not always easy to come by, particularly if you have specialist requirements such as period costumes or wigs. Don't underestimate the time, difficulty and expense involved in locating and accessing these. For workshop sessions, rehearsal props and costumes are usually very satisfactory for giving you the feel of the real thing – and they're much easier to obtain.

- **Lights, sound, special effects**: if you are intending to use these, you will need to plan and probably take advice, as there will be health and safety issues involved here.

The most important thing with the use of all these resources is not to make assumptions, but to plan thoughtfully.

# DEVELOPING DRAMA SKILLS

Whatever experience of drama and theatre you have had prior to starting this course, as an AS student, it's important that you continue to build your drama skills. The next few pages outline some of the key areas you should be working on throughout the course:

- imagination
- research
- voice
- movement
- communicating with the audience.

This section is very relevant whether your main interest is in acting, writing, or the visual and technical side of theatre, as it will help you to gain a greater understanding of how drama and theatre work. Even if you are not performing, you need to understand how performers work.

## Practitioner note

Stanislavski, the 19th-century Russian director, actor and teacher of acting, said that actors needed to act 'as if' the situation of their character was real. In other words, they had to enter imaginatively into the mind of the character. This may sound obvious to us now, but it's an important point to remember. See page 154 to find out more about Stanislavski and the 'magic if'.

## Imagination and research

Your imagination is the product of your experiences. These can come from first-hand experiences, such as through your senses of touch, smell, sight, and through observation (looking at people, architecture, historical costumes or objects, for example), or through second-hand experiences, such as books, films, visual art and photography. To develop your imagination, you need to have an active, inquiring mind. Don't just look at people or things, but try to let your imagination enter their reality. Imagine what it is like to be them. Imagination shouldn't be a vague, abstract thing – it should be about making things outside your immediate experience as real as they can be.

For example, what was your grandparents' life like when they were the age you are now? If you had to play the role of one of your grandparents (playing them at the age you are now) answers to the questions below (and others) would help you to get into the role imaginatively.

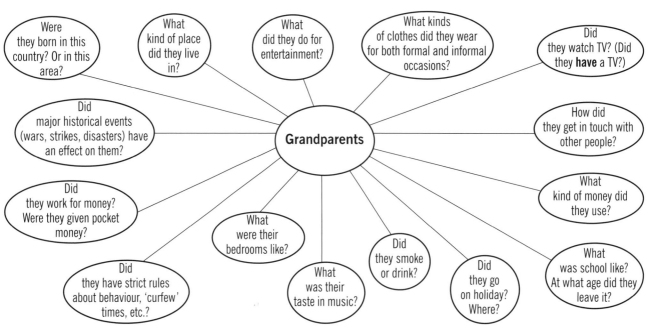

## Types of research

Researching the character of someone known to you may be easier because you can talk to them or to people who know them, as well as looking at photographs, letters, documents, and so on. Researching a character in a play will make you look for other sources of information, and will almost certainly make you use your imagination in a positive way. For example, if the character you are playing is a murderer, how do you enter his or her mind? Assuming that you have never murdered anybody, you might still have had murderous thoughts (perhaps if you had to kill a big spider). You can build on your own memory bank of feelings and experiences to help you to enter the mind of the character imaginatively.

This is the kind of research which actors do all the time – observing how people behave in real life, talking to people, exploring their own memories – and they link this to how a character in a play behaves. It might not be what you think of as academic research (you're not using a library or the internet), but it's an important part of an actor's preparation to play a role. Designers and directors need the same ability to observe life and to explore their imaginations so that they can create something believable on stage.

Research can take a number of different forms, which are explored below:

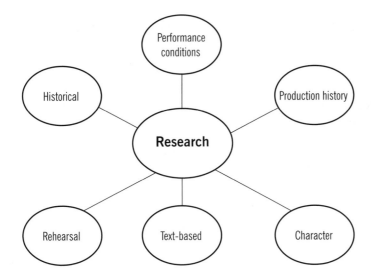

Rehearsing is in itself a kind of action research, although it would not find a place in any academic book about research techniques. For actors and directors, it's a time when they explore their own resources and see what can be made from them. Often this involves a traditional printed text (the script of a play), but in a devised production, it more frequently involves other approaches, which depend on the creativity of the team.

The point of research for you as an actor, is to give your imagination a firm foundation, not just to give you ideas to copy. Often your director will have done a great deal of research as well, which is helpful – but discovering things for yourself is more powerful.

**Key term**

character

**Tip**

If you talk to people as part of your research, be sensitive to the fact that there are some things they might not want to tell you about. People who have lived through wars are sometimes reluctant to talk about their experiences. You might have to find other sources of information to fill out gaps to enable you to imagine what their lives really were like.

**Historical research**

Historical research can help you to understand what it was like to be alive at a particular time as a member of a specific kind of society.

- You could find books which deal with social history to get relevant information about, for example, the position of women in the society of the time, or attitudes to ethnic minorities, to crime and punishment, to family life, and so on.

- You could research into the costumes, furniture and artefacts of the period to enable you to enter imaginatively into it. Bear in mind that period costume is very important in determining how actors move on stage.

- If you're acting in a play that deals with specific historical events, you could find out more about those events, for example the First World War in *The Accrington Pals* or the 17th-century witch trials in *The Crucible*. Remember, however, that they are not intended to be absolutely historically accurate; they are plays, not history lectures.

- If you're acting a role from recent history, you could talk to people who lived through that period or were involved in events of the time; for example, listening to stories from your parents or grandparents.

## Activity 1

Read the extract opposite from Act 1 Scene 3 of *The Accrington Pals* by Peter Whelan and think about what research you could do into the play. For example:

a) How much was £4 worth in 1914? Is May trying to give Tom a morning's takings from her fruit stall, or her life savings? It makes a huge difference to what is going on between them.

b) When Tom bites an apple from her stall, is he taking something which was scarce or valuable at the time? It makes a difference to the intention of his action.

c) More generally, what would happen to Tom if he decided not to go (to 'chuck it', as he puts it)?

d) Would he really go to 'clink' (prison)? How long for?

e) Was it socially unacceptable for an unmarried man to sleep under the same roof as an unmarried woman without someone else being present in the house?

f) Is May being oversensitive or difficult in sending out a message to Tom?

Research into these areas can really help to inform an actor about how to play the role.

See page 19 for some information about this play. In this extract, Tom is just about to leave with the Accrington Pals regiment to train as a soldier in the First World War.

| | |
|---|---|
| TOM: | Shall I chuck it? |
| MAY: | What? |
| TOM: | Shall I not go? |
| MAY: | And go to clink? |
| TOM: | I could run my head against that wall? |
| MAY: | This is the mood you've put me in. It's no use me standing on that platform waving a hanky and singing Auld Lang Syne or God Save the King. I don't feel especially proud of myself and I wish I could do otherwise. |
| TOM: | Shall I be able to drop in … on leave? |
| MAY: | Providing Eva's with me and you're prepared to sleep on the sofa. But not if the house is empty. Not again. |
| TOM: | I must thank you for taking me in and all that. |

MAY *takes an envelope out of her pocket and thrusts it at him.*

| | |
|---|---|
| MAY: | Put this in your pocket. |
| TOM: | What is it? |
| MAY: | Put it away. |
| TOM: | Not if it's money. |
| MAY: | It's four pounds, that's all. |
| TOM: | Take it back. |
| MAY: | I wanted to give you something. |

TOM *stares at her. The bugle gets louder and louder as it passes the end of the street.* TOM *suddenly tries to embrace her but* MAY *is able to respond. She pushes him away.* TOM *can't give in and struggles with her but* MAY *is frantic and strong. As the bugles blare they keep up this silent wrestling with each other. Finally* TOM *breaks away.*

| | |
|---|---|
| TOM: | Yes, you'll give me money! Yes, you'll give me money all right! |

*He goes to the stall, takes an apple, bites it. Then he takes the envelope she gave him and slams it down on the stall. Then goes.*
MAY *is left trembling at what they have done.*
*Blackout.*

## Original playing conditions

Knowing what the original playing conditions were (which will include the stage form in use – see the section on 'Performance spaces' on pages 147–152) can help you to imagine the effect the playwright intended the play to have on the audience. You, or your director, may choose to present it differently, but you will understand the playwright's original vision. For students interested in design, a study of the original playing conditions can be particularly rewarding. Think about the following aspects:

- **Inside or outside?** We're used to theatres inside buildings, but the ancient Greeks and Romans built their theatres with no roofs as outdoor spaces. (We still have open-air theatres such as at Regent's Park in London or The Minack Cliffside Theatre in Cornwall, but these are now exceptions to the general rule.)

- **Theatre size and auditorium shape**: in ancient Greek theatres the audience of up to 15,000 were seated in a huge semi-circle. Some modern 'fringe' theatres have an audience capacity of about 45 and have flexible seating arrangements, while the Theatre Royal in Drury Lane, London can accommodate 2,237 audience members on four levels, all facing the proscenium arch stage.

- **Stage shape, size and features**: in his lifetime, most of Shakespeare's plays were played on thrust stages (approximately 13 metres wide and 8 metres deep). Some early 18th-century theatres (proscenium arch) had stages about 18 metres wide and almost 20 metres deep. On the other hand, London's only permanent in-the-round theatre, the Orange Tree in Richmond, has a 5 metre by 5 metre stage. Some stages have permanent features, like the upstage balcony and the trapdoors of the Elizabethan theatre, or the elaborate machinery of some Victorian theatres, which allowed the staging of shipwrecks, horse races, etc.

- **Set**: some theatres (such as most large West End venues) are built to accommodate large sets; most have fly-towers to enable backcloths and scenery to be lowered on to the stage. In other theatres (such as the Orange Tree, mentioned above) there is no requirement for large items of scenery – but the design of the floor will be important.

- **Stage technology**: ancient theatres had no lighting systems. Early indoor theatres used candles, and later theatres used oil lamps and gas lighting systems, but the first electric system was installed in the Savoy Theatre, London in 1881. Similarly, until the development of sound recording technology in the 1920s, all sound effects were produced mechanically – and music had to be live.

- **Actors**: in ancient Greek and Elizabethan periods, only men were actors. In some cultures, actors are regarded as 'suspect'. For example, when women were first allowed to appear on the English stage in 1660, it was hard to find well-spoken actresses as no 'respectable' woman would go on the stage.

- **Audiences**: it is likely that only male citizens attended performances of ancient Greek tragedy. The audience in the Elizabethan theatre was socially very mixed, although the very poor could not afford to go and the very rich paid actors to perform in their houses or palaces. During the Restoration period (from 1660), audiences were mostly from the higher social classes. In the 21st century in the UK, audiences vary in age, class and ethnicity from theatre to theatre – and even from show to show.

### Tip

Finding out about how a play has been produced and acted since its original performance can be fascinating and give you useful ideas about playing a role:
- For relatively modern plays, some productions have been preserved on video or DVD, and you may have access to reviews.
- For earlier plays, your research may involve reading books of theatre history or accessing reviews written at the time. *Equus*, for example, was originally staged in 1973, but there will be plenty of reviews of the 2006 revival starring Daniel Radcliffe (of *Harry Potter* fame).

THOMAS TALLIS SCHOOL LIBRARY

## Text-based research

When you're acting a role, it's important that you understand the words you are saying and any references you are making. If you do not have a full grasp of what you are saying, it won't sound convincing. Read the following extract from *The Crucible*. How much of the language do you understand on a first read?

> In this section from Act 3, a witchcraft trial is interrupted by the hysterical behaviour of some of the young girls, who are prosecution witnesses. See page 19 for some more information about this play. One early piece of research you could do is to check what a 'crucible' is and think about why the play has that word as its title.

| | |
|---|---|
| **MARY WARREN:** | *(turning on the girls hysterically and stamping her feet)*: Abby, stop it! |
| **GIRLS:** | *(stamping their feet)*: Abby, stop it!! |
| **MARY WARREN:** | *(screaming at the top of her lungs and raising her fists)*: Stop it! |
| **GIRLS:** | *(raising their fists)*: Stop it!! |

*(*MARY WARREN*, utterly confounded, and becoming overwhelmed by* ABIGAIL*'s – and the girls' – utter conviction, starts to whimper, hands half-raised, powerless, and all the girls begin whimpering as she does.)*

> Do you know what 'utterly confounded' means? You would need to know if you were playing Mary.

| | |
|---|---|
| **DANFORTH:** | A little while ago you were afflicted. Now it seems you afflict others; where did you find this power? |
| **MARY WARREN:** | *(staring at* ABIGAIL*)*: I have no power. |
| **GIRLS:** | I have no power. |
| **PROCTOR:** | They're gulling you, mister! |
| **DANFORTH:** | Why did you turn about these past two weeks? You have seen the Devil, have you not? |
| **HALE:** | *(indicating the girls)*: You cannot believe them! |
| **MARY WARREN:** | I... |
| **PROCTOR:** | *(sensing her weakening)*: Mary, God damns all liars! |
| **DANFORTH** | *(pounding it into her)*: You have seen the Devil, you have made compact with Lucifer, have you not? |
| **PROCTOR:** | God damns liars, Mary! |

> Are you sure what 'afflict' and 'gulling' mean in this context?

> Do you understand the expression 'made compact with Lucifer'?

You may be able to guess the meanings if you don't already know, but be careful about making assumptions. Sometimes words change their meaning over time. For example, the word 'naughty' as used by Shakespeare, is the equivalent of our word 'evil'. So the intention behind the phrase 'Thou naughty knave' is much more aggressive than it immediately appears to us – this is important for an actor to know.

# Voice

Voice is a vital tool in acting and you need to work at it to become a more effective performer. If your voice becomes stronger and more flexible, it will extend the range of your acting. You may also have picked up habits, which make your voice less effective (like muttering or talking too quickly); developing your voice involves weeding these out and 'finding' your voice.

The characters you play will all have their own distinctive ways of speaking. How would the voice of a young girl on her first date and very nervous be different from that of an authoritarian schoolteacher? Or an elderly, housebound man from a smooth salesman? The more flexible your voice is, the more you can bring vocally to these roles. Remember, though, that the voice should not be 'stuck on'; it has to come from your imaginative creation of the character and your belief in it.

## What is voice?

'Voice' and 'speech' are different. Certain parts of your body work to produce the voice and other parts produce the speech:

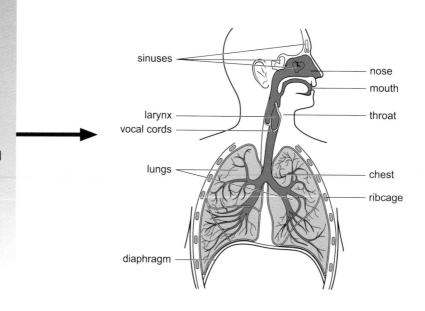

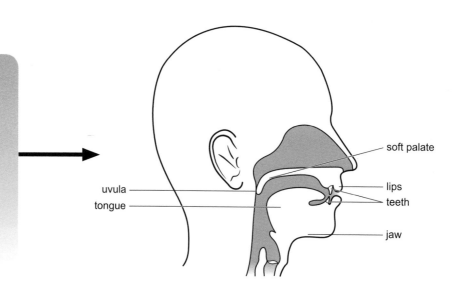

> **Tip**
>
> While it's good to understand how your body produces voice, remember that your voice is tied up with who you are, how you're feeling and your self-image: in many ways, your voice is your identity.

> The body has 'resonators' (partially enclosed air-filled spaces) which act as amplifiers for the sound. These are the chest, throat, mouth, nose and the sinuses. Actors sometimes talk about a 'chest voice' (lower, fuller sound) and a 'head voice' (brighter, sharper sound). You develop the range of your voice through the use of both. Breathing is a vital part of voice production. The power and control of your breath come from the diaphragm, the ribcage and the lungs. These produce a column of air which passes through the voice box (the larynx) in which sound is produced by the vibration of the vocal cords. This produces the pitch (the note).

> The 'speech' organs are those which produce the vowels and consonants which make up all words and sounds:
> • lips
> • teeth
> • tongue
> • jaws
> • soft palate
> • uvula.
> Different positions of these produce the different sounds.

# How do you develop your voice?

Do regular exercises – daily if possible – to build up the power and range of your voice and the precision of your speech. For example, the muscles that you use to produce your voice need to be strong enough for you to project your performance: you need to be able to make yourself comfortably heard in large acting spaces. Remember that projection is not the same as shouting; shouting damages the voice and destroys the credibility of the character you're creating.

## Warm-ups

It's really valuable to warm up your voice as well as your body before a working session of devising or rehearsal. The routine below is a basic suggested warm-up:

1. On hands and knees stretch your spine by arching it upwards (with head down) and then arching it downwards (head up). Do this ten times.

2. Stay on your hands and knees and breathe in deeply, expanding your ribcage as you fill up with air. Open your mouth wide and release on a sigh. Do this ten times.

3. Lie on your back, with a book or a cushion supporting your head, and your knees pulled up. Take a deep in-breath to a count of five, then sigh out. Increase this to 10, 15 and 20. Repeat several times.

4. On your back or standing, part your teeth, close your lips and hum, pushing the sound towards your lips. You should feel vibrations in your face. After you have done this a few times, open your mouth on an 'ah' sound as you breathe out, working your lips and jaw at the same time.

5. Close your mouth and move the tip of your tongue quickly round inside it, in a darting movement, trying to touch all the points inside your mouth. Then imagine that you have a piece of very sticky toffee in your mouth and chew it.

6. Yawn extravagantly!

7. Run through all the consonants in the alphabet, repeating them in a rhythmical way (e.g. 'bu-bu-bu-bu-bu-bu-bu-bu-bah; cu-cu-cu-cu-cu-cu-cu-cu-cu-cah) and building up the volume from the first 'bu' to the final 'bah'.

8. Walk round the room, saying a few tongue twisters, getting faster and faster, for example:

   A big blue badly bleeding blister

   A lump of red leather, a red leather lump

   The crisp crust crackles crunchily

   Six thick thistle sticks

   Frisky Freddy feeds on fresh fried fish

   If a dog chews shoes, what shoes would he choose to chew?

   How high his Highness holds his haughty head.

**Key term**

warm-up

**Taking it further**

You'll find many more exercises in specialist voice books such as *Voice and the Actor* by Cicely Berry (Virgin Books, 2000); *The Need for Words* (Methuen, 1994) and *The Actor Speaks* (Palgrave, 2002) by Patsy Rodenburg; and *The Voice Book* by Michael McCallion (Faber, 1998).

**Tip**

It's important never to feel tension on stage. Although the **situation** may be tense, tension in your body (especially in the shoulders and the neck) can prevent your voice from expressing itself fully. When actors talk about being 'relaxed', they **don't** mean being casual. They mean getting rid of the unproductive tensions, which divert their energy from its proper purpose.

## Movement

Just as speaking on stage needs practice, so too does movement. You may think that movement is obvious and natural, but in fact you have to **learn** to be natural on stage. It can be too easy to jiggle around, move without purpose and not know what to do with your hands.

Many of the same basic principles apply to movement as to voice. Movement comes from:

- an imaginative creation of the character and the circumstances

- a body which is trained and fit, and is therefore more flexible as an instrument for expressing purposes and emotions.

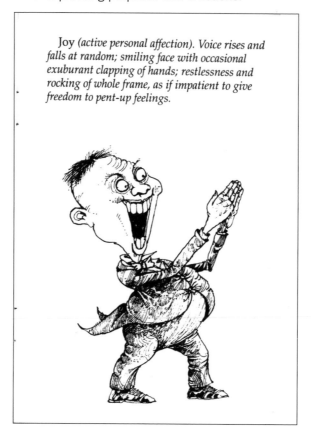

*Joy (active personal affection). Voice rises and falls at random; smiling face with occasional exuberant clapping of hands; restlessness and rocking of whole frame, as if impatient to give freedom to pent-up feelings.*

The words above the cartoon to the left are taken from a real and well-intentioned booklet, giving advice to actors (the cartoon was added as a joke many years later). The idea behind the words is clear; if you find the 'right' movement and gestures, you will communicate a particular emotion to the audience.

There are certain general characteristics of emotional states. For example:

- people stricken by grief tend to hunch up and cover their faces

- people who are excited and happy tend to have a more expansive, open body shape.

Actors need to be specific, though, and to find the right way of moving and gesturing for their character in the precise situation which the performance demands.

Your performances will involve you in creating a character (possibly more than one character). This character will have a distinctive way of speaking and a distinctive way of moving. By making this character's movement convincing and credible, you will create a more effective performance. If you are creating more than one character, you will be able to demonstrate that you can distinguish between them by the range of your movement skills.

## How do you develop your movement skills?

To develop your movement skills, you make yourself more flexible, fitter and more aware of your body as an instrument. Firstly, you need to lose bad habits and tensions. Then you should try to develop a state of relaxation, which enables you to make proper use of your body to express the purposes and intentions of the character. Relaxation is nothing to do with feeling 'chilled' or 'mellow'; it's to do with eliminating all the negative tensions which hold you back.

Develop a physical warm-up routine, but keep varying it to stop you getting bored. It's useful to do the physical warm-up **before** you do your voice warm-up. If you have a reasonably open space to work in, try the basic routine outlined below:

1. Find a centred position: stand with your feet the same distance apart as your hips and sway gently (not moving your feet) until you find a good balance point. Your head should feel as though it's lengthening out of your spine, not being pushed forward or back.

2. Now, let your head drop gently onto your chest and gradually continue to 'roll down' your spine, letting your knees bend at the same time. Let your arms hang loose. Now, breathe in and stretch up (again gently), reaching up with your arms and your whole body. Repeat this several times.

3. Return to your centred position. Roll your shoulders in a large circle, first forwards, then backwards, making sure that nothing else in your body tenses up.

4. Keeping your feet rooted, make a series of arm swings across your body, making sure that your neck and shoulders remain relaxed. Don't forget to breathe with the movement.

5. Jog on the spot, shaking all the parts of your body that will shake – hands, wrists, elbows, shoulders, torso, and so on.

6. Fix a spot in another part of the room with your eyes and walk purposefully there. When you get there, turn and fix another spot in a different part of the room. Walk purposefully there in a different way, at a different speed, and so on. Make sure that you don't collide with other purposeful actors!

7. As a group, play a warm-up game, such as Zip-Zap-Boing! This is a 'passing-on-the-action' game and needs to be played at enormous speed:

   • For a 'Zip', you clap your hands to your left. (A nominated person starts with this.)

   • You can also 'Zap', which means you clap your hands pointing them at someone across the circle. (It can't be someone next to you.)

   • The third possibility is a 'Boing'. You jump in the air and make an outwards circle with both your arms. This reverses a 'Zip', so that the 'Zip' now has to go to the right – until it's interrupted by a 'Zap' or another 'Boing'.

   Important rule: you can't 'Boing' after a 'Zap'. Anyone who gets it wrong, or is too slow, is out. This is a good one for getting your energy levels up.

## Creating character through movement

You'll be aware that you can recognise people you know by their movement at the other end of a long corridor or a long way down the street. Spend some time observing any member of your group or of your family, or just watch people going about their business in a town or on a bus or train. What is distinctive about the way they move and gesture? What factors affect the way they move? Think about:

- age
- gender
- occupation
- social status
- physical appearance
- medical history.

What do you know about their particular current situation that will affect movement? Have they just missed a bus? Have they got a new job? Have they had a row with a loved one? Have they a new pair of shoes? You need to bring together all the essential information about your character and then see how you can create this person in your imagination.

## Communicating with the audience

Communication is important because audiences have to be able to 'read' a play in performance. As a performer or designer, and as part of a team, your job is to make sure that you communicate the meaning of a play to the audience.

To give a clear performance:

| Do | Don't |
|---|---|
| • be vocally and physically clear | • fidget on stage |
| • make sure you know the play well | • speak inaudibly or unclearly. |
| • make sure you understand your own role in the play's structure. | |

Think about what your character's motivation is on stage:

- What are you there to get? This could be a simple physical thing, such as a drink or a letter, or a more complex thing such as the admiration of another character.
- What obstacles are in the way of this? For example, perhaps the family disapproves of drinking, the letter is locked in a drawer or you know that the other character thinks you're a fool.
- Is there one overarching objective that your character has that motivates everything they do in the play? Focusing on your character's objectives should give your performance clarity.

For more about objectives, see the section about Stanislavski on page 154.

**Tip**

When you're developing a character from a play, you need also to think about the period of time they are living in. Don't forget that your movement on stage will be affected by the costume which your character is wearing. If you're wearing thick, heavy skirts, or carrying a sword, or wearing a fat-suit, you'll need to rehearse with the real costume or with a rehearsal costume which is similar to it so that you can find the appropriate movement.

# Unit 1: Exploration of Drama and Theatre

## What you need to know

**Unit 1: Exploration of Drama and Theatre**

- is worth 40% of your AS mark (20% of the total A level marks)
- is internally assessed (marked by your teachers) and externally moderated (by Edexcel).

### Assessment objectives

Unit 1 is assessed against Assessment objective 2 and Assessment objective 4. See page 4.

## What you have to do

You have to study and work on **two plays** in detail, exploring them through **practical activities** and writing up your findings in a set of **Exploration Notes**. You will draw together your ideas, experiences and discoveries about the texts to put in these notes. The plays will be chosen by your teacher and will be published texts by known playwrights that are contrasting in period and genre.

Your work on these plays will be a mixture of reading, discussing and analysing the text, research and practical activities. The timing of these activities will vary through the course – at times you may be doing a lot of close study of the text, and at other times extensive practical work. At least one of the texts must be explored using the ideas of a recognised '**theatrical practitioner**'. This means someone (or a group of people) whose ideas about plays and theatre have had an influence on how people work and think in today's theatre.

You also have to see and evaluate **a live theatre performance** – that is a performance which you have seen live as a member of the audience; plays on video/DVD do not count. This may be one of the two plays which you are exploring through practical activities, but it may be a completely different play.

## How are you assessed?

- Your teacher will assess your practical work over a number of sessions. One of these sessions will be recorded on video or DVD and sent to the moderator.
- You need to submit an individual set of Exploration Notes (maximum 3,000 words), based on the study and practical exploration of the two plays.
- You need to submit a written evaluation of the live theatre performance that you see (maximum 1,000 words).

## Unit 1: At-a-glance summary

| Material to be worked on | Assessment requirements | Percentage of Unit 1 marks allocated |
|---|---|---|
| Two plays | Textual study, research, practical sessions | 42% |
| | Exploration notes (maximum = 3,000 words) | 33% |
| One live theatre performance | Evaluation (maximum = 1,000 words) | 25% |

## How will this book help you with Unit 1?

The plays that you study for Unit 1 will have been chosen by your teacher, as there are no prescribed texts. In the pages that follow, almost all the examples come from 15 plays that represent a wide range of period and genre to show you how the exploration and evaluation processes work and how you can apply these to the plays you explore and see live.

You may well be familiar with some of these plays; others you won't have heard of. Below are some brief details about each of them to give you some context for the discussion that follows.

**Key term**

genre

*The Trojan Women* by Euripides (415 BC). Ancient Greek tragedy. The Greeks have conquered Troy (after the deception of the Trojan Horse). The action takes place in the smoking ruins. The Trojan men have all been killed and the surviving women of the royal family are about to be put on ships to Greece, where they will be slaves.

*Romeo and Juliet* by William Shakespeare (1590s). Elizabethan tragedy. Against a background of a continuing feud between two of the most important families in Verona (the Montagues and the Capulets), Romeo and Juliet, only children of the heads of the two families, meet by chance and fall deeply in love. Though they marry in secret, fate and the feud between their families conspire to bring about their deaths, both by suicide, after which their parents end the feud.

*Macbeth* by William Shakespeare (1606). Macbeth and Banquo, two victorious Scottish generals, are returning from battle when they are met by three witches, who predict that Macbeth will be King. This leads him, with the help of his wife, to murder the current King (Duncan) and to take the throne. To remain king, he embarks on a reign of terror in which many others are murdered. Eventually Lady Macbeth commits suicide and Macbeth, realising the witches deceived him, is killed in battle by Macduff, whose wife and children he has had killed. Malcolm, Duncan's son, regains the throne.

*The Beggar's Opera* by John Gay (1728). This was a ground-breaking play in which the conventions of the newly established form of opera were brought down to earth by the use of popular songs and a cast of London low-life characters. The main plot features the (mainly) undignified contest between Polly Peachum and Lucy Lockit to claim Captain Macheath as husband, while he tries to avoid being hanged.

*The Seagull* by Anton Chekhov (1896). Russian playwright Chekhov called it a 'comedy' but it ends in a death, and comic and tragic elements intertwine in this realist play. The main plot concerns the relationships between Konstantin, his mother Arkadina, her lover (the writer Trigorin) and the young aspiring actress, Nina. It is notable for the depth and complexity of its characters. Although a failure when first produced, a later production by Stanislavski for the Moscow Art Theatre established it as a brilliant piece of theatre.

*Pygmalion* by George Bernard Shaw (1913). A comedy, although without a happy ending. The story of Eliza Doolittle, the 'guttersnipe' flower-seller and her transformation at the hands of Professor Henry Higgins to a society lady is well known, especially through the musical adaptation *My Fair Lady*. The themes include how language affects character and perception, social mobility and the relationships between men and women.

*The Threepenny Opera* by Bertolt Brecht (1928). This is Brecht's version of John Gay's *The Beggar's Opera* (see above). Although much of the story and the main characters remain, Brecht has a different aim from Gay: to show that the underworld of crime and the representatives of capitalist society collude to support each other and their mutual interests. There is still much humour in the play and Weill's musical score is excellent.

*A Streetcar Named Desire* by Tennessee Williams (1947). This gritty realist drama with expressionist elements and set in a run-down area of New Orleans is, among other things, a powerful exploration of raw sexual attraction between an uncultured man with animal instincts and a desperate fading beauty, close to breakdown.

*The Crucible* by Arthur Miller (1953). This play deals with the events of the witch-hunt in Salem, Massachusetts in 1692, during which 19 innocent people were tortured and hanged as witches. Miller changes some facts for his purposes, including the ages of Proctor and Abigail (historically, 60 and 11, respectively). The play was intended to refer to the contemporary anti-communist activities of Senator McCarthy and the House Un-American Activities Committee.

*A Raisin in the Sun* by Lorraine Hansberry (1959). The title is a quotation from a poem: 'What happens to a dream deferred? Does it dry up like a raisin in the sun?' and the play is about the final refusal of a poor black family in 1950s Chicago to defer their dream. Having come into some insurance money, Mama buys a house in a white area and her son, Walter, although tempted to back down for the offer of money, eventually asserts his right to go and 'comes into his manhood' by doing so. It was the first play by a black woman to be performed on Broadway.

*Equus* by Peter Shaffer (1973). Based on a true incident of an adolescent boy who blinded a number of horses with a metal spike, Shaffer's play explores the psychology of both the boy (Alan) and his psychiatrist (Dysart). It was one of the first plays to make nudity acceptable for artistic purposes.

*Translations* by Brian Friel (1980). The play is set in the fictional village of Ballybeg, Donegal in Ireland in 1833. The action takes place mostly in a 'hedge-school' (a school for adults) run in basic conditions in a barn by Hugh (in his sixties) and his son Manus. The locals learn basic skills, but also Latin and Greek. English soldiers are mapping the local countryside, giving mostly English names to local places. They are unable to communicate with the Irish, and there is some local resentment to them. Yolland (a young English officer who falls in love with both the local countryside and with Maire) goes missing, presumed murdered by some locals.

*The Accrington Pals* by Peter Whelan (1988). This play, set in Accrington, Lancashire, during the First World War, places relationships between men and women and ideas about how life should be lived against the background of war. Historically, the 'Accrington Pals' regiment lost more than 600 of its 700 men in the Battle of the Somme (1916). The play shows the effect of this disaster on the women of a tightly-knit community.

*Our Country's Good* by Timberlake Wertenbaker (1988). In 1787 the first batch of criminals to be deported to Australia left England by boat. The play recounts the extraordinary (but basically true) story of how the convicts mounted a production of *The Recruiting Officer*, a popular comedy of the time. Wertenbaker uses the events to stage a genuine debate about the purpose of punishment and the way that theatre can be a civilising and redeeming force.

*Prayer Room by* Shan Khan (2005). Set in a college prayer room that has to be shared by Jews, Muslims and Christians. Through the tensions which inevitably arise, the play explores the nature of religious intolerance and its consequences. It is often very funny and the dialogue reflects the speech of many young inner-city people (hence there is a great deal of casual swearing which some may find offensive).

# PRACTICAL EXPLORATION AND EXPLORATION NOTES

See page 67 for the live performance evaluation part of Unit 1. What you learn about how drama and the theatre work in this section will help with evaluating what you see performed live.

There are two areas for you to cover in this part of Unit 1:

• taking part in activities exploring two play texts practically, as well as through reading and research

• writing up your findings in your Exploration Notes.

The diagram below sets out the elements that you will be expected to explore and to write about in your Exploration Notes. These elements overlap and it is likely that in each session you will cover more than one of them.

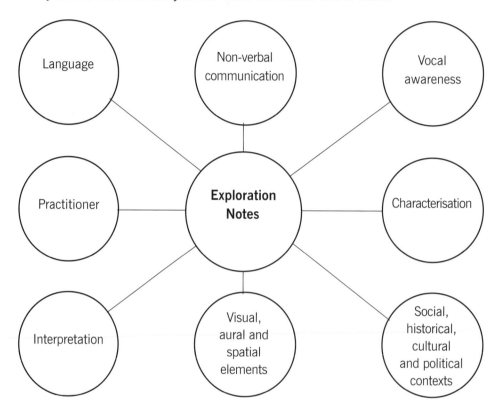

Each of these elements has a section of this book devoted to it (pages 31–66). It is intended to give you an overview of what the practical exploration of a text might mean and how activities might relate to each element, and to give you material to write about for your Exploration Notes.

## What does 'exploring a text' mean?

We're all familiar with the idea of the explorer – someone who goes into territory which is unfamiliar to them and comes back with new discoveries. Exploring a text is the same; you discover by doing something, often practical. Your discoveries should throw new light on the text for you, so that you understand more fully how it works (or might work) on stage.

Exploring a text practically means that you can try different ways of performing it, for example emphasising different aspects of character in your acting, experimenting with changing the acting space, using vocal effects, or techniques which you may have come across before such as 'thought-tracking'.

**Key terms**

technique
thought-tracking

In this example, four groups of AS students are engaged in exploring Shakespeare's *Romeo and Juliet*. Read through the brief description of what one session involves for each group.

## Group A

Group A is working in an area of the Drama Studio. They have read Act 3 Scene 5 and are concentrating on the middle section, lines 65–205, where Juliet is being told by her mother and father (with the Nurse present) that her wedding to Paris has been arranged (they do not know that she has already married Romeo). They are exploring the ideas of gender and of parental authority in the play. They agree on a simple staging for the scene and read it through, scripts in hand, discussing the situation and the feelings of the characters as they do so. They run the scene, trying to give it the right intensity of feeling. They then swap roles, so that males are playing the female parts and vice versa. They discuss how they react to changes in gender and anything new they noticed about the text. They then go back to the original casting and improvise a version of the scene. Again they discuss how their improvisation was different from the previous ways of performing the scene. They write down their thoughts about the session.

> **Key term**
>
> improvisation

## Group B

Group B is in another part of the Drama Studio, exploring ways of staging the balcony scene (Act 2 Scene 2). They want to see if there are alternative methods of staging which might work in a more experimental production. With both actors standing on the floor, they perform the scene varying the distance between them. They then try it standing back to back. Then they place Juliet in a strong light, with Romeo in the darkness. Finally they try the scene with Juliet on a high stage block, with Romeo crouching on the floor. Each time they try it a different way, they discuss what effect the changes have had. Finally, they write down their thoughts about the session.

## Group C

Group C has been given copies of the rehearsal scenes which Bertolt Brecht wrote for the actors playing Romeo and Juliet. These are designed to make the actors see their roles differently, to make them 'stand aside' from their roles in line with Brecht's ideas about 'Verfremdung' (translated as 'distancing' or 'alienation'). They read through the two rehearsal scenes and then (as Brecht intended) through the balcony scene. They discuss how the experience has expanded or altered their ideas about the characters. They then write down their thoughts about the session.

> **Taking it further**
>
> For more on Brecht, see pages 50 and 153. Brecht's rehearsal scenes can be found in the *Romeo and Juliet* New Casebook, by R.S. White (Palgrave Macmillan 2001).

> **Key terms**
>
> alienation
> Verfremdung

## Group D

Group D has been in the Learning Resources Centre researching the original playing conditions of the Elizabethan playhouse. They have been reading about the shape and size of the stage, the position of the entrances and exits, and the position and likely height of the balcony. They have learnt about the time of day when performances originally took place and the kind of audiences who came to see them. They are going to report their findings to the rest of the group and see how they might use the information in future.

## Assessment requirements

## Practical activities

As you can tell from these examples, there is a large range of possible practical activities that can be used for exploring plays. You might spend whole sessions concentrating on voice or movement (or other aspects of non-verbal communication, such as mime). The exploration of character is likely to be a significant aspect of your work, but you will also explore the effects of different ways of staging scenes (visual, aural and spatial elements) and of interpreting the text in practice. You will also explore at least one of your two chosen texts by putting into practice the ideas of one or more practitioners (see page 66).

Your teacher will assess your contribution to these practical activities over a number of sessions; one session will be recorded on video or DVD and sent to an external moderator. The table below shows the criteria your teacher will be using to award marks for your practical exploration of your two texts in Unit 1. Pay particular attention to the words and phrases that have been underlined.

> Your practical exploration is assessed against Assessment objective 2: Demonstrate knowledge and understanding of practical and theoretical aspects of drama and theatre using appropriate terminology. See page 4.

| Level of response | Mark range |
|---|---|
| Student's practical exploration of the texts is outstanding. Involvement and creativity in all practical tasks is consistently committed and focused. They are able to demonstrate accuracy and comprehensive understanding of the themes and issues in both texts. | 21-25 |
| Student's practical exploration of the texts is excellent with sustained engagement in all practical tasks. Their detailed knowledge and understanding of the main themes and issues in both texts is communicated effectively through all practical activities. | 16-20 |
| Student's practical exploration of the texts is good with clear engagement in a range of practical activities. They are able to demonstrate a good grasp of the texts, main themes and issues through the confident application of practical activities. | 11-15 |
| Student's practical exploration of the texts is adequate with some engagement in practical activities. They may be stronger on one text than the other and may not always be able to demonstrate their understanding clearly in a practical workshop. | 6-10 |
| Student's practical exploration of the texts is limited. They often misunderstand the focus of a practical activity or are unable to communicate their intentions. Interaction and cooperation with others can be inconsistent. | 0-5 |

**Examiner's tip**

Notice the emphasis on being 'consistently committed and focused' and 'sustained engagement'. You need to maintain your effort and concentration through all the practical activities, getting as much as you can out of them. You need to aim at a 'comprehensive understanding' of both of your chosen texts so that you become an expert on them.

Notice these **key words and phrases**:
involvement
creativity
committed
engagement
knowledge and understanding of themes and issues.

# Exploration Notes

Your Exploration Notes need to be based on the notes which you have kept all the way through this part of Unit 1. You need to keep notes on each practical session in which you're involved. You will also have research notes, and you may well have background notes handed out by your teacher. Your final Exploration Notes, which you build by drawing on all your other notes, must be no more than 3,000 words. There is no tolerance on the word limit – your work will not be marked beyond the 3,000 words – so be very careful to stick to it. The notes need to record your ideas and reflections about what you have learnt about the texts and their potential on stage through your practical activities and research. Remember that the point of the exploration is to understand the texts better – not just an understanding of the words (the 'written text'), but of how the play might work in performance (as a 'performance text' – see page 74).

The table below shows the criteria your teacher will use to mark your Exploration Notes, with some of the important words and phrases underlined.

| Level of response | Mark range |
|---|---|
| Student's Exploration Notes show an outstanding knowledge and understanding of both texts explored. Practical observations are embedded in their notes, which are accurate, concise, analytical and well-researched. | 17-20 |
| Student's Exploration Notes show an excellent understanding of both texts explored. There will be supported examples of the student's own practical work and this will be shown in accurate, detailed comments. | 13-16 |
| Student's Exploration Notes show a good understanding of the texts explored. There will be a balanced response towards both texts with clear references to the student's own practical work. | 9-12 |
| Student's Exploration Notes show an adequate understanding of the texts explored. There may be a tendency to regurgitate class notes and the work may be bland and repetitive. There will be very little sense of the student's own practical exploration. | 5-8 |
| Student's Exploration Notes are limited in terms of content and understanding. There will be limited connection to the student's own exploration work and possibly errors and inaccuracies. | 0-4 |

Notice these **key words and phrases**:
knowledge and understanding of both texts
practical observations
accurate
detailed
analytical
well-researched.

Your Exploration Notes are assessed against Assessment objective 2: Demonstrate knowledge and understanding of practical and theoretical aspects of drama and theatre using appropriate terminology. See page 4.

**Examiner's tip**

Notice the emphasis on how well you have to know and understand both your chosen texts. If practical observations are 'embedded', it means that they are used to make a larger point. The top category requires your notes to be 'analytical' (so you're analysing the texts by considering what you've learnt about them through your practical work) and 'well-researched', pointing out that your own research on the texts is important.

## What goes in the Exploration Notes?

All the elements on the left-hand side of this table are required evidence in your Exploration Notes. The activities listed in the right-hand column are suggestions, not exhaustive lists – there will be many more possibilities.

| Elements to provide evidence of your exploration | Examples of activities which might be involved |
|---|---|
| Language (see page 31) | Sessions on speeches or short sections in which the focus is on the features of the language used, such as the sound and rhythm. You might experiment with different ways of delivering speeches. There will be strong links with vocal awareness. |
| Non-verbal communication (see page 39) | Sessions in which you explore the essential features of a scene through movement and mime, or explore the nature of a character through experimenting with a range of movement and gesture. Links with characterisation. |
| Vocal awareness (see page 43) | Voice sessions in which such features as pace, pitch, pauses and volume can be applied to sections of the text to experiment with how meaning can be communicated in different ways to an audience. Strong links with both language and characterisation. |
| Characterisation (see page 49) | Sessions in which you explore imaginatively the background to the character, making use of 'given circumstances'. |
| Social, cultural, historical and political context (see page 53) | Some of the work for this area may be research-based, but remember that the research has to be of practical use in performance. For example, your understanding of the relevant political context might lead you to experiment with a characterisation based on a modern politician. |
| Visual, aural and spatial elements (see page 57) | A session experimenting with simple lighting and sound effects can demonstrate how the atmosphere of a scene can be changed to create a different effect for the audience. Experiments with use of space to create meaning. |
| Interpretation (see page 62) | Interpretation will affect all areas of a production. A session might concentrate on playing what seems to be a serious scene as comedy to discover if there are elements which might contribute to a more complex interpretation of the scene. |
| Response to a practitioner (see page 66) | A session on the ideas of Stanislavski might experiment with a range of objectives (intentions or aims) for characters in specific scenes, showing how different objectives can change the nature and balance of the scenes. |

### Activity 1

Look back to page 21 at the work being done by the four groups on *Romeo and Juliet*. Read through the details on each group and see if you can link their activities to the elements in the table above. In the table below, Group A's session has been partially completed for you.

| Group | Elements covered |
|---|---|
| A | Characterisation (by swapping roles and studying the effect) Language (by becoming aware of the differences in the language used in their improvisation and the language of Shakespeare's text) |

## Exploration Notes: capturing the information

You will compile your notes over several months. You need to have a system to make sure that you 'capture' everything relevant. Your system needs to help you to retrieve the information and put it together for your final version. There are several ways of doing this and you can devise your own. The form on the next page offers just one of many possible ways of recording the details of your practical work, research and discussions.

### Activity 2

Use the headings from the Exploration Notes form on the next page to write down notes from a practical session you've been involved in early in the course. Make the 'Outline details of session' notes as soon as you can – ideally towards the end of the session or just after. Give yourself a little time to think about the session and then write the 'Reflections' notes. Check with your teacher if you're not sure that you're writing useful material. Recording a few sessions in this way will get you into the habit of doing it well when you come to your work on the texts.

## Building up your Exploration Notes: the sequence

**1. Capture the information.** Note down the main activities you work on and your findings from them.

**2. Review all your material.** This means reading through everything with close attention. Your material may include your session notes, your research notes and hand-outs from your teacher. You need to read through all these, noticing sections and points which link with each other.

**3. Group information under main points.** These main points will become the most important sections of the final version of your Exploration Notes. For each main point make a list of where you can find the supporting information. (This will be easy if you have used a clear system of recording your sessions.)

**4. Write a first draft.** Concentrate on building up a paragraph for each main point, with clear supporting evidence.

**5. Check your draft against the criteria.** Check that you have covered the eight elements and that you are within the word limit (3,000 words).

**6. Create a final draft.** Edit your first draft to create a final draft, adjusting it to the word limit and adding any necessary information to cover the eight areas. Add a brief introduction and conclusion.

**7. Check again and adjust.** Check your final draft, considering all the previous factors and making sure that the links between sections are smooth.

These are your page numbers (i.e. this is page 12 of your notes).

Make sure that you 'capture' the main activities of your practical or workshop session.

This is where you capture your thoughts – the most important section for putting together your final version. Underline or highlight sections which link to the 'elements' at the bottom.

Use the 'Reminder' box at the bottom to check through your notes for relevant points. Put the number of the element against the highlighted section to make it easier to see when you're going back over your notes.

These are links with other pages of your notes – here you are reminding yourself that there are useful similar points on pages 7 and 9.

| Page no.: 12 | Exploration Notes | | Date: 12/3 |
|---|---|---|---|
| Element links (highlight notes) | Text(s): A Streetcar Named Desire | | |
| | **Outline details of session** | | |
| | Character session, focusing on movement and voice. Looking at Blanche, Stanley, Stella and Mitch. Took each one in turn, miming their daily activities, imagining their working environment. Then what objects they would use. We varied the level of effort, then the size of the gestures. Found a vocal noise (not words) to go with the actions. Explored their activities when not at work – Stanley bowling, Mitch with his mother, Blanche in the bath, Stella organising baby clothes, etc. Selected one character and asked to say which animal our character would be. Then explored movement, gesture, sound, playing the character as the animal. Looked at text, found a phrase for each character to repeat. I chose 'Be comfortable is my motto' (Stanley), 'Sometimes – there's God – so quickly!' (Blanche), 'You need somebody. And I need somebody too.' (Mitch) and 'When he's away for a week, I nearly go wild!' (Stella). Tried these in different ways, expressing different feelings, imagining different situations. In pairs, selected short scenes from the play and acted these out, concentrating on voice and movement. | | |

**Reflections (with supporting details)**

| | |
|---|---|
| 2 | Miming Stanley's work, realised how hard he works physically and how this must affect his everyday movement. This goes with |
| 3 | volume – when I was experimenting with his 'vocal noise' it felt in character to be loud and let the voice come from the chest. Chose |
| 2 | Stanley for 'animal' work and played him as a gorilla. This felt right, but I wondered about playing the 'softer' parts of the text, when he's showing his love for Stella. But gorillas can be gentle |
| 2/4 | so I tried a 'softer' kind of movement, which seemed to fit. I found Stella the most difficult. It was hard to imagine how she spends her days. Wondered if her character is not as clear as the other |
| 4 | main ones. Does she depend so much on Stanley that she lives in his shadow? Is she quite passive? Check text again. Chose the first scene between Stanley and Blanche to act – and played Blanche! Kathy played Stanley, using my 'gorilla' character. Powerful movement, but all clear and precise. I found |
| 2/3/4 | that I immediately developed a seductive voice for Blanche and used flirting movements. |

**Reminder of required elements**

| Link with pages: 7 and 9 | 1. Language | 2. Non-verbal communication | 3. Vocal awareness | 4. Characterisation |
|---|---|---|---|---|
| | 5. Social, cultural, historical and political context | 6. Visual, aural and spatial elements | 7. Interpretation | 8. Response to practitioner |

# The writing-up process

## What counts in the word limit?

As the word limit is very strict (3,000 words), you need to be clear about what will be counted. The following **don't** count:

- the words of the play text if you're submitting an annotated script (for example, a scene you've worked on with notes in the margins)
- list of references or bibliography (any sources you've consulted)
- diagrams and sketches.

The following **do** count:

- quotations which you use in your writing
- all your own words in your Exploration Notes
- the words you use to explain diagrams and sketches.

> Make sure you acknowledge quotations by showing clearly where you've found each one.

## Diagrams and sketches

Including diagrams and sketches in your Exploration Notes is useful, especially when dealing with the set or spatial issues. Your annotations on them will communicate how you were thinking about the text or a practitioner. If you choose to use these, make sure that they are in the right place to link with the point you're making and that they convey information clearly.

## Using your notes

Once you've got all your notes, you need to look over them and then base your main points on them. Look at the following sample notes which are from different working sessions on *Romeo and Juliet*.

| 2/4 | We had to look at all the scenes between Romeo and Juliet. R and J only have four scenes together (when they are both alive) and two of these scenes are quite short. Reading through their scenes with Jason made me realise how whirlwind their romance is. Their first meeting must be electric for the relationship to move so fast. We improvised (just in movement) their first sight of each other, staging it so that they suddenly see each other across a crowded room. We found by timing their meeting, using crowded and then empty space, we could produce a sudden feeling as though fate had thrown us together. |
|---|---|

> Remember that the numbers refer to the elements as they are numbered on the form on page 26.

| 2<br><br>4 | The theme of today's session was 'personal pressures' (on R and J). In our 'freeze-frame' work we created 'snapshots' of first R and then J, trying to show their relationships with other individuals/groups. We used space, physical shape, gesture and facial expression. Romeo came out as quite a loner – closest to Mercutio, but distant from his parents. Our freeze-frames of Juliet showed that she was distressed by the rejection of her parents and towards the end felt betrayed by the Nurse. |
|---|---|

| 1<br>4<br><br>3 | In our work on language, we looked at the balcony scene. In our reading of the text we focused on the imagery. We tried to make it physical, so the bigger the image, the bigger the physical response. So 'It is the East and Juliet is the sun' was a 'big' image, needing an extravagant gesture to go with it. It was surprising to find that Juliet was more often cautious in her language, while Romeo used more extravagant images. She does use 'big' images, though, like 'My bounty is as boundless as the sea/My love as deep'. Then we read the scene again, taking out the big gestures, but trying to make our voices do the work, using range, pace and projection that felt right. This certainly made the scene between them more intense. |
|---|---|

| 8<br><br><br><br><br><br><br>4<br>7 | We worked on versions of Brecht's 'practice scenes' which he wrote for actors to play before working on the balcony scene. They both play scenes in which they are inconsiderate to their servants, so that they can focus on getting what they want. I really became aware of the fact that both R and J could be seen as rich, privileged young people. In both scenes, they regard the lives and the worries of their servants as far less important than their own. It made me think again about whether we should feel sympathetic to R and J, or whether we should also see them as self-indulgent. Brecht wants us to think about the society and not just the individuals. |
|---|---|

## Activity 3

Even if you don't know *Romeo and Juliet*, you can try this exercise. Take the four extracts and combine them to write about 200 words, putting together clear information about the characters of Romeo and Juliet and their relationship.

## Introductions and conclusions

Don't spend too long on your introduction or conclusion, and don't repeat information from your main points in them. In your introduction you need to introduce the plays you have explored, but you don't need to go into any detail about the plot. In your introduction you can give a brief overview of what you have learnt and in your conclusion you can show how the exploration has been a personal journey for you.

The important thing is to save your words for exploring the eight elements with reference to your plays.

# Exploration Notes: the final version

Here are two extracts from final versions of Exploration Notes. Both have been given a detailed commentary to highlight their strengths. After this, there is an activity for you to try on your own.

There are two possible approaches to structuring your Exploration Notes: you can make main points about your first text and then go on to your second text, or you can write about both texts at the same time. Both approaches are fine – there are no additional marks for comparing the two plays. It will probably depend on how you have worked on the practical activities. Take the advice of your teacher.

In Extract 1, the student is writing about one of the chosen texts (*Equus*); in Extract 2, the student is dealing with both texts (*Equus* and *Pygmalion*).

### Extract 1

Visual, aural and spatial elements make a huge contribution to a production of Equus. Peter Shaffer describes the set in detail and the stage directions show how effectively it is used in sequences like the end of Act 1, when Alan 'rides' Nugget, with the circle in the centre of the stage spinning around with them on it, and spotlights shining on them. (The 'Equus' noise, made by the cast vocally in the background, helps to build this scene up to its climax.) In our session we found that the scene could be staged very effectively with Alan standing on a high stage block, gripping onto the raised hands of the actor playing Nugget kneeling below him.

Lighting the scene with a single spotlight from below (actually, we used a powerful torch which we could move around) isolated Alan in the middle of the space. I became very aware of how simple effects of both lighting and sound (we built up the 'Equus' noise as well) can create a powerful focus, really concentrating the audience's attention on a sequence. This part of the play is very important in letting us into the private life of Alan and showing us his 'act of worship' so the use of staging, lighting and sound effects need to contribute to making it a powerful experience for the audience, who need to share Alan's experience at this point, so that they can understand his horrific act of violence later in the play.

**Commentary:** The writer makes it clear from the beginning that the main point being discussed is 'visual, aural and spatial elements' (one of the eight elements). She identifies examples of all three of these, showing how they all contribute to the dramatic effect of the sequence (the single spotlight (or torch), the 'Equus noise' and the isolation of Alan on a single stage block). She links her practical experience of staging this sequence to the way it is described in the text, showing how the same effect can be achieved by a different, simpler staging. She shows how her practical experience has helped her to understand the dramatic impact of this sequence in the play, mentioning how the effect of the sequence on the audience is important to an understanding of both Alan and the play as a whole. The writer could have added an annotated diagram to illustrate clearly what she means.

### Examiner's tip

The quality of your written communication will be taken into account when your work is marked. This includes clarity of expression, the structure and presentation of ideas, and grammar, punctuation and spelling. Therefore, make sure you check your work carefully; don't just spell-check, but read through, looking for the errors that spell-check doesn't pick up (there/their, your/you're, etc.). Be particularly careful to spell all drama and theatre terminology correctly. Don't use words that you don't fully understand (avoid the temptation to make your language seem more 'educated' if you're not sure about the vocabulary).

**Extract 2**

We used the techniques of Stanislavski to explore characterisation in both of our texts. I found that applying the two ideas of 'given circumstances' and 'imagination' helped me to understand the characters I was working on from the inside. I chose Alfred Doolittle (Pygmalion) and Martin Dysart (Equus). They are both middle-aged men (or older), so some imagination was necessary for me!

Compiling a list of 'given circumstances' from the two texts helped me to see that although Doolittle is a comic character, he has a life outside the play which you can explore and which helps you play the character. In a 'hot-seating' session, I talked about his six previous 'wives', his work as a navvy, and the way he has brought up Eliza ('a lick of the strap now and again' - p. 47). I also imagined the kind of place in which he lived and his relationship with Eliza's 'sixth stepmother' (p. 29).

With Dysart, when I improvised a movement and mime sequence of him in his home, I found imagining the objects which he and his wife have brought home from their Greek holidays helpful in exploring his reactions to his love of the classical world and the fact that she doesn't share this love. (I mimed picking up the Chianti-bottle lamps and the china condiment donkeys (p. 62), showing my dislike of them.) Imagining his empty relationship with his wife helped me to understand how important his work has become to him.

With both characters, Stanislavski's techniques improved my understanding of the characters and made it easier for me to play them.

**Commentary:** The focus on characterisation (one of the eight elements) is clear from the start. Details of how two aspects of the chosen practitioner's work were explored are clearly given (hot-seating, movement and mime improvisation). Points are helpfully supported by brief quotations from the text, with page references (details of the editions of the plays used need to be given in a bibliography at the end). Examples from both plays are used to show how Stanislavski's ideas of ways of working on characterisation helped the writer to understand the texts better.

Again, the paragraph stays focused on the main point and uses clear evidence from both practical activities and the texts. In this example, clear knowledge of the ideas of the chosen practitioner is also shown.

### Activity 4

Choose one main point from your notes on one of your texts to build a paragraph of your own.

Make sure that you:

• stick to the main point

• use examples from your practical activities

• show how your understanding of the text(s) has been helped by your practical work.

Writing the Exploration Notes will take you time, but you should find it an absorbing activity, which helps you understand both the plays and the ways in which they can come to life on stage.

# Exploration Notes: the eight elements

The following pages look in more detail at the eight elements that you are required to write about in your Exploration Notes. Each section draws on examples from the plays listed on pages 18–19 to explain what each element means in a drama and theatre context and to show you how you can apply what you read here to the plays you are exploring.

## Language

The phrase 'the language of drama' is often used (just in the way 'the language of music' or 'the language of film' are used) to mean all the ways in which drama communicates – through visual elements such as set and costume, as well as through physical elements such as movement and mime. This section is concerned only with the spoken word on stage. Later sections deal with other elements of 'theatrical language'.

To help you understand what kinds of features you should be looking for in the language of your plays for Unit 1, read through the extract below from *The Beggar's Opera*, then read the information on the next page.

> This extract is from Act 2 Scene 13 of *The Beggar's Opera* by John Gay (1728). Macheath (a highwayman) has been imprisoned and condemned to death. Polly is married to him and Lucy is pregnant by him. Each woman feels that she has a better claim on him than the other.

| | |
|---|---|
| MACHEATH: | Was there ever such an unfortunate villain as I am? |
| LUCY: | Was there ever such another villain? |
| POLLY: | O Macheath! Was it for this we parted? Taken! Imprisoned! Tried! Hanged! I'll stay with thee till death. No force shall tear thy dear wife from thee now. What means my love? Not one kind word – not one kind look! Think what thy Polly suffers to see thee in this condition. |
| MACHEATH: | *(Aside)* I must disown her. The wench is distracted. |
| LUCY: | Am I then bilked of my virtue? Can I have no reparation? Sure, men were born to lie and women to believe them! O villain! Villain! |
| POLLY: | Am I not thy wife? Thy neglect of me, thy aversion to me too severely proves it. Look at me. Tell me, am I not thy wife? |
| LUCY: | Perfidious wretch! |
| POLLY: | Barbarous husband! |
| LUCY: | Hadst thou been hanged five months ago, I had been happy. |
| POLLY: | And I too. If you had been kind to me till death, it would not have vexed me. And that's no very unreasonable request (though from a wife) to a man who hath not above seven or eight days to live. |
| LUCY: | And art thou then married to another? Hast thou two wives, monster? |
| MACHEATH: | If women's tongues can cease for an answer – hear me. |

In an extract such as this, you might explore some of the aspects considered below and see what these communicate about the characters. You may not find all of these elements in your texts; look at the examples from different plays over the next few pages to see what other features of language you might look for in your plays.

## How much each character says

It's useful to look at the characters who appear to be dominating the dialogue and ask if this means that they are more powerful in the situation on stage (or feel that they are more powerful). Lucy and Polly dominate this section of the scene as they compete with each other in insulting Macheath. Characters who say the most are not always the most powerful, however. Often silence can be more powerful.

## Punctuation

Punctuation often provides clues about the feelings and intentions behind words. For example, Polly's and Lucy's early speeches are full of exclamation marks and question marks. The exclamation marks (always a sign of intensity) show their strong feelings towards Macheath. The number of unanswered questions suggests that they are giving Macheath little opportunity to answer – although he probably has little that he is able to say in his defence.

## Rhetoric

The term 'rhetoric' covers a wide range of uses of language which we associate with making speeches. We preserve the word in 'rhetorical question' – the kind of question in a speech which requires no answer. Polly's 'Was it for this we parted?' is a rhetorical question; we know that she is implying the answer 'No'. Where else in this extract can you see similar rhetorical questions?

## Repetitions

Another type of rhetorical device is repetition, for example in Polly's 'Not one kind word – not one kind look'. The word 'villain' is used four times (each character uses it, but Lucy's and Polly's meaning is more aggressive and insulting than Macheath's self-pitying use). 'Wretch' and 'monster' provide some variety of insult later on. There is also an interesting repetition of rhythm and grammar, when Lucy's 'Perfidious wretch!' is echoed by Polly's 'Barbarous husband!' This indicates how they are beginning to work together as a team, as it has become clear to them that Macheath will not simply choose one of them. Note the exclamation marks as well.

## Asides

Asides are lines or short speeches delivered directly to the audience; the convention is that the other characters on stage cannot hear them. Often this has the effect of making the audience feel privileged and closer to the character. Here, for example, we may feel that Macheath is a lovable rogue, being 'got at' by the two women. Sometimes, especially in melodramas, asides have the opposite effect, letting the audience know the villain's evil plans.

## Activity 5

Now read the extract below from *Equus*. This is a much more modern piece and the language is very different from that in *The Beggar's Opera*.

It's clear that Frank dominates the dialogue. But what can you tell about his character from the way he speaks? Dora (Frank's wife) and Alan have much less to say; what can you tell about their relationship with Frank and with each other from the way they speak?

Make notes on the use of language in this scene. Then compare your points with the notes at the top of the next page in Activity 6.

This extract is from Act 1 Scene 6 of *Equus* by Peter Shaffer (1973). Frank is the father of the 17-year-old Alan. Alan and his mother, Dora, have just bought a television for the first time. Frank has come home to find them watching it.

FRANK *stands up and enters the scene downstage on the circle. A man in his fifties.*

FRANK:     *(To* ALAN*)* It may not look like that, but that's what it is. Absolutely fatal mentally, if you receive my meaning.

DORA *follows him on. She is also middle-aged.*

DORA:     That's a little extreme, dear, isn't it?

FRANK:     You sit in front of that thing long enough, you'll become stupid for life – like most of the population. *(To* ALAN*)* The thing is, it's a swiz. It seems to be offering you something, but actually it's taking something away. Your intelligence and your concentration, every minute you watch it. That's a true swiz, do you see?

*Seated on the floor,* ALAN *shrugs.*

     I don't want to sound like a spoilsport, old chum – but there really is no substitute for reading. What's the matter; don't you like it?

ALAN:     It's all right.

FRANK:     I know you think it's none of my beeswax, but it really is, you know… Actually, it's a disgrace when you come to think of it. You, the son of a printer, and never opening a book! If all the world was like you, I'd be out of a job, if you receive my meaning!

DORA:     All the same, times change, Frank.

FRANK     *(reasonably)*: They change if you let them change, Dora. Please return that set in the morning.

ALAN     *(crying out)*: No!

DORA:     Frank! No!

### Activity 6

Compare your comments on the extract from *Equus* on the previous page with the following points:

Frank talks assertively, in statements; he is convinced of the correctness of what he is saying and treats opinions as if they were facts ('there really is no substitute for reading'). He uses old-fashioned jocular expressions ('none of my beeswax', meaning 'none of my business') which make him seem outdated, like some of his views. A word like 'swiz' (or 'cheat') is old-fashioned 'polite' slang. In a similar way, he calls his son 'old chum'. Dora and Alan are reduced to monosyllabic responses in the face of his uncompromising attitudes.

## Using language for a purpose

In real life, we are always using language for a purpose – to praise, to insult, to persuade, to amuse, to encourage, to threaten, and so on. When you're acting a role in a play, you need to find the character's purpose. The words and the way they're put together into phrases, sentences and whole speeches will relate to a specific purpose in a specific situation in the play. You need to understand what you are saying very clearly, so that you can say it with real purpose and conviction.

Language in plays is for speaking out loud. This makes it different from language in novels, magazines, and so on. Hesitations, rewordings, sudden breaking-offs, ungrammatical phrases and sentences – these can reflect a character's thought patterns.

### Activity 7

Read the extract opposite from *Our Country's Good* and answer these questions.

a) Think about the situation. Ralph is an officer in the army. His job is to be in charge of the convicts who have been transported to Australia as punishment for their crimes in England. Meg is a convict. On the surface, he is in a position of power and she has none. How would you expect her to be talking to him?

b) What do you notice about the kind of language that Meg uses? Look at the individual words. Do you recognise all of them? If you don't, why might that be? What about her grammar? How does she address Ralph?

c) How is Ralph's language different from Meg's? Do his words and expressions reveal his attitude to her? How does he address her?

d) Overall, how does the use of language show what is going on in the scene between them? Looking at the balance of power between the two characters, how does each use language to gain power over the other?

*In* RALPH's *tent.* MEG LONG *is very old and very smelly. She hovers over* RALPH.

| | |
|---|---|
| MEG: | We heard you was looking for some women, Lieutenant. Here I am. |
| RALPH: | I've asked to see some women to play certain parts in a play. |
| MEG: | I can play, Lieutenant, I can play with any part you like. There ain't nothing puts Meg off. That's how I got my name: Shitty Meg. |
| RALPH: | The play has four particular parts for young women. |
| MEG: | You don't want a young woman for your peculiar, Lieutenant, they don't know nothing. Shut your eyes and I'll play you as tight as a virgin. |
| RALPH: | You don't understand, Long. Here's the play. It's called *The Recruiting Officer.* |
| MEG: | Oh, I can do that too. |
| RALPH: | What? |
| MEG: | Recruiting. Anybody you like. *(She whispers.)* You want women: you ask Meg. Who do you want? |
| RALPH: | I want to try some out. |
| MEG: | Good idea, Lieutenant, good idea. Ha! Ha! Ha! |
| RALPH: | Now, if you don't mind – |

*(*MEG *doesn't move.)*

| | |
|---|---|
| | Long! |
| MEG: | *(frightened, but still holding her ground)* We thought you was a madge cull. |
| RALPH: | What? |
| MEG: | You know, a fluter, a mollie. A prissy cove, a girl. |

This extract is from Act 1 Scene 5 of *Our Country's Good* by Timberlake Wertenbaker (1988). The young Lieutenant Ralph Clark has arrived with the first group of convicts to be transported to Australia. He wants to impress his Captain by producing a play with a cast of convicts and has arranged auditions for them. Meg turns up uninvited.

## Types of language in drama

Language is subtle and can express all sorts of shades of meaning. There are a few obvious 'rules'; for example, if a character shouts, he or she may be angry, frightened, in pain, frustrated, shocked or in many other states of mind.  As a student of drama, you have to be sensitive to various features of the language which help you to analyse the characters, their relationships and the situations in a play. Playwrights choose their words carefully and with purpose; you need to pick up the clues to see what these purposes are.

The areas on page 36 will help you to think about language in drama, and to identify the types of language in the plays you are exploring.

## NATURALISTIC – NON-NATURALISTIC

| Naturalistic | Non-naturalistic |
|---|---|
| The language imitates the features of recognisable, everyday speech, especially of characters whom we would recognise as being working-class or middle-class. | The language may be literary – highly organised and polished, carefully balanced, using a range of vocabulary not in everyday use by most people. It may be stylised or 'heightened' in various ways to achieve particular effects. |
| Example:<br><br>She's not going back to teach school! In fact I'm willing to bet you that she never had no idea of returning to Laurel! She didn't resign temporarily from the high school because of her nerves. No, siree Bob, she didn't! They kicked her out of that high school before the spring term ended – and I hate to tell you the reason that step was taken! A seventeen-year-old boy – she'd gotten mixed up with!<br><br>*A Streetcar Named Desire* by Tennessee Williams, Scene 7 | Example:<br><br>It will be done. I will whisk these waters into a turmoil<br>And the Aegean shores will be littered with the Grecian dead.<br>Go now, Goddess Athene, to great Mount Olympus and<br>From those heights you may watch the Greek fleet sink into oblivion.<br>Be warned you mortals who violate the temples of the gods<br>And the sacred tombs of the dead for in these acts lie your own destruction.<br><br>*The Trojan Women* by Euripides, Prologue |

## INFORMAL – FORMAL

| Informal | Formal |
|---|---|
| Links with naturalistic. May make use of slang, swearing, omit words, employ 'ungrammatical' sentences. Sentences are often simple in structure, although they may be rambling. | Uses Standard English, with conventional grammar. Uses 'educated' vocabulary. Sentences are usually longer, more complicated and more carefully organised. |
| Example:<br><br>Yeah, but nah – it ain't that. It's like that space-dust shi- space-dust stuff – s'only way I can say it. S'like poppin' in my head – fizzy, know what I mean. Sparklin'. You know that stuff? Space-dust.<br><br>*Prayer Room* by Shan Khan, p.21 | Example:<br><br>What is a statesman's responsibility? To ensure the rule of law. But the citizens must be taught to obey that law of their own will. I want to rule over responsible human beings, not tyrannise over a group of animals.<br><br>*Our Country's Good* by Timberlake Wertenbaker, Act 2 Scene 2 |

## PROSE – VERSE

| Prose | Verse |
|---|---|
| Prose is the medium of most modern drama. Words are in the order of normal speech. Lines can be of different lengths on the page. Although prose speeches may use different speech rhythms, they do not normally use a regular rhythmical pattern. Prose is used for naturalistic dramas (although at times for non-naturalistic dramas as well). | Verse and poetry are different, although poetry is usually in the form of verse. Dramas in verse are usually 'heightened', taking them away from naturalism. Verse features repeated rhythms and often employs rhyme. Most of what Shakespeare wrote is in 'blank verse' – unrhymed lines with an underlying rhythm and a standard length. |
| Examples:<br><br>See the extracts from *Our Country's Good* and *A Streetcar Named Desire* above. | Examples:<br><br>See the extracts from *The Trojan Women* (above) and *Romeo and Juliet* (below). |

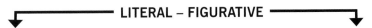

**LITERAL – FIGURATIVE**

| Literal | Figurative |
|---|---|
| In literal language, the words say what they mean plainly; there can be little disagreement about the surface meaning. If a character says 'I am going out and I may be some time', the surface meaning is clear. The context in which a line like this is said may give it dramatic meaning, however. (This is the line said by Captain Oates as he left the tent on Scott's Antarctic expedition. He had chosen to go outside and die so that the others stood a chance of survival without him.) | Figurative language makes use of 'figures of speech' – ways of using language more creatively and inventively. There are many 'figures of speech'; they often have specialised names. The use of images (metaphors, similes, personification) is common, but look out for understatement, exaggeration, puns, euphemisms, epigrams, aphorisms and paradoxes, as well as the use of irony. |
| Example:<br><br>This is Mary Warren's deposition. I – I would ask you to remember, sir, when you read it, that until two week ago, she were no different than the other children are today. You saw her scream, she howled, she swore familiar spirits choked her; she even testified that Satan, in the form of women now in jail, had tried to win her soul away…<br><br>*The Crucible* by Arthur Miller, Act 3 | Example:<br><br>Come, night; come, Romeo; come, thou day in night;<br>For thou wilt lie upon the wings of night<br>Whiter than new snow upon a raven's back.<br>Come, gentle night; come, loving black-browed night;<br>Give me my Romeo; and, when I shall die,<br>Take him and cut him out in little stars…<br><br>*Romeo and Juliet* by William Shakespeare, Act 3 Scene 2 |

## The world of the play

All plays, from pantomimes to tragedies, create their own 'worlds' with their own atmospheres and 'rules'. Reading, watching and acting in plays open the doors to these 'worlds' and we enter into them in our imagination. Language experts tell us that people 'see' their world through their language (for example, the more words you have for different types of snow, the more types you are able to perceive). By studying the language used in a play (naturalistic, formal, poetic, dialect, etc.), you can understand more about the world of the play and how your character fits into it, if you're acting a role.

For directors and designers, studying the language is important too. The kind of world which is being created by the language needs to be reflected in the visual elements of the play, for example, and in the way you encourage the characters into their roles and help build their relationships with each other and with the audience.

**Activity 8**

Think about a play you know well. What pictures does it create in your mind? What feel does it have? (For this exercise, it's better if you haven't seen a film of it.) Are there parts of the language you remember? How do these contribute to the pictures in your mind?

The lines in the diagram below are from Act 1 Scene 2 of *A Raisin in the Sun* by Lorraine Hansberry (1959). The Walters are a poor black family, living in Chicago. Ruth is married to Mama's son Walter, who has unrealistic dreams of setting up in business (he's a chauffeur at the moment). Ruth has discovered that she is pregnant (unexpectedly) and has just returned from seeing a doctor.

## Text and sub-text

Especially in modern naturalistic plays, there is a great deal going on under the surface of the words which are being said out loud. Like the iceberg with its bulk under the water line, most of the meaning may be implied by the tone in which something is said (or the fact that something isn't said) rather than by the words on the page. As a student and as an actor, you need to be very aware of the sub-text (see page 34 about using language for a purpose). Look at the following example from *A Raisin in the Sun*.

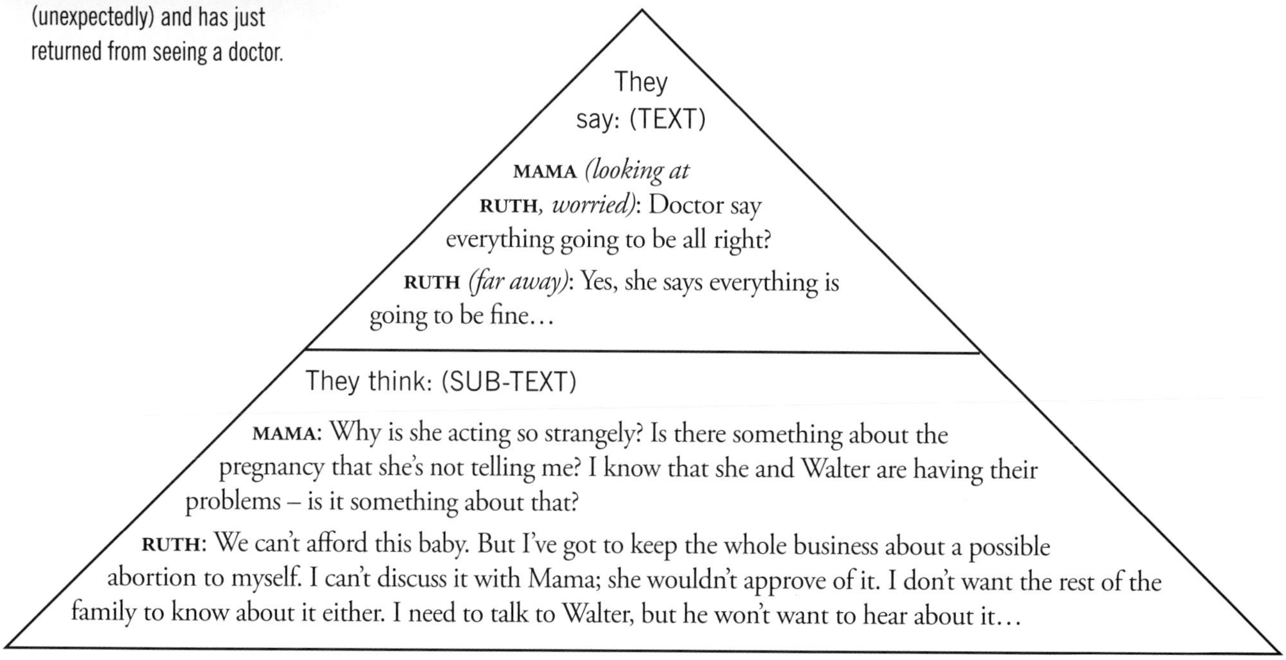

They say: (TEXT)

MAMA *(looking at* RUTH, *worried)*: Doctor say everything going to be all right?

RUTH *(far away)*: Yes, she says everything is going to be fine…

They think: (SUB-TEXT)

MAMA: Why is she acting so strangely? Is there something about the pregnancy that she's not telling me? I know that she and Walter are having their problems – is it something about that?

RUTH: We can't afford this baby. But I've got to keep the whole business about a possible abortion to myself. I can't discuss it with Mama; she wouldn't approve of it. I don't want the rest of the family to know about it either. I need to talk to Walter, but he won't want to hear about it…

**Key term**

sub-text

**Activity 9**

Read through a section of one of your texts. Find an example of the use of sub-text (a character thinking something different from the words he or she is saying).

Make up the words that he or she is actually thinking. Why is the character saying not these words (the sub-text), but the words of the text?

# Non-verbal communication

The language of theatre is about more than spoken language. Some plays have no spoken words at all. Non-verbal communication refers to any form of action on stage which conveys meaning to an audience. This will include: gesture, facial expression, movement, mime, tableaux (sometimes called 'freeze-frames', 'photographs' or 'still images'), physical theatre, and dance and mask work.

## Exploring non-verbal communication: off the text

There are many ways of exploring a role physically. This section gives some possible examples of ways into character and situation through physical means.

The following two activities use *The Crucible* to explore the non-verbal communication of a character, but can be applied to any text you are studying. The subsequent three activities are generic and can be used for any play.

### Activity 10

a) John Proctor is a farmer who has to work hard to get his land to yield crops. He is living in a time (1692) before farming has become mechanised, so most labour is done with simple tools and with the hands. Devise a short mime sequence in which (in character) you work on digging the ground, planting, reaping and repairing a wooden fence. Be precise in imagining the tools which you are using and in simulating the effort which these tasks take.

b) Now play John Proctor towards the end of the play, when he has been confined to jail for some months and has been kept in chains. Devise another short sequence in which he sits, stands, eats some bread, takes the few paces which he is able to, and tries to look out of the cell window. Again, concentrate on the physical effort.

What do you observe about the different types of movement? How does this exercise make you feel about the character and its development?

### Activity 11

Mary Warren is a maidservant, working for the Proctors with heavy physical duties to perform. Imagine her at three different points:

a) before the play has started

b) when she has become (as she sees it) an important 'officer of the court'

c) after Elizabeth and John Proctor have been sent to jail.

Devise a short sequence in which she cleans the floor, using a bucket of water, a broom and a handbrush. Repeat this for each of the three different points, thinking about how her physical movements are affected by her state of mind. What differences were you aware of between the three sequences?

**Taking it further**

Look at Samuel Beckett's *Act Without Words 1* where the printed text is entirely stage directions.
A few years ago, the company Derevo won a Fringe First Award for new writing for their performance at the Edinburgh Fringe Festival, despite the fact that no words were spoken during the whole performance (and, therefore, there was no 'writing' in the usual sense of the word). The judges said that the performance had spoken 'the language of theatre'.

**Key terms**

action
freeze-frame
physical theatre
still image
tableau

## Activity 12

Take one of the plays you are studying for Unit 1 and imagine that a group of characters meet on neutral territory (a park, for example). They greet each other, without saying anything, just relying on physical means and facial expressions. Their physical bearing will reflect the period in which the play is set and their social background (e.g. the late 19th-century Russian gentry will behave differently from 1940s working-class English characters). You may not be clear about the precise social conventions of the time, but use your body and face to reflect an attitude and to respond to the greetings which you receive.

What non-verbal communication took place? What degree of formality was there? Was there physical contact (e.g. shaking or kissing hands)? How did your physical behaviour change as you greeted different characters?

## Activity 13

**Status**. Some characters are considered to be 'socially superior' to others, such as kings and queens having a much higher status than servants. Characters can acquire status, for example achieving success, power or money. Sometimes in a play status isn't clear-cut, however, or changes as the play moves on. Allocate the characters from a play in your group and improvise a scene in which they are engaged in an activity. Doubling-up characters can be very interesting for comparing notes at the end. Take a pack of playing cards from which all the court cards and aces have been removed and get everyone to choose an unseen card. The card reflects your status, with ten being the highest and two the lowest. Play the scene according to your card's status, focusing on the physical elements, showing your attitude to yourself and to the other characters. This can be repeated trying a different status which is either random or given to each character.

Was your character comfortable with the status allocated? How did this make you behave physically? Did you become aware of parts of the character which 'grew' physically during this exercise? What difference did it make physically when you changed status?

**Key term**

doubling-up

**Practitioner note**

Objective is a term used by 'Stanislavski' (see page 52). Bertolt Brecht wrote about the idea of Gestus (sometimes referred to as 'geste'). This refers to the way that a gesture or action on stage can convey an attitude, often reflecting aspects of class or society (see page 153).

## Activity 14

**Pursuing an objective**. An 'objective' is what a character wants. It should be positive (such as 'I want to leave the room' not 'I don't want to be here') and should motivate the character to action. Take a situation from one of the plays you are exploring in which one character is playing a strong objective that can be expressed physically. Play the scene out physically, exploring different ways of trying to achieve your objective.

Did the range of movement you explored give you any insights into the character? Is there the potential for aggression in them or was the movement softer and more persuasive? Which kind of movement was most successful and hardest to resist?

# Non-verbal communication: using the text

The language of theatre is recorded in printed plays in two ways: the dialogue and the stage directions. This section deals with working with stage directions.

In Shakespeare's time plays were what happened on stage. Printed texts sometimes followed, but often didn't. If they did, the stage directions were virtually non-existent or implicit (that is, implied in the text). In *Macbeth*, for example, when Lady Macbeth returns from smearing blood on the grooms' faces, there is no stage direction to show that her hands are covered with blood, but her line 'My hands are of your colour' clearly implies this.

When plays became an activity for readers as well as a live audience (or when playwrights wanted to indicate that they were reacting against conventional methods of staging), stage directions became much more important in the printed text. Plays published in the late 19th century and afterwards usually have much more detailed and extensive stage directions.

### What do stage directions tell you?

Stage directions deal with four main areas:

- the nature of the set and the positioning of doors, furniture, etc.
- technical effects (lighting, sound, special effects, etc.)
- movement or gestures of characters
- the thoughts or states of mind of characters and sometimes the delivery of specific lines.

### Do stage directions matter?

In modern plays, stage directions are often those from the original production. Information about the set will be interesting to directors and designers, but will not necessarily be copied. Similarly, actors and directors may have their own ideas about the movement of characters on stage or the delivery of particular lines. As a student of the plays, you need to treat stage directions as an important source of information. You may choose to do things differently, but you should be able to say why.

## Activity 15

On the next page are stage directions from three plays. Read through these examples and say how useful you think they would be in helping you with the non-verbal communication of the role. What scope is there for your own interpretation? For example, when Konstantin places the dead seagull at Nina's feet, what is the gesture intended to mean? How does he perceive it? How does she perceive it? How does the audience 'read' it? How many different ways of interpreting that stage direction can you find (in action) so that it means subtly different things? How else could you convey physically Mama's emotions as she leaves her home? What do you make of the stage direction 'Eliza's beauty becomes murderous'? Is this helpful to an actor? How else would you convey her frustrated rage?

### The Seagull

*Enter* KONSTANTIN, *hatless, with a gun and a seagull he has killed.*

| | |
|---|---|
| KONSTANTIN: | You're alone? |
| NINA: | Yes, I'm alone. |
| | (KONSTANTIN *lays the seagull at her feet.*) |
| | What does that signify? |
| KONSTANTIN: | I had the dishonour to kill this seagull today. I'm laying it at your feet. |
| NINA: | What's the matter with you? *(Picks up the seagull and looks at it.)* |

### A Raisin in the Sun

MAMA: *(waving* RUTH *out vaguely)* All right, honey – go on down. I'll be down directly.

RUTH *hesitates, then goes.* MAMA *stands at last alone in the living-room, her plant on the table before her as the lights start to come down. She looks around at the walls and ceilings and suddenly, despite herself, while her children call below, a great heaving thing rises in her and she puts her fist to her mouth, takes a final desperate look, pulls her coat about her, pats her hand and goes out. The lights dim down. The door opens and she comes back in, grabs her plant, and goes out for the last time. Curtain.*

### Pygmalion

HIGGINS: Yes: that's what drives me mad: the silly people don't know their own silly business. *(Rising)* However, it's over and done with; and now I can go to bed at last without dreading tomorrow.

ELIZA*'s beauty becomes murderous.*

PICKERING: I think I shall turn in too. Still, it's been a great occasion: a triumph for you. Goodnight. *(He goes.)*

HIGGINS *(following him)*: Goodnight. *(Over his shoulder, at the door)* Put out the lights, Eliza; and tell Mrs Pearce not to make coffee for me in the morning; I'll take tea. *(He goes out.)*

ELIZA *tries to control herself and feel indifferent as she rises and walks across to the hearth to switch off the lights. By the time she gets there she is on the point of screaming. She sits down in Higgins's chair and holds on hard to the arms. Finally, she gives way and flings herself furiously on the floor, raging.*

HIGGINS *(in despairing wrath outside)*: What the devil have I done with my slippers? *(He appears at the door.)*

LIZA *(snatching up the slippers, and hurling them at him, one after the other with all her force)*: Here are your slippers; and may you never have a day's luck with them!

## Vocal awareness

This section is about applying your voice to your work on texts. It will also make you more aware of what to observe in the performances of actors when you are evaluating the live theatre performance as part of your work for this unit.

## Your character's voice

Read this extract from *Translations* in a group, or by yourself, as an individual exercise. There are four speaking and three non-speaking characters in the extract, but the focus is on how Lancey is using his voice.

**Tip**

Look back to pages 12–13 for general advice about using your voice and for a basic warm-up routine. It's good to begin practical sessions with a vocal and physical warm-up.

| | |
|---|---|
| OWEN: | And I'll make no other introduction except that these are some of the best people of Baile Beag and – what? Well, you're among the best people in Ireland now. *(He pauses to allow* LANCEY *to speak.* LANCEY *does not.)* Would you like to say a few words, Captain? |
| HUGH: | What about a drop, sir? |
| LANCEY: | A what? |
| HUGH: | Perhaps a modest refreshment? A little sampling of our aqua vitae? |
| LANCEY: | No, no. |
| HUGH: | Later perhaps, when – |
| LANCEY: | I'll say what I have to say, if I may, and as briefly as possible. Do they speak any English, Roland? |
| OWEN: | Don't worry. I'll translate. |
| LANCEY: | I see. *(He clears his throat. He speaks as if he were addressing children – a shade too loudly and enunciating excessively.)* You may have seen me – seen me – working in this section – section? – working. We are here – here – in this place – you understand? – to make a map – a map and – |
| JIMMY: | Nonne Latine loquitur? |
| | HUGH *holds up a restraining hand.* |
| HUGH: | James. |
| LANCEY | *(To* JIMMY*)*: I do not speak Gaelic, sir. *(He looks at* OWEN.*)* |
| OWEN: | Carry on. |
| LANCEY: | A map is a representation on paper – a picture – you understand picture? – a paper picture – showing, representing this country – yes? – showing your country in miniature – a scaled drawing on paper of – of – of – |
| | *Suddenly* DOALTY *sniggers. Then* BRIDGET. *Then* SARAH. OWEN *leaps in quickly.* |
| OWEN: | It might be better if you assume that they understand you – |
| LANCEY: | Yes? |
| OWEN: | And I'll translate as you go along. |

This extract is from Act 1 of *Translations* by Brian Friel (1980). Captain Lancey, an English soldier in charge of a map-making exercise in Southern Ireland, is addressing some local inhabitants, trying to explain what he is doing. He does not speak the local language (Gaelic), but is being helped by Owen (whom he mistakenly always calls Roland), a local originally, but who has spent years in England. The play is set in 1833.

## Factors affecting voice

Read the notes which follow. When you've read and discussed them, read the extract on page 43 again, concentrating on how these factors would affect your voice in playing the scene.

The major factors that will affect how the actor playing Lancey uses his voice in this scene are those outlined below.

> *Translations* is a play which has language as one of its main concerns. In the play we realise quite quickly that although the Irish characters are speaking in English, they are really speaking in Gaelic. This becomes clear when the English and Irish talk, without being able to understand each other. It's a bold and effective theatrical device.

| Character |
|---|
| The voice will relate to the character's background, education and experience. |
| Brian Friel provides this character note on Lancey's first entrance: '*CAPTAIN LANCEY is middle-aged; a small crisp officer, expert in his field as a cartographer, but uneasy with people – especially civilians, especially these foreign civilians. His skill is with deeds, not words.*' So we can see that he is a specialist, an army man, ill at ease in social or public situations. We might assume that the army has been his life and that he enjoys its security and its strict regimes. We can tell that he has not studied Latin (which any well-educated man of the time would have) as he thinks that Jimmy is addressing him in Gaelic. |

**Key terms**

given circumstances
realist

| Situation/given circumstances |
|---|
| The character's background and the situation he or she is in will affect how the lines are delivered. |
| Lancey has been sent to a rural part of Ireland in order to make a proper map of the territory (an 'ordnance' map was originally a map made for military purposes). Their equipment has been interfered with by some locals who, to differing degrees, resent the English presence in the country. Horses have been killed (and later, one of the soldiers is killed). This, and the fact that he cannot speak the native language (Gaelic) makes him uneasy. He is on 'their' territory, as this scene takes place in a 'hedge-school', a disused barn where they gather for classes. He does not recognise their hospitality and their willingness to listen, because he is tense and suspicious. |

| Style of play |
|---|
| In plays in the realist tradition where we can accept the reality of life on the stage as recognisable, actors' voices will reflect that reality. In other styles of play we might expect to use a voice which involves a way of speaking a 'heightened' language. |
| *Translations* is a realist play, so we expect recognisable characters and ways of speaking. |

| Objective/intention |
|---|
| What is the character's objective or intention? How will that come across in their voice? |
| Lancey expresses his objective clearly: 'I'll say what I have to say, if I may, and as briefly as possible.' He wants to deliver his message about what the army are doing, to do so as acceptably as he can (note 'if I may') and to get away (he doesn't want to delay or get socially involved by accepting a drink). |

**Applying your voice to the character**

Once you have recognised all these factors, it becomes easier to decide how you can apply this vocal awareness to a performance.

In your work on the character, you will need to fill in missing information, building imaginatively and logically on what the text gives you. For example, we can assume that Lancey is not an upper-class character, but there is no clue to whether or not he speaks in an English regional accent. Given the contrasts between the Irish accents and the English in the play, you might choose to opt for RP (Received Pronunciation), but a regional accent might help him to sound even more out of place here.

The following elements are important in finding your character's voice:

- pitch (the note)
- range (how high and low your voice will go)
- pace (the rate or relative speed)
- use of pauses
- tone (which relates to the attitude of your character and his or her relationship with the person who is listening)
- volume
- articulation (how clearly you pronounce the words).

All these will be influenced by the four factors discussed on the previous page. For example in speaking to the locals, Lancey's **pitch** might be higher than usual and his **range** narrower, reflecting his anxiety about the situation. Although he wants to get it over with, he will be dutiful about delivering his message, so his **pace** will be slow and it's clear that his **pauses** reflect his anxiety as well as his determination to make himself clear. His **tone** (which will express his attitude to his listeners) will be formal; he wants to make a speech, not engage in conversation. His **volume** may be rather too loud for the space and situation, reflecting his desire to make himself clear (the old joke about English people believing that foreigners will understand them if they shout loudly at them is relevant here!). His **articulation** will be distinct, again because he wishes to make himself clear.

## Activity 16

a) Once you've considered all the factors affecting character and situation, read the extract on page 43 once more and discuss how effectively these factors were conveyed by the use of the voice.

b) Now take a scene from one of the plays you are studying for Unit 1 and go through the same process: focusing on one character, make notes on character, given circumstances, style and objective, and how these factors will influence that character's pitch, range, pace, use of pause, tone, volume and articulation.

## Sub-text

Sub-text is to do with objective/intention (see pages 38 and 40). Stanislavski wanted his actors to play the sub-text, not the text; that is, the intentions which lay behind the words and which were often different from (or in complete opposition to) the words on the page. You need to consider sub-text, as it will make all the difference to how you apply your voice in any acting situation.

### Activity 17

Read this extract, also from *Translations*. There are two characters, Yolland (an English soldier) and Maire (a local Irish girl who works on a farm). After reading it through once, look at the notes about the scene on the next page and then read the extract again, focusing on the sub-text and how this affects the way in which the lines are delivered vocally.

YOLLAND:  Maire.

*(She still moves away.)*

     Maire Chatach.

*(She still moves away.)*

     Bun na Abhann? *(He says the name softly, almost privately, very tentatively, as if he were searching for a sound she might respond to. He tries again.)* Druim Dubh?

*(MAIRE stops. She is listening. YOLLAND is encouraged.)*

     Poll na gCaorach. Lis Maol.

*(MAIRE turns towards him.)*

     Lis na nGall.

MAIRE:   Lis na nGradh.

*(They are now facing each other and begin moving – almost imperceptibly – towards one another.)*

     Carraig an Phoill.

YOLLAND:  Carraig na Ri. Loch na nEan.

MAIRE:   Loch an Iubhair. Nachaire buidhe.

YOLLAND:  Machaire Mor. Cnoc na Mona.

MAIRE:   Cnoc na nGabhar.

YOLLAND:  Mullach.

MAIRE:   Port.

YOLLAND:  Tor.

MAIRE:   Lag.

*She holds out her hands to* YOLLAND. *He takes them.*

It is clear in this extract that the surface of the text reveals little (especially as it is incomprehensible to anyone who does not speak Gaelic). But what is going on between the characters is a love scene. It is like a courtship ritual in which the Englishman's (Yolland's) showing his love of the sound of the place names in Maire's language (Gaelic) becomes a love offering to her, which she gradually accepts. It's interesting to note how the words become shorter (monosyllabic towards the end) as they presumably approach each other, focusing on each other, rather than the words they are saying.

The actors' voices will reflect this sub-text and won't just be a list of Irish place names; that would make no sense at all in the context of the scene. Their voices will be soft, gentle, exploratory, relishing the sounds of the place names. There will also be a progression vocally in the scene as they gain confidence in the reaction to each other. The stage direction uses the word 'tentative' to describe Yolland's speech at the beginning of this extract; by the end, we can assume that there is a shared confidence and security between them.

## Stage directions

It's always worth noting what the stage directions say (and imply) about how lines are delivered. While you may not always agree, they will be a factor in deciding how to use your voice effectively. See also pages 41–42.

### Activity 18

Look through the stage directions in one of the plays you are studying for Unit 1 and see if any of them suggest or imply how you might deliver a line or a speech.

## Actioning

Actioning is a useful technique to consider in the context of vocal awareness. In essence, it's putting into action the idea that every sentence the character speaks is delivered with a specific intention – and that the intention will change from sentence to sentence. The actor defines in a word (an active verb) his or her character's intention in saying that sentence. So it might be: I abuse, I belittle, I liberate, I revitalise, I admire, I bewitch, I compliment, I value, I compel, I unsettle, I frustrate, I denounce – or many other possibilities.

### Activity 19

Take a speech of several lines delivered by a character in one of the plays you are studying for Unit 1. See if you can decide on a precise 'action' for each sentence. Then try to deliver the speech in the ways you have decided.

The more precise the action (or the intention), the clearer your use of your voice in the delivery.

## Space, stage form and projection

One of your most important duties as an actor is to be heard by your audience. You will need to take into account the size of the auditorium in which you are playing, its acoustics and the stage form.

Projection is using the strength of your voice so that you can be heard comfortably by all the audience members. Audiences don't like straining to hear actors and have no way of turning the volume up. Projection is not shouting, but using the power of your vocal equipment effectively. Sustained shouting is also uncomfortable for an audience and damages actors' voices.

Broadly speaking, the bigger the auditorium, the more you will have to rely on your power of projection. In addition, you will need to be aware of the acoustics of the space:

- Hard surfaces will reflect sound, making it reverberate.
- Soft surfaces (like stage curtains) will 'soak up' sound, making it harder for you to be heard.

Stage form is also relevant: if you are performing in a proscenium arch theatre, you will probably find it easier to make yourself heard than if you're playing in-the-round, where you will have audience behind you and to your sides. See pages 147–152 for more detail on different stage forms.

Part of your vocal awareness will be your skill in adapting to different playing conditions.

### Key terms

in-the-round
proscenium arch

### Activity 20

In a group, experiment with the effect of placing an audience in front of you and in-the-round. Try to maintain your projection at the same level and see how comfortable the audience finds your audibility.

## Other uses of the voice

Any performance may make other demands on your voice: you may be required to undertake choral speech (*The Trojan Women*), to sing (*The Beggar's Opera* or *The Threepenny Opera*), to scream (*The Crucible*), or to make animal or 'atmospheric' noises (*Equus*). You may be required to learn new accents (*Translations*, *The Accrington Pals*, *A Streetcar Named Desire*).

You may also be involved in productions in which actors use their voices to make sound effects. Sometimes these may be substituting for real sounds (for example, actors creating a sound environment of an airport or a supermarket with their voices) or for a non-realistic effect (a sinister or ghostly atmosphere).

All these will involve interesting aspects of your use of voice and increase your vocal awareness.

# Characterisation

Your ideas about character in the texts you are studying will be drawn from both dialogue and stage directions, and developed in practical activities. It is important to read the text closely, with attention and with a strong sense of how it might appear in performance. The following extract is from *The Seagull* by Chekhov. It has been annotated to show what clues about the characters might be gathered from an initial read through.

> In this scene Nina (a young girl) has just ridden hurriedly across from her father's and stepmother's house on a neighbouring estate to give a solo performance in a short surrealist play which Konstantin (slightly older than her) has written.

**NINA:** My father and his wife won't let me come here. They say you're all Bohemians... They're afraid I might run off to be an actress ...But it's the lake that draws me here, like a seagull ... My heart's full of you. *(Looks round.)*

> Nina is worried about the attitude of her father/ stepmother, suggesting a strict upbringing.

**KONSTANTIN:** We're alone.

**NINA:** I think there's someone there.

*(They kiss.)*

**NINA:** What sort of tree is that?

> Nina is easily distracted from the kiss.

**KONSTANTIN:** Elm.

**NINA:** Why does it have such a dark colour?

**KONSTANTIN:** It's evening – everything looks dark. Don't go early, please don't.

**NINA:** I can't stay.

**KONSTANTIN:** Supposing I came to your house, Nina? I'll stand in the garden all night and look up at your window.

> Konstantin is in love with Nina. He feels like making excessively romantic gestures.

**NINA:** You can't – the watchman will see you. Treasure's not used to you yet – he'll bark.

> Nina is more practical – or less keen than Konstantin is.

**KONSTANTIN:** I love you.

**NINA:** Shh...

**KONSTANTIN** *(hearing footsteps)*: Who's that? Is that you, Yakov?

**YAKOV** *(behind the improvised stage)*: Sir.

**KONSTANTIN:** Stand by. Time to start. Is the moon rising?

**YAKOV:** Sir.

**KONSTANTIN:** Have you got the spirits? And the sulphur? When the red eyes appear there must be a smell of sulphur. *(To* NINA*)* Go on, then, it's all ready. Are you nervous?

> Konstantin is authoritative with the servant, Yakov, and obviously keen to make the production of his play successful.

**NINA:** Yes, very. I don't mind your mother, I'm not afraid of her, but you've got Trigorin here ... When I think of acting in front of him I'm terrified, I'm ashamed ...He's a famous writer ... Is he young?

> Nina is in awe of the writer, Trigorin, but less so in relation to Konstantin's mother, who is a famous actress.

**KONSTANTIN:** Yes he is.

**NINA:** Such wonderful stories he writes!

**KONSTANTIN** *(coldly)*: I wouldn't know. I haven't read them.

> Konstantin seems jealous of Trigorin and his success as a writer. He may also resent the fact that Nina is enthusiastic about them.

**49**

## What is character?

The playwright David Mamet maintains that there is no such thing as 'character' in plays; there are only words on the page. Because an actor speaks these words on stage, the audience forms an impression of an actual person. The 'character' is, in fact, an illusion. This should alert us to the idea that character may be less obvious than we think it is. Many television viewers who watch soaps find that the characters in them seem as real (or even more real) to them than the people they meet every day. But these characters do not exist. Character is always constructed by a playwright and then interpreted by an actor on stage or screen.

### Stanislavski and the realist view of character

Much of modern acting is influenced by the teachings and work of Constantin Stanislavski (1863–1938). He was living and working at a time when the modern study of psychology was developing. Character was seen as being complex and multi-layered, with the psychology of individual characters worth exploring. Characters, for example, might not say what they mean (sub-text is relevant here) or they might have complex motives. This is sometimes referred to as 'psycho-realism'. To us, this realist approach may seem obvious because we are so used to this way of thinking about character. However, in plays written before the second half of the 19th century, it is much more common to find characters who are stereotypical – or even allegorical (Gluttony, for example). We tend to think of stereotypes as bad, but it would be better to think in terms of what is appropriate for a certain style of play.

### Brecht and character

Bertolt Brecht (1898–1956) admired Stanislavski's work, but had a different view of character in drama. He saw character as being determined by circumstances. So each scene might demonstrate a rather different character, depending on the situation. He also wanted actors to distance themselves from the character they were playing, so that they could, as necessary, stand outside the part and comment on it, for example through song. (Brecht still used many of Stanislavski's techniques during early rehearsals, as some identification with the character was necessary, to be able to become distanced from it later.)

### Artaud and character

Antonin Artaud (1896–1948) also thought that the portrayal of complex characters with psychological depth was not a significant element of the kind of theatre that he desired to establish. His 'theatre of cruelty' demanded a style of playing in which the actor's voice and body were highly trained and flexible, but in which subtle character playing was out of place.

### Craig and character

Edward Gordon Craig (1872–1966) also felt that the actor was only one element in the language of theatre. In one essay he puts forward the idea that the actor should be an 'Uber-marionette' (that is, a kind of 'super puppet') rather than a complex and real human being.

The point here is that certain texts, and the study of particular practitioners, may involve you in considering alternative ways of approaching character. It is likely, however, that much of your work will be involved with an in-depth study of aspects of character in drama. The next two pages will help you with ways of achieving this.

For more information on Stanislavski, Brecht and Artaud, see pages 153–154. For more on sub-text, see page 46.

**Taking it further**

Find out more about the Method of Lee Strasberg, which was based upon some elements of Stanislavski's system and shares its concern with a detailed investigation of character.

▲ Artaud

# Characterisation and given circumstances

In building your characterisation, it is important to begin with 'the given circumstances'. This comes from the work of Stanislavski and is invaluable for actors, directors and designers. The given circumstances include all the facts given in the play, the background, geographical and time setting, the conditions of life, and the story of the play. Stanislavski also said that the director's interpretation, with the circumstances of the particular production (such as the design and the technical effects), should be included.

**Considering the given circumstances for your character**

In addition, you can look in more detail at some aspects which relate to your character. This can be done under four headings:

- What are the facts about my character?

- What does my character say about himself or herself?

- What do other characters say about my character?

- What does my character say about other characters?

Let's look at how you might apply this to the character of Blanche in the first scene of *A Streetcar Named Desire*.

| | |
|---|---|
| What are the facts about my character? | Daintily dressed, out of keeping with the setting. Has a 'delicate beauty'. Sister of Stella Kowalski and therefore sister-in-law of Stanley. A schoolteacher, from Laurel, Mississippi. Lived in a large house called Belle Reve ('beautiful dream') on a plantation there. Drinking a lot at the moment. Smokes. Very tense (shaking and panting). Shocked by the cramped conditions in which her sister is living. Her parents and other relatives ('Margaret and Cousin Jessie') are now dead. Was married when young to a boy who died. |
| What does my character say about herself? | Claims that she has not put on an ounce of weight in ten years. Says she has been given 'leave of absence' from her job because of her nerves. The job had a 'pitiful salary'. Says that she can't be alone. Says that she fought for Belle Reve, but that it is now 'lost'. |
| What do other characters say about my character? | 'I never had your energy' – Stella. 'It's just incredible how well you're looking' – Stella (wearily). |
| What does my character say about others? | 'I never had your beautiful self-control' – about Stella. 'You're all I've got in the world' – about Stella. |

Characters may not always tell the truth about themselves or others. Stella is merely being polite in saying how well Blanche is looking (she says it 'wearily' and later 'dutifully'). It's important to record the information, however, as it will be useful in interpreting your character's relationship with others.

## Activity 21

Working in pairs or a small group, take one of the minor characters in one of your plays and put together a chart like this for that character's given circumstances. (Remember that there are more general aspects of given circumstances which you won't be covering in this chart.)

## Characterisation and imagination

Once you have gathered all the information about your character that the text offers, you will still be left with gaps. For example, in the extract from *The Seagull* on page 49, Nina refers to how her father and stepmother don't wish her to visit Konstantin and his family, as they disapprove of their 'Bohemian' lifestyle. In the rest of the play we learn very little about Nina's parents, and they never appear on stage. If you were playing the part of Nina, however, you would need to have a very strong sense of who these characters are and what your life is like living with them. (Later in the play, Nina leaves home, tries to become an actress and has an illegitimate baby. Her father and stepmother reject her.)

As an actor playing Nina, you would need to **imagine** these characters, your home life and your relationship with your dead mother (who is mentioned by Nina in the play), because they are so important to the way your character behaves in the play. Your imagination must be based on the given circumstances in the text; however, there would be no point in imagining that Nina has a wicked uncle who beats her, for example, as this has no basis in the text and would distort the character and her motives.

### Practitioner note

Stanislavski encouraged his students to use imagination in this way – a creative and reflective activity, based on the text.

### Activity 22

When you have gathered all the information you can for the given circumstances of your chosen character, work in pairs or groups again to imagine what relevant parts of the character's life are like. Imagine off-stage characters or incidents in their past which help to develop your sense of characterisation.

## Creating objectives and units

Again, 'objective' is one of Stanislavski's terms. It's an invaluable tool in acting and thinking about character. An objective is what a character wants (see the earlier section on communicating with the audience, page 16). It needs to be positive, to lead to action and to be achievable (even if it is not actually achieved by the character). A character will have a 'through-objective' which lasts right through the play (with Nina it might be 'I want to be a successful actress').

There will be smaller and more immediate objectives (for example, 'I want to impress Trigorin with my acting'). There will be a number of these, one after the other, in the play. These are called 'units'. A character will never stop having an objective, which will lead to the achievement of the 'through-objective'. Having a clear understanding of what your character wants will help your awareness of the characterisation and enable you to give a focused performance.

### Tip

There are three main areas of characterisation to write about:
- **text**: what the text tells you about the character
- **production**: how you will play this character in a production (or how you think it should be played)
- **reception**: what the intended effect is on the audience – how you want it to be received.

### Activity 23

Take the character you have worked on in the two previous activities and, in the same pair or group, work out a series of objectives for an act or scene of the play. These should all begin 'I want…'. Then discuss what you think the character's through-objective is and try to put it in words.

# Social, historical, cultural and political context

It's important that you are clear about what is meant by social, historical, cultural and political context. An example from everyday life may help.

See page 91 of Unit 2 for more on these four areas of context.

**Social context**: who travels on buses? Is it a true cross-section of society? Does this vary with region and time of day? Who works on buses?

**Historical context**: what stage of development is public transport at historically? Have services declined in recent years? Have they increased? Has car ownership had a progressive impact on public transport use?

**Taking a bus journey**

**Cultural context**: how is the culture of the local area (or the nation) affected by the ability of individuals and groups to travel relatively cheaply and easily? Does travelling by bus make participation in various 'cultures' (sport, leisure, music, film, theatre) easier?

**Political context**: central government public transport policy – is public transport being subsidised? Local government policy – are there bus lanes to make the journey easier? Is there local subsidy for young/old/disabled people? Is it 'greener' to travel by bus than by other means?

The point is that everything we do is done in these contexts. The meaning of the word 'context' should have become clearer from this example. You could think of it as background or surrounding circumstances.

## Activity 24

Try placing the following activities in the four contexts:

a) buying a cup of coffee

b) going to a cinema.

Plays are no different; they exist in these four contexts. In studying your plays, you need to be aware of what these contexts were at the time the play was written, as this will affect your view of the text, the playwright's intentions, the situations in the play and the characters. In addition, a play's production may place it in other contexts which affect your view of it. Notable examples are 'updated' versions of Shakespeare's plays, such as the 1996 film version of *Romeo and Juliet*, directed by Baz Luhrmann and starring Leonardo DiCaprio and Claire Danes.

## Identifying contexts

From the example of a bus journey, you will see that not everything falls into neat divisions. A context which you may see as cultural will overlap with social. Political contexts may well be closely tied up with historical contexts; for example, the history of the supply of coffee to this country is closely linked to political power and influence. Are economic and religious issues political, social or cultural? They can, of course, be all three.

The important thing for you is to identify significant background contexts which are relevant to the texts which you are studying. This information will affect a director's, designer's and actor's view of the play and will have an influence on its production. It's important to know (as far as we can) how the original audience would have received the play – not so that we can copy it ('museum theatre'), but so that we can understand it better.

### Activity 25

Take one of the plays you are studying for Unit 1 and think about the four areas of context. Create a table like the one below and write in your initial thoughts. Remember that there will be overlap, but that it is more important to capture the ideas than to worry about the strictness of the categories.

| Context | Areas which seem important | Research needed (and possible sources) |
|---------|----------------------------|-----------------------------------------|
| Social | | |
| Historical | | |
| Cultural | | |
| Political | | |

### Types of historical contexts

Don't forget that part of the 'historical' context will be the original playing conditions – that is, the type of theatre, the actors, the audience, the production values, and so on.

Some plays are written to take place in their own time; the events of *Pygmalion*, for example, seem to take place in 1913 and the events of *Equus* in 1973. They are contemporary plays, dealing with issues that are relevant to that time (and which will remain relevant to later times). *Prayer Room*, first performed in 2006, deals with issues about religious intolerance immediately relevant to us.

Many plays, however, deal with historical events. These include a great many of Shakespeare's plays (*Richard II*, *Richard III* and *Henry IV*). *The Accrington Pals*, *Our Country's Good* and *The Crucible* are all based on historical events. Plays based on history, however, are not usually about history. They use history as material to create dramas which matter to us now, often because they reflect contemporary concerns and problems. (It may come as a surprise to learn that the real Macbeth was quite a good king, who ruled Scotland successfully for 17 years. Shakespeare knew this, but was creating something very different with the material at his disposal.)

### Tip

All of the following may be valuable resources for research: notes/introduction in your copy of the text, websites, history textbooks, newspaper archives, biographies, art/photography books, films/documentaries, journals/magazines, literature of the period, books on period costume, maps – and don't forget your teachers!

## *The Crucible* and the four context areas

Some plays can be seen as having a 'double' set of contexts: the contexts in the world of the play and the contexts at the time it was written. The following pages explore the example of *The Crucible*.

### Context as seen in the play (1692)

All the characters in *The Crucible* are taken from history, even though there are some significant changes made by Arthur Miller. He studied the original trial records in the museum at Salem, Massachusetts. Directors, designers and actors need to understand the contexts of 1692.

| | |
|---|---|
| **Social context** | Religion affects everything in this community. Society revolves around the church both as an idea and as a building. The only buildings where people can meet outside their own homes are the church and the tavern. The society is rule-governed; Reverend Hale asks Proctor to recite the ten commandments as evidence that he is a good member of society. It's a rural community, where people are isolated; it takes time for news to travel. However, it's also a small society, where people know each other's business. People also genuinely believe in witchcraft.<br>The broader social context is concerned with the rebuilding of a society by the Puritans after they had decided to leave England behind and establish a 'new world' where they could live according to their principles. Religion can be seen as the foundation of their social life. |
| **Historical context** | In 1692, the Royal Charter of the region had been withdrawn. This meant that the sense of security of being under the direct supervision and care of the King of England had gone. With this, all original entitlements to land had been cancelled, so the community was living in a great deal of suspicion and fear – suspicion that neighbours would steal their land and fear that their survival might be at risk. This context is clear in the play in the attitudes of Giles Corey and Thomas Putnam to land. |
| **Cultural context** | Again, the culture is largely defined by religion. There is no evidence of art or performance; the girls will be whipped soundly just for dancing, and even more soundly for dancing naked (a detail invented by Miller). There is a culture of hard work and even entrepreneurship; Thomas Putnam is keen to take advantage of the circumstances to expand his land ownership. These were people who had to fight for survival, using their skills and wits. However, there is evidently a counterculture of drunkenness, laziness and petty crime (Sarah Good, for example). Tituba also represents a counterculture; as the sole black character in the play, coming from Bermuda rather than from Europe as everyone else's family had, she is exploited by the young girls (who get her to 'summon spirits' by voodoo magic) and suspected by the adults. |
| **Political context** | Politics, as seen in the play, is local or regional and again largely defined by religion. The 'meeting' held at the church is the governing body and there seems to be an element of democracy in the way the society is run; votes are held on the way money is spent, for example. There is a clear legal system laid down, with Boston as its regional centre (Hathorne and Danforth, the Deputy Governors of the province, come from there). Politically, America is a young country, establishing its own systems. |

**Context at the time of writing (1953)**

It's well known that Arthur Miller used the story of the Salem witch trials as an allegory; we are intended to see the parallels with events of his own time. Audiences who saw the play's first production in 1953 would have 'received' or 'read' it in the context of their own time, so it would be important for you to know about that as well.

| Social context | Much of American society in the 1950s was deeply suspicious of Communism and feared it as a challenge to its way of life. More than invasion by Russia, the other world superpower, people feared 'the enemy within' – Communist sympathisers who would gain control secretly of important American institutions and change the 'free' and democratic society they knew. |
|---|---|
| Historical context | Senator Joe McCarthy headed a Senate Committee named the 'House Un-American Activities Committee' (HUAC). He saw its job as being to hunt down Communist or left-wing sympathisers and to root them out. Many public figures, including actors and film-directors, were brought before this committee (the proceedings were televised nationally) and asked if they were Communists and to name anyone they knew who was a Communist. If they refused to do so, they were presumed to be 'guilty'. The parallels with the Salem witch trials are clear. Although eventually discredited, McCarthy ensured that some actors and directors never worked in Hollywood again. |
| Cultural context | This links closely with the above box. Communism was seen (by many, not by all) as an evil, secretive force – effectively, like witchcraft, the work of the devil. Communism's rejection of organised religion confirmed this view for many, who also maintained the importance of protecting American culture against this evil force. |
| Political context | There is an international dimension to this: two alternative political systems, Communism and Capitalism, were in conflict in a period known as 'The Cold War'. Inside America, anyone with left-wing views might be identified as a 'red' or a 'commie' by those with right-wing views. This period is sometimes referred to as the 'Red Scare'. |

**Other contexts**

*The Crucible* has been seen all round the world in the last half-century, often by audiences who have no idea of the context in which it was seen in 1953. Arthur Miller points out that it has often been produced in countries just before, or just after revolutions, when it seems to strike significant chords. When it was produced in Communist China, it was seen as referring to the Cultural Revolution of the 1960s, in which the young Red Guards tortured, humiliated and killed those who had been previously in power over them – the power given to them corresponding to the power given to the previously powerless girls in the play.

## Activity 26

Take one of your Unit 1 texts. Decide whether it has a single or a double context. Make a list of questions about all the contextual information which it would be useful to find out in one, or both, contexts. Group the questions on your list under the four context headings: social, historical, cultural and political.

## Visual, aural and spatial elements

Visual, aural and spatial elements are important aspects of the 'language of theatre' which appeal particularly to the senses of sight and hearing.

**Visual**: everything the audience sees: this includes set, props, costume, makeup, masks, lighting and some special effects

**Aural**: everything the audience hears apart from dialogue: this includes sound effects (live and recorded), music (live and recorded), choral work, vocal sound, recorded dialogue and some special effects

**Spatial**: the use of space, including the acting and audience areas, the actor/audience relationship, proxemics, grouping, use of levels

Understanding of these elements is vital to directors and designers, and also to actors and reviewers. In your own practical work there are likely to be limitations on the extent to which you can explore complex settings, lighting states, sound effects, and so on. However, often very simple visual, aural and spatial effects can be strikingly effective on stage and you should try to explore the effects of these in your practical sessions. You will be able to observe and write about the effects of these elements in your evaluation (review) of a live theatre performance (see page 67). The remainder of this section consists of examples of the effective use of visual, aural and spatial elements.

## Visual elements: the set

### Activity 27

Compare this photograph of a set for *Translations* with Brian Friel's description at the beginning of the play given on the next page. How closely does the set follow Friel's description? What has been added or taken away? What is the overall effect achieved by the visual appearance of the set?

The hedge-school is held in a disused barn or hay-shed or byre. Along the back wall are the remains of five or six stalls – wooden posts and chains – where cows were once milked and bedded. A double door left, large enough to allow a cart to enter. A window right. A wooden stairway without a banister leads to the upstairs living quarters (off) of the schoolmaster and his son. Around the room are broken and forgotten implements: a cart-wheel, some lobster-pots, farming tools, a battle of hay, a churn etc. there are also the stools and bench-seats which the pupils use and a table and chair for the master. At the door a pail of water and a soiled towel. The room is comfortless and dusty and functional – there is no trace of a woman's hand.

## Visual elements: costume

In *Pygmalion*, when Eliza comes to live at Higgins' house, her clothes are so battered and dirty that they are burnt and she is given a bath and new clothes by Mrs Pearce, the housekeeper. Her father, Alfred Doolittle, turns up in pursuit of her – or, rather, he tries to get money out of Higgins for 'selling' her to him.

| HIGGINS | *(handing him a five-pound note)*: Here you are. |
|---|---|
| DOOLITTLE: | Thank you, Governor. Good morning. *(He hurries to the door, anxious to get away with his booty. When he opens it, he is confronted with a dainty and exquisitely clean young Japanese lady in a simple blue cotton kimono printed cunningly with small white jasmine blossom. Mrs Pearce is with her. He gets out of her way deferentially and apologises.)* Beg pardon, Miss. |
| THE JAPANESE LADY: | Garn! Dont you know your own daughter? |
| DOOLITTLE: | Bly me! Its Eliza! |
| HIGGINS: | Whats that? This! |
| PICKERING: | By Jove! |

*(DOOLITTLE, HIGGINS, PICKERING — exclaiming simultaneously)*

The effect of the costume (and, of course, the bath) transform Eliza so that she becomes unrecognisable, not only to Higgins and Pickering who were speaking to her a few minutes before, but also to her father.

### Activity 28

Consider how a costume (or a costume element, such as a hat or a scarf) would affect the impression given by any character in one of the plays you are studying for Unit 1. What would the effect be on the other characters in the scene, and on the audience?

## Visual elements: props

The kind of props which are used (along with costumes) can determine the style of a production and can have a powerful effect on the audience. When Konstantin brings on the dead seagull to lay at Nina's feet (see page 42), the appearance of the seagull will affect both Nina's and the audience's reaction. If it appears bloodied and partly shot away, our reaction will be different from if it appears undamaged and a perfect (although dead) example.

Some props acquire a symbolic value. For example, in *A Raisin in the Sun*, the plant's dogged survival in difficult conditions becomes linked in our minds with Mama herself. The plant is first mentioned in the play the first time that Mama appears and so is closely associated with her:

> She goes through the room, goes to the window, opens it, and brings a feeble little plant growing doggedly in a small pot on the window-sill. She feels the dirt and puts it back out.

It is no surprise that the last thing that Mama does in the play is to come back to 'rescue' the plant which has meant so much to her.

### Activity 29

Discuss in your group any prop which has an important presence on stage in one of your plays. Discuss precisely its appearance and what effect you wish it to have on stage.

## Visual elements: special effects

Special effects can range from very complex to fairly simple examples, such as the following effect from *Prayer Room* by Shan Khan; a concealed blood bag is punctured by the actor, and the effect on stage is startling.

> **BUNCE:**  Shit – look at that – I'm alright! *(Pointing to the gun)* S'that thing real?
>
> *A pool of red blood oozes across* BUNCE's *shirt – everyone notices.*

The following effect from *The Seagull* can be designed to impress the audience or to appear laughable. This is an important decision for the director and designer, as it affects how sympathetic we then feel to Konstantin when his mother's reaction to the effect makes him call a halt to the performance in which Nina is the sole actor.

> *Two red spots appear against the background of the lake*
>
> **NINA:**  Here comes my mighty adversary, the Devil, now. I see his fearful crimson eyes…
>
> **ARKADINA:**  There's a smell of sulphur. Is there supposed to be?
>
> **KONSTANTIN:**  Yes.
>
> **ARKADINA**  *(laughs)*: I see – it's an effect.
>
> **KONSTANTIN:**  Mama!

A more spectacular effect occurs in *A Streetcar Named Desire*:

> The night is filled with inhuman voices like cries in a jungle. The shadows and lurid reflections move sinuously as flames along the wall spaces. Through the back wall of the rooms, which have become transparent, can be seen the sidewalk. A prostitute has rolled a drunkard. He pursues her along the walk, overtakes her and there is a struggle. A policeman's whistle breaks it up. The figures disappear.

This is complex to achieve well, but the effect is to create a visual image of the nightmare that is in Blanche's mind. You may be able to think of more simple, but equally effective, ways of achieving this effect.

Many atmospheric and dramatic effects may be achieved by lighting quite simply; if you are able to, experiment with these in your practical sessions. Similarly, playing scenes with particular kinds of makeup, or with masks, can have marked effects and you should experiment with these as well.

## Aural elements: recorded effects and recorded music

The stage direction above from *A Streetcar Named Desire* shows how a sound collage can contribute to a sharp change of atmosphere. Every sound cue, whether 'atmospheric' or 'functional' needs to be carefully considered and to provide precisely the effect required in the production. For example, the 'clank of chains' heard from outside at the end of Act 2 of *The Crucible* when Elizabeth is arrested, must suggest both the right weight and the right distance from the house to be effective.

Music can be extremely powerful (as film producers have discovered). The effect of the music described here at the end of *Our Country's Good* as the convicts, after all their trials and tribulations, finally begin their performance, can bring tears to the audience's eyes:

> And to the triumphant music of Beethoven's Fifth Symphony and the sound of applause and laughter from the First Fleet audience, the first Australian performance of *The Recruiting Officer* begins.

Introductory and closing music can be particularly important in establishing atmosphere and in closing the performance. Experiment with the use of music to introduce the beginning and ending of the plays you are studying for Unit 1.

## Live effects and live music

Live effects need to be rehearsed carefully. Live music in musical productions such as *The Beggar's Opera* and *The Threepenny Opera* is generally much more effective than recorded music, and good musicians can vary their playing sensitively to reflect subtle changes in particular performances. Some effects are easier to create and time live; for example, when the footsteps of Higgins and Pickering are heard on the stairs at the beginning of Act 4 of *Pygmalion*, it may be more effective for the actors concerned to make these themselves (given the right steps and landing area off stage).

It's interesting to experiment with the cast making vocal effects live (see Vocal awareness on page 48) and some plays require this. For example, Peter Shaffer provides this note for *Equus*:

> References are made in the text to the Equus noise. I have in mind a choric effect, made by all the actors sitting round upstage, and composed of humming, thumping and stamping – though never of neighing or whinnying. This noise heralds or illustrates the presence of Equus the God.

## Activity 30

Experiment with providing live effects (vocal and made with objects) for an appropriate section of one of your texts. Even though you might decide that it is not appropriate for a production, it may have the effect of highlighting some aspect of the play for you.

## Spatial elements

The section on stage forms (pages 147–152) will give you ideas about how playing in different 'shapes' may affect your performance, as well as your relationship with the audience. This will also be affected by the size of both your playing space and the auditorium, however. This needs to be taken into account when considering the staging of scenes. It may well be possible to stage a version of *The Trojan Women* with a large chorus on a small in-the-round stage, but it may well present problems not present on a larger thrust stage, for example. The use of different levels on stage (by using stage boxes, for example) can create potentially 'strong' areas for performance and more interesting groupings on stage.

### Proxemics

This might appear to be a complicated term, but it's a simple idea. It is used to refer to the positioning of characters on stage and the distance between them. The 'blocking' of a production is very concerned with creating the right spaces between characters to express their relationship and feelings towards each other at particular points. It's interesting to experiment with this and almost any scene between a small number of characters will provide you with fruitful material. Try playing scenes over different distances (moving chairs further apart, or simply standing further away – and then coming very close to each other). See what effect this has on how your character plays the scene and how you feel as an actor.

### Examiner's tip

Remember that you can explore the use of sound effects to add meaning to a text. For example, an inappropriate sound or something surprising can be used to create comedy. This works well in a farce or in pantomime.

### Taking it further

For a very specific (and exciting) use of space, read the note on 'The Setting' at the beginning of *Equus*, and then see how it is used, particularly in Scene 21, at the end of Act 1.

### Taking it further

Two scenes to look at for this are: *The Beggar's Opera* Scene 13 and *The Threepennny Opera* Scene 6; in both Lucy and Polly compete for the imprisoned Macheath, who is also present in the scene.

### Key terms

blocking
proxemics

## Interpretation

### What does 'interpretation' mean?

An interpreter of foreign languages works between people, making what one is saying comprehensible to the other. The interpreter is conscious of the original speech or text, but is also conscious of how to construct a different version of it so that not just the literal meaning of the words, but also their spirit and intention are conveyed to the listener. Of course, the interpreter may put his or her own 'spin' on it, or even distort the original meaning completely.

Anyone interested in music is familiar with the idea of interpretation. Many modern songs exist in multiple, often very different, versions, covered by a range of different individuals and groups. To take one example: Leonard Cohen wrote and recorded *Hallelujah* in 1984. It has been recorded by at least 47 other artists and groups, including Jeff Buckley, Bono, Bob Dylan, k.d.lang, Street to Nowhere, Enrique Morento (a flamenco version in Spanish), and John Cale (in the film *Shrek*). Cohen himself recorded a very different version of the song on his 1994 album, *Cohen Live*. Apparently, the song as written by Cohen has 15 verses and he uses a different selection and combination of verses at different times when he sings it live.

Apply this to a drama text. In what ways can we discuss 'interpretation'?

| Are there selecting decisions to be made? |
| --- |
| There may be different versions of the text to choose from. |
| For example, *The Crucible* has a scene between Acts 2 and 3 which Miller inserted for the national tour after the play's initial Broadway run. It features a conversation in the woods between Abigail and Proctor the night before Elizabeth's appearance in court. There are three different printed versions of the first scene of *Our Country's Good*. How do we decide which version to choose? |

| Does the text need to be cut or adapted? |
| --- |
| Texts may need to be cut because the length seems excessive for the performance occasion. |
| Minor characters may be cut to suit the casting required by a particular company of actors. Whole scenes may disappear, or appear in a different order. It is rare to see the full 4.5 hours of *Hamlet*, for example. |

| Are there additions? |
| --- |
| Sometimes movement or mime sequences may be added before or during a performance; text may also be added. |
| One production of *The Crucible*, for example, showed a wordless scene of the girls practising their 'voodoo' rituals in the woods before starting the text of the play in Act 1. |

| What period or style will the visual elements reflect? |
| --- |
| The set, costume and prop design may reflect a period of time which is different from the original setting. |
| *Romeo and Juliet* may be transferred to 1990s America, for example, or *The Beggar's Opera* to the modern-day underworld of London (there may be difficulties in the text to overcome with any updating, however). |

| What will the style of acting be? |
|---|
| The style of acting may vary. For example, it may rely on the techniques of physical theatre, or the stillness and precision of Japanese Noh theatre. The interpretation of character will be important. |
| For example, could you imagine a Romeo who is played as self-centred and spoilt and just wants to get his own way? This may be unlikely, but he is a privileged and rich young man, with plenty of leisure time on his hands, so there may be elements of this in his character which could be emphasised in performance. |

## The director and interpretation

All this leads us back to the director, the central figure in today's theatre. When a director has decided on their interpretation, what do they do? For Unit 1, of course, you are not expected actually to take on the role of director, but in your group you will need to think about the kinds of choices which a director would have to make in interpreting the text. You should be able to explore the effects of different directorial decisions on interpretation in your practical sessions.

The first thing to realise is that you cannot be free of interpretation. Some production decisions may be more obvious than others. It may seem obvious to have Elizabethan costumes for *Romeo and Juliet* or late 19th-century costumes and furniture for *The Seagull*. These are certainly more conventional choices, but if you take them, you are already interpreting the production in a particular way. They become default choices, but they are choices all the same.

Respect for the text (and for the playwright's intentions) is a much debated issue. Is it the duty of a director to deliver, as closely as he or she can, a version of the play which the playwright would have approved of? Or is it the director's job to use the text as a way of presenting a specific audience on a specific occasion with a stimulating and entertaining experience which will have them buzzing as they leave the theatre? At one end of this you can see the danger that we get 'museum' theatre which leaves the audience cold; and at the other end we may get a self-indulgent piece of theatre which uses the text as an excuse to explore the preoccupations of an individual director.

There are no right answers here. We're in a fascinating area of human activity where 'interpretation' is a vital and negotiable area. Theatre reviewers will disagree about whether a director's interpretation is 'valid', 'justified', timely', 'relevant', 'idiosyncratic', 'inconsistent', 'poorly thought through' or a thousand other terms.

Look at the example of a recent production that follows and see what you think.

## The Podrozy *Macbeth*

Under the title *Macbeth: Who is That Bloodied Man?* and directed (in English) by the Polish director Pawel Szkotek for the group Biuro Podrozy, this production appeared for the first time in Britain at the Edinburgh Fringe Festival in 2007.

The venue was the large quadrangle of the 'Old College', part of Edinburgh University. The large gravelled central area is enclosed by 18th-century buildings, with stone staircases and balconies. Inside this was a square area closed off by metal barriers of the kind used to channel crowds at football matches.

Five wooden pillars, like tree trunks and about 3 metres tall, were placed at intervals in the centre. (It was an open-air production.) The audience were on three sides, standing throughout, with a huge metal structure forming the fourth side in the acting area. The production started at 10 p.m.

The performance opened with loud operatic music and singing from a female figure in black, who stood in among the audience just off one side of the acting area, but elevated high above them. Three figures in long black dresses appeared on stilts (between 4 and 5 metres high) and strode round the acting area, lighting candles at the top of the pillars with flaming torches. Shortly after, soldiers dressed in long leather coats and Nazi-style helmets appeared on old motorbikes (some with sidecars) and rode round, spraying the gravel as they did so. These eventually included Macbeth and Banquo.

The vertical structure made of metal sheets changed shape and purpose from time to time (with parts of it forming horizontal structures and ramps) so that it became both the inside and outside of Macbeth's castle. At one point Macbeth opened a large metal door to find the hanged figure of his wife inside it. At another point a maid hung out (for washing) the blood-soaked sheets in which Duncan had been murdered. Banquo and Fleance (on a motorbike) were pursued by the two murderers (also on motorbikes) in a prolonged chase scene around the acting area. A naked captive (possibly the previous Thane of Cawdor) was driven on, lying flat in a low metal cage attached to a motorbike.

The witches (in increased numbers) featured at several points in the play, always on stilts. A wordless scene between Fleance and Macbeth took place (after Banquo's murder) in which they played happily together.

At the end of the play Macbeth and his throne went up in flames inside his castle, with Fleance rescuing the crown from his head through the flames with a metal pole.

The production lasted an hour and used less than a tenth of Shakespeare's text, with much of what there was delivered in voiceover. Some lines (a poem) which were not by Shakespeare were also added at the end. The character of Macduff was cut completely and the role of Malcolm hardly featured.

▲ Biuro Podrozy performers, Edinburgh 2007

While it is impossible to judge a production fully without having seen it, try to answer the following questions on the basis of the description on page 64:

- Do you think this is a valid interpretation of Shakespeare's *Macbeth*?

- Do some of the visual effects (such as the witches on stilts) seem effective to you? Why?

- Can it be justified to cut so much of the text and still call it *Macbeth*?

- Would Shakespeare have approved? Does it matter?

## Writing about interpretation

The Podrozy *Macbeth* is an example of a radical directorial interpretation. Your own work and the productions you see may be less radical, but choices of interpretation will be necessary. You will be dealing with interpretation when you write your evaluation of a live production (see page 67), but you will also be concerned with levels of interpretation when exploring your texts practically and when writing your Exploration Notes.

You will be able to write about the following areas:

- the production as a whole: as with the Podrozy *Macbeth*, this will include all areas of production – any cutting of the text, visual, aural, style, etc. It is more likely that you will focus on these when writing your evaluation of a live performance

- particular scenes

- moments: there are often particular moments in performance which carry great dramatic weight; these frequently relate to decisions by characters

- characters and relationships.

**Tip**

You are required to evaluate the merits of both of your chosen texts and to **consider their worth in society today**. The ways in which texts are interpreted can often affect how audiences perceive them and how they relate them to their own lives.

### Activity 31

a) Choose a short scene or extract from one of the plays you are studying for Unit 1. Read it again closely and discuss what effect you think it should have on the audience. Perform it so as to achieve this effect. Then discuss how you could vary the scene to produce a different effect, for example make one of the characters appear less sympathetic or raise the 'emotional temperature' of the scene. Note the ways in which you tried to achieve this effect and the reactions of those watching.

b) Select a 'moment' (which may last several seconds, or even a minute) and see how you can interpret it in performance to convey different meanings to an audience. (For example, the moment in Act 4 of *The Crucible* where Proctor tears up his confession. Is it sudden and impulsive or a considered and measured decision?) Moments when characters exit are often worth looking at, as these often relate to decisions.

c) Select a scene from one of your texts which has a small number of characters – two or three, if possible. Explore the use of pace, timing and space to see how these can become reflections of your character's feelings and attitudes, and the ways these affect your relationship in the scene. Prepare two different versions and then play these for other students in your group. Listen closely to their reactions and make notes accordingly.

## Working with a practitioner

There are some individuals and groups who have had an enormous influence on the way drama has changed and developed. These 'practitioners' (that is, people who have 'practised' the art of theatre) have often built up their theories through a lifetime of experience of working in, and thinking about drama, and have made a unique contribution to theatre practice.

At least one of the plays you explore for this part of Unit 1 must be studied in the light of a recognised influential practitioner. This might be an individual such as Artaud, Boal, Brecht, Craig, Grotowski, Stanislavski, or a company such as Complicite, Kneehigh, DV8, Moscow Art Theatre. Your practical activities will vary according to your chosen practitioner, but you will have to learn about their theories through reading and research as well as by applying the ideas and techniques to your practical work. See pages 21, 40 and 50 for just a few ideas of how practitioners' theories and techniques might influence your work.

You will need to carry out your own research into whichever practitioner you are studying. You'll find references to other books and websites where you can find more information on some key practitioners on pages 153–155. If you are studying a practitioner or group not included in this book, your teacher will direct you to information sources.

Some general reference books that you will find useful are:

- *The Director and the Stage* by Edward Braun (Methuen, 1982)

- *History of the Theatre* by Oscar G. Brockett and Franklin J. Hildy (Allyn & Bacon, 2007)

- *Drama and Theatre Studies* by Sally Mackey and Simon Cooper (Nelson Thornes, 2000)

- *Fifty Key Theatre Directors* by Shomit Mitter and Maria Shevtsova (Routledge, 2005)

- *The Routledge Performance Practitioners* series, which includes books on Boal, Brook, Grotowski, Meyerhold, Stanislavski and Strasberg among others

- *Twentieth Century Actor Training* by Alison Hodge (Routledge, 1999)

It's not surprising that there's a huge range of ideas about theatre and acting expressed by a large number of practitioners. They have often worked with their own companies of actors in different areas of the world. Some, like Stanislavski and Strasberg, are very concerned with the processes which actors go through in preparing themselves. Some, like Brecht and Boal, are politically motivated and are interested in how the audience may be involved and affected. Some, like Craig, have views about the whole 'stage picture' and how all the production elements contribute to it.

The kind of activities which you become involved in will depend on which practitioner you study. You may explore ways of working on character, voice, movement, mime, staging, lights, sound, costume – or any of the elements which go to make up theatre. Your teacher will be your guide, but you will be able to undertake additional research for yourself.

# Evaluation of a live theatre performance

The requirements for this part of Unit 1 are outlined below:

'Evaluation': the following pages deal in detail with this, but as the word suggests, the idea of seeing the 'value' of a performance (its good and bad points) is a part of evaluation.

'Live theatre' means being in an audience watching live performers on stage (i.e. not film/video/DVD).

An 'informed audience member' is a person who goes to the theatre with a good knowledge of how theatre productions work, and of the play in question.

Your evaluation is worth 10% of the total of the available AS marks.

- Experience live theatre as an informed audience member.

- Write an evaluation of a live theatre performance; the maximum word limit is 1,000 words.

- In writing this, you must show that you have 'a working knowledge of production values and be able to make critical and evaluative judgements'.

'Production values': this is a term which originally comes from the film industry, where it refers to how much money has been spent and what it has been spent on. From this, especially in theatre, it comes to mean where the emphasis has been put in relation to cost (e.g. is the set complicated and huge, but the costumes cheap and ill-fitting?). From your point of view, it refers to all the aspects which contribute to the production and how these work together.

'Critical and evaluative judgements': these are informed opinions, based on knowledge and sensitive reactions to the performance; judgements will be balanced and considered, avoiding extremes.

'Working knowledge' means that you have knowledge that you can make practical use of (in this case, of how a theatre production works).

**Tip**

Although you only have to submit one evaluation for your teacher to assess, it is sensible to practise your skills before you have to undertake the 'real' evaluation. Watching a play on video/DVD can be a useful warm-up as you can stop the performance and discuss aspects of it, but it's also very valuable to watch several live performances.

Your evaluation will be similar to a theatre review in a newspaper or on television or radio but will involve more in-depth analysis. Most reviews in national newspapers (look in *The Guardian*, *The Independent*, *The Times*, *The Daily Telegraph* and *The Financial Times* for daily reviews, and in *The Observer*, *The Independent on Sunday* and *The Sunday Times* for reviews looking back (selectively) over the previous week) are shorter than 1,000 words – the average is more like 300 to 400 words – so you will deal with and analyse in detail more aspects of the performance you have seen (see pages 73–74 for the aspects you will be expected to cover). Looking at examples of reviews in the media will be helpful, but remember that your evaluation has to meet a specific set of criteria (see page 75). The next page looks at the functions of a review. The pages that follow show how you can approach your evaluation of live theatre.

## What are the functions of a review?

A review should perform the following functions:

1  to provide factual information about the production
2  to give the reader information about the nature of the production
3  to place the production in a context
4  to evaluate the production.

Below is a review of a performance by the senior theatre critic of *The Scotsman*, Joyce McMillan. The performance is *Macbeth: Who Is That Bloodied Man?* by the Polish group, Biuro Podrozy (see page 63). Read through the review and see how it fulfils the different functions. The text has been divided and  numbered to show how it meets each point above.

---

¹ [MACBETH: WHO IS THAT BLOODIED MAN?

\*\*\*

OLD COLLEGE QUAD (VENUE 192)

10 p.m. until August 27th]

² [Nothing much has changed, in the aesthetic style of the fabulous Polish group Biuro Podrozy, since they first astonished Edinburgh audiences a decade ago with their Carmen Funebre, inspired by their horror at the war in former Yugoslavia. It's still the same mind-blowing combination of fire, music and huge, sinister stilt-walkers looming from the darkness;] ⁴[and this year they bring it to bear on a brief 75-minute version of *Macbeth*,] ²[played out in the superb setting of Old College Quad, with its grand, looming walls of dark stone.

As versions of *Macbeth* go, this one often seems more confused than illuminating.] ²[There's a Banquo but no Macduff, a coronation scene but no banquet; and Macbeth dies not in battle – although there is a memorable evocation of a battle engine rattling with the skulls of his slain enemies – but by locking himself up in his fortress and setting it on fire, after discovering Lady Macbeth hanged by her own hand.

The text is largely reduced to the odd scrap of booming voiceover, and the First World War-style battlefield motorbikes used to transport the cast around splutter and skid on the deep gravel surface of the quadrangle.]

⁴[In the end, though, the show has two memorable assets. There's a fabulous score, sung live by a soprano perched high on a wind-blown ladder; and there is that visual imagery, mad, wild and beautiful. The sight of eight great stilt-walkers in single file suddenly emerging on to the stage, touched by an eerie blue light, and representing all the generations of kings descended from Banquo, is almost worth the ticket price in itself; and helps to confirm Teatr Biuro Podrozy's status as one of those inimitable companies whose work, once seen, is never to be forgotten.]

---

It's not always easy (nor necessary) to separate descriptive comments from evaluative comments; reviewers often combine them. For example, when the reviewer says: 'The text is largely reduced to the odd scrap of booming voiceover', the comment is clearly both descriptive and evaluative.

### Activity 1

Find a review from a local or national newspaper. Highlight the text with four separate colours, using the four categories above.

## Approaching the evaluation of live performance

There are four main stages in the evaluation of live performance:

1. preparing

2. attending the performance

3. reflecting

4. writing-up.

## Preparation

Think about the preparation stage in two sections:

- background (or long-term) preparation

- preparation for the specific performance.

### Background preparation

Everything you do on the course will be part of your preparation for this section. You will bring to it all your experience of performance, and your thoughts and ideas about plays and productions.

In your practical work, much of what you do is concentrated on creating some kind of performance from a text; other members of your group or your teacher (or sometimes an audience) will then judge your success. In other words, you are working on this model:

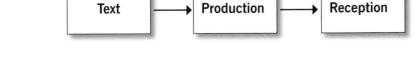

In your practical work, you are focusing on the production element, interpreting the text. The reception element is then up to other people, who may give you feedback on how successful you were in realising your intentions in performance. (Some of this reception may be obvious to you straight away. If, for example, you intended a piece of stage business to be really funny, but it falls flat in performance and no one even sniggers, you will be aware that your production has not been successful at that point.)

When you are evaluating a live production, you are looking through the other end of the telescope: you are the receiver and you are trying to evaluate the success of the production by looking at your own response to it and trying to see how it matches what was intended – and assessing the theatrical means by which the production team intended to achieve it, as they interpreted the text.

So the work which you have done creatively and practically will help to give you insights into the practical and creative work of the production team which you are now observing.

**Preparation for the specific performance**

You will not be going to this performance as an average member of the audience. Remember that you have to be an 'informed' audience member and that you need to be more aware and alert to what is going on in the performance, and be able to place it in a context. There are more ways in which you will need to prepare for going to the performance, however.

If the production which you are going to see is one of the two plays you are exploring practically and writing about in your Exploration Notes for this unit, then you will have been involved in a great deal of preparation already. If you are seeing a production of a different play, then you will need to have a reasonable knowledge of it, to have read and discussed it and to have thought about its possibilities in production terms. Even if you are seeing a completely new, unpublished play, there are still ways in which you can prepare.

The table below outlines some possible areas of research you can carry out on the play as preparation.

| Playwright | New or established? |
| --- | --- |
| | Previous plays? |
| | Is there relevant biographical information about him/her? |
| Genre of play | Is the genre identifiable? |
| | What do you know/can you find out about it? |
| | Do you know other plays of this genre? |
| Historical setting | When was it written? |
| | Is its setting contemporary with this (i.e. is it set at the time it was written)? |
| | What do you know about the period in which it is set? |
| Director/company | Are either of these well known? |
| | Are they known to have a particular approach or style? |
| | What has their previous work been? |
| | Are they influenced by any particular practitioner? |
| Venue | Is it an established venue? |
| | Does it have a reputation for a certain kind of theatre work? |
| | Have you been there before? |
| Publicity | What messages do you pick up from the posters/flyers/website/mailshots? |
| | How do text and image combine? |

## Activity 2

A useful way of preparing is to create your own production conference, although it will only work if everyone involved has a good knowledge of the text of the play. Follow the process explained below.

Every production has a production conference. This is an important event in which key decisions about the production are taken or confirmed. The key personnel are present and able to give their views in discussion about how the show will be presented.

In practice, the views of some of the key personnel will have more weight than others (for example, the director is likely to have most say); for the purposes of your production conference, however, everyone should have opinions which are listened to carefully.

Allocate roles: Director, Set Designer, Costume Designer, Props Designer, Makeup Designer, Lighting Designer, Sound Designer, Production Manager, Stage Manager.

With the Production Manager acting as the Chair of the meeting, discuss how you will approach the production, remaining in role and representing your particular area. A Lighting Designer, for example, may have views about the atmosphere of a particular scene and how it might be created.

Your agenda:

1. Why are we doing this production at this time? What do we want to 'say' to the audience members who come to see it?

2. What are the important themes we are dealing with?

3. Are there aspects which we want particularly to emphasise?

4. Visual, aural and spatial aspects: what do we want from the setting? Will it be realistic or abstract? Will we change the historical period? Why? Which stage form will be appropriate? What will be the contribution of costume, props and makeup? What effect do we want the sound to have (overall and at particular points)?

5. Practicalities: are there scenes/sequences which may create challenges for the stage management (for example, quick changes of set, difficult pieces of set construction, special effects)?

6. Summing-up: draw together your views about the production you have been planning.

**Tip**

Remain open-minded. You may have some brilliant ideas for a possible production of the play, but don't let them blind you to the alternative ideas which other members of the production team have come up with for their interpretation of the play.

Don't expect to agree! The point of the activity is to place yourself in the position of those who have been responsible for taking decisions about the production, so that you are more prepared to evaluate their choices. (Note that a real production conference wouldn't work like this, as a great deal of previous planning would already have been done.)

## Attending the performance

On the day of the performance, it is worth revising your preparation just before you go, so that you raise your awareness of the possibilities of the production. You will also find the advice below useful.

- Be aware of the whole experience; keep your brain active from the moment you enter the theatre.

- Get a programme (or get one to share if they're expensive). This will be your source of essential information about the cast, director, designer (you'll need their names) and possibly the playwright, the company and the director's view of the play. Some programmes (for example, those at The National Theatre) contain articles about the historical background or the theatrical context of the first production.

- Concentrate on the **experience**. Be sensitive to your reactions to the performance. Try not to make lots of notes during the performance – if you do this, you won't be watching and concentrating. As much as possible, make notes before, during the interval (if there is one) and immediately afterwards (see page 73).

- This isn't about box ticking. You need to be aware of all the elements which make up the performance (see below), but it's not a shopping list. You need to be aware of your reactions to how these elements are combined to create effects on you. Remember that you are working back from the effects to the interpretation of the creative team of the original text, looking at how this interpretation is being put into practice.

| What? | How? | Why? |
|---|---|---|
| What were the effects of the production decisions on you as a member of the audience? | How were these decisions put into practice in the performance (sometimes called 'the performance text')? | Why were the decisions about interpreting the (printed) text taken? |

**Making notes before the performance**

At the theatre, but before the performance begins, make some notes about:

- **the space**: the acting area, the audience area, the actor/audience relationship

- **the atmosphere**: pre-show sound and lighting; foyer displays relevant to the show

- **the set**: you may be able to see the set and its architectural features (doors, windows, etc.) as well as its furniture, use of colours, etc. before the performance begins. Lighting may be focusing on particular features to draw your attention to them

- **the programme**: you won't need to make actual notes about this, but you may want to make some mental notes about the information given in it.

## Making notes in the interval and after the performance

The following is a reminder list of all the aspects of performance to consider.
There are many other questions which could be asked; this list points to some
significant areas, but your own awareness will prompt other questions.

| Spatial | Acting area | Does this change during the performance? Are there uses of the height or depth, for example? |
|---|---|---|
| | Actor/audience relationship | Does this remain constant? Do actors use the audience space? |
| Visual | Set (this includes scenery) | Where would you place it on the 'realistic to non-realistic' scale? Is it a single set, allowing for the representation of different locations? Are the entrances/exits well placed? Is there a strong sense of period style? Are the colours strong, muted, etc.? Does the set seem to be making a statement about the play? Are there different sets for different acts? Does each setting make a statement? |
| | Costume | Apply the last four questions above to costume. Do costumes reflect the characters? Are some characters made to stand out, for example by the use of colour or style? If characters have more than one costume, is there some evident progression being marked by the changes? |
| | Props | Do these blend in with the set, giving a consistent visual impression? Are there particularly significant props and are these effectively designed and used? |
| | Lighting | Is the performance generally brightly or dimly lit? How does this vary from scene to scene? Is it effective in contributing to the atmosphere of particular scenes/moments? Is use made of particular colours/angles? Are there special lighting effects? |
| Aural | Recorded sound | Is background sound used? Does it affect the atmosphere? Are 'functional' sound effects (e.g. cars arriving) effective? |
| | Recorded music | What kind of music is used? Is it well chosen and effective? Does it create a sense of period or atmosphere? Does it add to particular sequences or moments? What kind of music is used in the interval (if any)? |
| | Live sound | Are any live sounds (doors slamming, footsteps, etc.) effective? Does the cast contribute vocally in any way to live sound? |

| Special effects | Pyrotechnics, smoke, etc. | If these are used, are they effective in creating atmosphere or moments of shock etc.? |
|---|---|---|
| Stage management | Scene changes | Are these effectively managed?<br>Are they consistent with the style of the production (e.g. done by the cast or stagehands in costume) or are they functional (stagehands in black)?<br>Do they seem to hold up the performance? |
| Acting | Interpretation | How does the actor's interpretation differ from your impressions from the text, if you have had the opportunity to read it beforehand?<br>Is there an overall acting style (this will affect the areas below)? |
| | Voice | What use is made of range, volume, etc. at different points? Do the voices suit the characters? Are accents used (and appropriate)?<br>Is the projection good enough? |
| | Movement | How do actors register their characters through movement and use of space? |
| | Relationships/interaction | Are these as you saw them from the text? Are there moments in which relationships are defined or changed? |
| Direction | This takes in all aspects of the performance | Are there sequences or moments when you are aware that the visual, aural and spatial elements (as well as the acting) have been arranged to create particular effects?<br>How significant are these sequences/moments in the overall effect of the performance? (Endings are especially important as they leave a final impression on the audience.)<br>Are you aware of pace and rhythm in the performance? |
| Audience | Audience reaction | You will be able to tell by laughter, applause, etc. how the audience in general is receiving the performance. |

## Writing up your evaluation

Let's look at some vocabulary first. A number of terms are fairly loosely used in general conversation and are usually clearly understood, but you should try to use them more precisely.

| Play | Generally used to mean the text (printed or not) which was created by the playwright (or company). |
|---|---|
| Text (or written text) | More specifically, the words on the page; with many plays, especially older ones, there may be different versions of the text. |
| Performance text | This is used to describe everything which happens in a particular performance (as distinct from a written text). It reflects a recent move towards 'performance study', separate from a study of the playwright's written text. |

| Production | A production may run for many performances (and occasionally, like *Les Misérables*, *Cats*, *Blood Brothers* or *The Mousetrap* in the West End, for thousands of performances). Essentially the features of the production, as conceived by the director and designers, will remain unchanged, even though actors may come and go. |
|---|---|
| Performance | A single occasion on which a specific audience meets in a specific venue to watch a specific cast perform. |
| Show | This vague term is used very generally to mean a play, musical, dance performance, revue, etc. and refers to both production and performance, as in 'Shall we see a show when we're in London?' It is also used more specifically to refer to a performance as in 'pre-show reception' or 'post-show discussion'. |

You will be writing about your experience of the **performance**, dealing with features of the **production** (or **performance text**), and relating them back to the **text**.

**Assessment requirements**

This table shows the criteria which your teacher will use to assess your work.

| Level of response | Mark range |
|---|---|
| Student's evaluation of a live theatre performance is outstanding. They are fully aware of a wide range of production values and are able to analyse the effect this may have on an audience. Supporting examples are detailed and reported with almost faultless accuracy. | 13-15 |
| Student's evaluation of a live theatre performance is excellent. Production values are clearly understood and their significance is both analysed and evaluated. Detailed examples are relevant and accurate. | 10-12 |
| Student's evaluation of a live theatre performance is good. They understand how production values contribute to the performance overall and are able to evaluate what they've seen with clear, detailed examples. | 7-9 |
| Student's evaluation of a live theatre performance is adequate. They are able to distinguish between the play and the production and comment on some aspects of what they've seen, making simple evaluative comments. | 4-6 |
| Student's evaluation of a live theatre performance is limited. They may have focused on the play rather than the production. It will be heavily reported with little, or no evaluation. | 0-3 |

> Your live performance evaluation is assessed against Assessment objective 4. See page 4 for more on this.

Notice these **key words and phrases**:

- production values

- analyse the effect

- evaluate detailed examples.

Remember to deal with **what** has been done, **why** it has been done and **how** effectively it has been done. You need to use details from the performance to prove your points. Your close observation of these details and your analysis and evaluation of them will gain you marks.

**Sample evaluations**

The following extracts from evaluations all deal with a performance of
*Macbeth*. There are two points being dealt with here: the lighting and the
style of acting. (Obviously there would be more to say about both areas when
considering the whole production.)

## Activity 3

Read each extract carefully and then do the following:

a) Place them in an order of merit from bottom to top, using the
assessment criteria on page 75 to help you judge what their strengths and
weaknesses are.

b) For each extract say what you think is good about it (or what contributes
to making it an effective piece of evaluation).

Compare your comments with those on page 79.

**A**

In all the scenes which were set outside the King's palace, the acting was naturalistic
in style, with characters such as Banquo and Fleance or Malcolm and Macduff
clearly having created a depth of character and pursuing obvious objectives. The
naturalistic style of lighting in these scenes reflected time of day and location.
These scenes contrasted with all the scenes set in the court of Macbeth, which
made use of harsh white, non-naturalistic lighting and the style of acting became
larger than life. When Macbeth delivered the 'Tomorrow and tomorrow and
tomorrow…' soliloquy in a crucified position leaning against the upstage wall, the
effect was symbolic of his state of mind and obviously not naturalistic.

**B**

The lights were very bright all the way through the scenes at the King's palace.
The lights for scenes set in other places were not as bright. In some scenes the
actors seemed to become larger and louder, so that I couldn't believe in them. In
other scenes they seemed to be acting normally.

**C**

The hard-edged and bright white lighting and the exaggerated style of acting
(with its uncomfortable loud vocal projection and expansive gestures) seemed
intended to produce the effect of a larger-than-life world in the King's court.
When the action moved to other locations, both the lighting and the acting style
became more naturalistic. The lighting made greater use of a range of colours
appropriate to the time of day and the actors' gestures and voices became more
acceptable as part of recognisable life.

**D**

In the scenes set in the King's palace the lighting was very harsh and white. It was
also evenly spread across the stage, so that no areas were highlighted.

**E**

> The bright, harsh and evenly spread lighting linked with the larger-than-life style of acting. The expansive gestures of the actors and the general level of projection (which was more forceful than needed in the space) both created an impression of an exaggerated world on stage.

**F**

> The style of acting varied from scene to scene. It was as though the director wanted us to feel that life outside the King's Court was more real, while life inside the Court was artificial. It would be a strain to live in a place where the lights were always so bright and people were always talking loudly and waving their arms about. This contrast in style was reflected in some of the details added by the director to the action. In the scene in which Banquo is murdered, just before the appearance of the Murderers, he kneels down and tucks the toy wooden sword which Fleance has been playing with into the boy's belt. Later, when Macbeth is given his sword by Seyton (when he is being prepared for the final battle) it is a similar shape to Fleance's, but too big for Macbeth, making him look inadequate.

## Structuring your evaluation

Gathering materials: what can you use to create your evaluation?

- preparation notes
- the text of the play
- the programme
- reviews (better not to look at these until you've arrived at your own views)
- your notes made before, during and after the performance
- discussions with others who saw the production.

Be careful about discussing ideas with others: while it can be valuable to share your memories and reactions to what you observed, you need to hold on to your own impressions.

You need to read through all your materials and then think about organising them. You are likely to have to draft and redraft before you feel satisfied with your evaluation. A simple structure is best, for example:

> **Examiner's tip**
>
> Remember that you have a maximum of 1,000 words for your evaluation. Anything you write over this limit will not be marked. Planning is important.

| Introduction | Very brief details of the production you saw: what, when, where, who (i.e. main cast, director, designer). |
|---|---|
| Overview | Brief account of your main impressions (e.g. how what you saw differed from your expectations). |
| Main points | A paragraph for each, making sure that you include **details from the production** ('production values') and that you **analyse the effects of these details** and that you **evaluate them**. Focus on some **key moments** in the production. **Make links** between aspects of the production wherever possible (e.g. how the visual aspects relate to the performances of the actors). The number of paragraphs will vary, but four or five will probably be enough. Remember that you can also use diagrams and illustrations. |
| Final summing-up | Keep this fairly brief and don't just repeat previous information. You might, for example, focus on one key moment which (for you) summed up the whole approach to the production. |

## Main points

You will earn most of your marks from this section of your evaluation because it's the longest and gives you most chance to fulfil the criteria. How do you decide on your main points? These need to be points which enable you to include a number of relevant details and to link aspects of the production. For example, it's unlikely that you would want to devote a whole 'main point' to the sound effects, unless they were exceptionally influential on the production. Look back to the headings suggested for your notes (pages 73–74) to check the areas which you should be covering.

Your choice of main points will be decided by your own main impressions, so it is impossible to give a template or definitive list of what they should be. However, they might include the following:

- the play's central relationship(s)
- interpretation of central roles
- the handling of a main theme
- the effect of the ways in which the visual elements combine
- the acting style
- specific major choices by the director (e.g. cutting/reordering the text, updating the period)
- the effect of staging decisions (e.g. playing in-the-round or traverse)
- actor/audience relationship (e.g. were you made to feel personally involved?).

### Activity 4

Remember that you're dealing with what?, how?, why? and how well? as questions. Look at the **main point** paragraph below and look for relevant supporting details, analysis and evaluation. The paragraph is evaluating a production of *The Crucible*. It's about 200 words long.

---

The production was staged in the round, in a small theatre (about 150 in the audience). The effect was that we were very close to the actors and felt closely involved in the action. In Act 4, when Proctor and Elizabeth meet in prison both had visibly aged and their costumes were dirty and torn. Being so close, we could see that their chains had left marks and scabs on their legs. Both the makeup and the costume were effective in creating the great sympathy I felt for them in their situation. Both remained upright and held their heads high, however, so the director seemed to want us to realise that they still had their dignity. Although the stage form allowed us to observe the effect of details like this, it created some blocking problems in Act 3 (the trial scene) when the number of characters on stage meant that important moments in the production were sometimes masked from parts of the audience. The lack of large scenery and the use of simple period props and furniture to establish locations meant that the production moved swiftly. A bed and a table effectively created Betty's bedroom in Act 1, with the effect of a window created by the lighting. On balance, the choice of the stage form worked well.

Notice that the paragraph sticks to the main point of the director's choice to stage the play in-the-round. Examples are given of where this worked both well and badly in the play – so the details are well observed and link to the main point of the paragraph. There is some analysis of the effect of the makeup, costume set and lighting. There is a clear evaluation of the overall effect of the director's choice.

## Comments on extracts on pages 76–77

**A** This shows evidence of good observation and makes links between the lighting and acting styles. The writer shows an understanding of the terms 'objectives' and 'naturalism'. A good supporting detail from the production is used. Although the writer is aware of the contrasts of style in the production, no conclusion is drawn about the director's reason for creating the contrast.

**B** This extract contains basic observations about the lighting and acting styles. The writer makes no links between them and draws no conclusions about why the contrasts have been created.

**C** This is 'tightly' written (the words are used effectively to pack in the information). The observations are clear and detailed (for example, the reference to lighting colours). The writer is aware that an intentional effect is being produced, but does not take the next step of drawing a conclusion about why the director created the effect.

**D** This is a basic observation about one aspect of the production, containing some useful detail ('evenly spread'). However, there is no comment on the purpose of the effect and no link is made with any other aspect of the production.

**E** This contains good observations and is quite 'tightly' written. The writer links the lighting and the acting styles, but doesn't comment on the contrast with other scenes in the production – nor draw any conclusions about the purpose of the effects.

**F** This links the points about the lighting and acting styles. There is a genuine insight into what the director's purpose was, even though there is some vagueness (for example, 'waving their arms about'). But there is also very good detailed observation, linking the details to the director's purpose.

**Tip**

The more practice you get, the better you will be at writing evaluations. See and discuss as many live productions as you can, practise making notes and writing them up into main points, and read the reviews of professional theatre critics.

# Unit 2: Theatre Text in Performance

## Assessment objectives

Half of the marks for Unit 2 are available for Assessment objective 1 and the other half for Assessment objective 3. See page 4.

## What you need to know

Unit 2: Theatre Text in Performance

- is worth 60% of your AS mark (30% of the total A level marks)
- is divided into two sections, A and B, which are equally weighted
- is externally assessed by a visiting examiner.

## What you have to do

You will already have had the opportunity to explore at least one of your two plays for Unit 1 and will have been introduced to ways of understanding and interpreting a theatre text. In Unit 2 you are going to use and develop the skills and methods you have learnt and apply them to a further two play texts that you will bring to life as a performer or designer.

- In **Section A** you are required to work on an individual skill either as a performer presenting a monologue or a duologue or as a designer offering a design skill in support of a performer.

- In **Section B** you are required to work as part of a group on a play in performance. You take on an acting or a design role in the performance of a published play. You are part of a group of between three and nine performers and perform in a play lasting between 15 and 60 minutes.

You can choose to be either a performer or a designer in each section: you do not have to offer the same skill in both Section A and Section B.

Your choice between acting or design skills will depend on your own strengths and which skills are taught in your school or college.

## How are you assessed?

For both sections your work will be presented to an appropriate audience and assessed by a visiting examiner.

In Section A, performers are assessed on vocal skills, movement skills and characterisation in performance, and on a written performance concept (maximum 500 words). Designers are assessed on their use of materials and equipment, the realisation of the design, the written design concept and the design documentation.

In Section B, performers are assessed on vocal skills, movement skills, characterisation and communication. Designers are assessed on their use of materials and equipment, the realisation of the design, the written design concept (maximum 500 words) and their interpretation of the director's concept.

## Unit 2: At-a-glance summary

| Section A | monologue/duologue/design skill | 50% of Unit 2 |
| Section B | contribution as performer or designer to group performance of a published play | 50% of Unit 2 |

# SECTION A

In Section A, you have the choice between being **either** a performer **or** a designer.

## What do you have to do if you choose to be a performer?

You have the further choice of **either** solo acting (on your own) **or** duo acting (in a pair with another actor).

- If you are a solo actor, you have to perform a **monologue** (a speech given by one actor) lasting no more than **two minutes**.

- If you act as part of a duo, you have to perform a **duologue** (a dialogue between two actors) lasting no more than **five minutes**.

You also have to write a **written performance concep**t of no more than 500 words that demonstrates your understanding of the role you have rehearsed.

More guidance on being a performer in Section A is given on pages 85–116.

More guidance on being a performer in Section A is given on pages 85–116.

> **Key terms**
>
> monologue
> duologue

## What do you have to do if you choose to be a designer?

You choose **one** of the following design skills:

- costume

- lighting

- mask

- makeup

- sound

- set and props.

Using the one design skill that you have selected, you will work with either one performer doing a monologue or two performers doing a duologue. You have to:

- produce a **design concept** for the whole of the play you have chosen

- realise the design for the section of the play shown to the examiner by the performer(s)

- produce documentation that shows how the chosen skill would work in the complete text

- prepare a ten minute presentation to the examiner

- produce a **written design concept** of no more than 500 words that justifies the approach you have taken as a designer.

More guidance on being a designer in Section A is given on pages 117–133.

More guidance on being a designer in Section A is given on pages 117–133.

Whether you choose to perform or design, the advice on planning on the next three pages will be useful to you.

## Planning your work for Section A

Planning your time for Unit 2 is of the utmost importance. To do well you need to make sure that you make good use of the time available to you.

The examinations for Unit 2 take place between February and June on a specific date arranged by your teacher with the visiting examiner; you will need to check with your teacher whether you will be examined on both Section A and Section B on the same day. Once an examination date has been fixed, it cannot be changed unless there are exceptional circumstances: think of the examination date as a performance date with the theatre booked and an audience having bought tickets – cancelling or altering the performance date is virtually out of the question.

In Section B, your teacher will be the director and will be responsible for organising rehearsals and setting and negotiating tasks. You will have to organise your time effectively in between rehearsals but the rehearsal process itself will be mapped out by your teacher/director.

In Section A, however, you are responsible for planning your own time. Your teacher may hold initial workshops with the whole class to provide you with ways of working and to give you advice and guidance about your choice of text. Once the work is underway, though, you will be working on your own (or with a partner some of the time if you perform a duologue or work as a designer with performer(s)). Your teacher will want to arrange progress reviews or tutorials with you while you are working on Section A, and will expect to see your work thus far and your plans for carrying it forward in order to make the examination deadline.

## Working backwards

The only effective way of planning your time is to work backwards from the examination (performance) date to the date that you are able to begin work on Section A. How long you should spend on this part of the examination will depend on a number of variables:

- the complexities of the chosen play either in terms of the acting role(s) or the design requirements

- the speed at which you work and are able to pace yourself

- your attention and concentration span: are you better at working in short bursts over several weeks or in large chunks of time in a shorter period of weeks?

- your own workload in relation to other subjects you are studying.

## Planning guide for Section A

What follows is a planning model based on a guide of 20 weeks, although this can be adapted to fit fewer or more weeks as required. Some of this time will be guidance from your teacher but the majority of it will be your own personal study and work. The important thing is that the activities and the proportion of time allocated to them should help inform your own project planning.

Week 0 is the week of the examination. More time is allocated towards the end of the process than at the beginning. However, you may want to complete the Section A work earlier to concentrate on Section B for the last two weeks, in which case you can reallocate the time to earlier weeks. The model assumes that you have already made your choice between performance and design, and between a solo or duo piece (for performers) or the different design skills.

| Week | Performers | Designers |
|------|-----------|-----------|
| 20 | Selecting and reading possible plays. | |
| 19 | Selecting and reading possible plays – making shortlist. | |
| 18 | Final selection of play and choice of monologue/ duologue – initial notes on given circumstances. | Final selection of play – initial notes on design requirements and ideas. Working with performer(s) |
| 17 | Reading and analysis of the play in terms of character's relationship to the whole and notes on contexts. Identifying questions for further exploration and research. | Reading and analysis of the play in terms of particular design requirements and identifying questions and areas for further exploration and research. |
| 16 | Contextual research. | |
| 15 | Contextual research. | |
| 14 | Experimenting with the character. Off-the-text work. Primary research (e.g. observation). | Produce initial sketches and a range of ideas based on the text and research findings. |
| 13 | Analysing the selected extract. Exploring vocal and physical techniques on the text. | Refine and select most appropriate ideas and produce a rationale for them. |
| 11–12 | Exploring and experimenting with the character within the extract. Using 'what if…' and other imagination techniques to bring the character to life. | Work designs up into workable plans and identify materials, equipment and construction/making techniques as appropriate within budget. |
| 10 | Learn lines and consolidate ideas so far. | Produce final drawings and plans and acquire necessary resources. Share ideas with performers. |
| 5–9 | Series of character building and technique development rehearsals. Identifying an objective for each rehearsal and keeping reflective notes on each. Introducing items of costume and props. Exploring different ways of using the space. Video recording your performance and analysing its strengths and weaknesses. Showing your work to your teacher and peers for feedback. | **Set/props**: model making process. **Masks**: mask making process. **Costumes**: costume making/sourcing/adaptation process. **Makeup**: trial makeup designs on models and make photographic recordings. **Sound**: recording, mixing, editing sound tape. **Lighting**: produce detailed scaled drawings (3D and 2D) of lighting design and rigging instructions. |
| 4 | Responding to feedback, refining and adjusting performance as appropriate and re-rehearsing it. | Presenting work to teacher and performer(s) for feedback. |
| 3 | Revisit contextual research and draft notes in preparation for your written performance concept. Continue to rehearse and explore performance. | Complete portfolio of ideas and sketches and select samples for final presentation. Continue with making process. |

| Week | Performers | Designers |
|------|-----------|-----------|
| 2 | Completion of written performance concept and submission to the examiner. Refine and reformulate performance ideas. Show rehearsed performance to teacher/peers for further feedback. Make sure each run-through is timed with a stopwatch to check the running time is within 90 to 150 seconds (for a monologue) or 270 to 330 seconds (for a duologue). | Completion of written design concept and submission to the examiner. **Costume**, **makeup** and **masks** should be at a stage where you are working with the performer(s) and showing the work under stage conditions for feedback.<br><br>**Lighting** and **sound** designers will need to rig or instruct technicians on the rigging of the lighting design and run technical rehearsals with performers.<br><br>**Set** designers will be finishing the set model and constructing – or instructing a construction crew to make – props/scenery for the performed extract. |
| 1 | Final performance preparation, including technical and dress rehearsals. | Final preparation for design presentation, including practice 'run-throughs'. Working with the performer(s). |
| 0 | Performance examination. | Presentation to the examiner. |

# BEING A PERFORMER IN UNIT 2 SECTION A

Whatever experience of acting you have already had, Unit 2 provides an opportunity to extend your abilities as an actor within the context of interpreting and presenting a character from a published play text.

In Section A the spotlight is very much on you as an individual. You will be acting to an examiner (and there may be additional audience members) with only yourself or one other person on stage. You are required to learn lines from a play and to make decisions about how to play a character based on the instructions and clues in the play. You will also have to research beyond the text to find out about things that relate to the play and to the character you are playing.

You will need to prepare yourself mentally and physically: acting is a complex skill that needs to be developed and perfected both from the inside (your thinking, your understanding, your feelings, your imagination) and from the outside (the way you use your voice and your body, the way you sound and the way you look, the way you react to other people and how they respond to you).

See pages 117–133 for advice on being a designer in Section A.

See the 'Developing drama skills' section on pages 6–16 for advice and activities that will help you develop your acting skills.

## Assessment requirements

You will be assessed as a performer on four areas, each of which carries a maximum of ten marks. Three of the areas assess your performance skills, and the final area of assessment is your written performance concept. These assessment criteria are the same whether you are performing a monologue or duologue. The grid below shows what is required for the **top mark band** in each area.

Your vocal and movement skills are assessed against Assessment objective 1: Demonstrate the application of performance and/or production skills through the realisation of drama and theatre. Your characterisation and written performance concept are assessed against Assessment objective 3: Interpret plays from different periods and genres.

| AO1 Vocal skills | An outstanding command of vocal skills is demonstrated, including clarity and use of pause, pace, pitch, tone, inflection and projection throughout the performance. |
| --- | --- |
| AO1 Movement skills | Student shows an outstanding ability to embody character and the ability to use gesture, poise and stillness with control and sensitivity. |
| AO3 Characterisation | There is outstanding understanding of the role and its context within the play. Characterisation is complete, consistent and fully committed to the style and context. |
| AO3 Written performance concept | The rationale shows an outstanding response to the chosen play in relation to its social, historical, cultural and political context. There is a comprehensive account of both the preparation process and the intended interpretation. |

## Selecting the play for Section A (performers)

The first decision you need to make as a performer is whether to work on a **monologue** or **duologue**. The considerations below can help your decision. It is important to discuss these issues with your teacher to ensure that you are playing to your strengths.

|  | Monologue | Duologue |
|---|---|---|
| Do you want to perform a monologue or a duologue? | When performing a solo piece you need to feel confident about taking the stage on your own. The audience's attention is entirely on you and any interaction is between you and them or with other characters on stage that are imaginary. | When performing a duologue you pair up with another performer in a piece requiring two actors. There is interaction with another character as well as the audience so you'll need to ensure that you work well with another actor. |
| What kinds of monologue or duologue might suit your talent and skills? | Do you want to perform a piece from a play specifically written as a monologue, such as *Shirley Valentine* by Willy Russell or *Via Dolorosa* by David Hare, or a significant speech by a character in a play? | Do you want to perform a piece from a play that is written as a two-hander, such as *Oleanna* by David Mamet or a scene written between two characters that can be identified within a whole play? |

Once you have made the decision to perform in **either** a monologue **or** in a duologue, work through the following suggested stages in the process of selecting suitable performance material.

## Where do you start?

Your time is valuable and you want to use it to work on the text rather than reading through play after play to find one that will suit you. Initial ideas of what you are looking for might come from:

- someone who knows you and knows about plays (principally this will be your teacher) and might be able to suggest plays that will suit you (or you and your partner for a duologue)

- your previous experience of studying plays and going to the theatre: you may already have discovered a playwright whose work you admire or a play you have really enjoyed which could form a basis for your search.

Write down a list of titles and playwrights' names from the process above, to help narrow the field in your search and track down copies of the plays.

## Create a shortlist

From these ideas, start building a shortlist of your top ten extracts (some might be from the same play). Be aware that you are unlikely to find a piece that is going to be right for you in every respect, so be prepared to make some compromises. Try your short-listed monologues or duologues out in a workshop session with the rest of the group, and ask for feedback from your teacher and from your peers. This will help you find out if more than one person or pair wants to do something from the same play. You may also spot something someone else has found that you prefer, and can use, if they drop it from their choice. It is a good idea to keep one piece in reserve in case your first choice does not work out.

## Ancient or modern?

A deciding factor for your choice of play might be when it was written. For example:

- Anything written before the 19th century will contain language which might initially sound unfamiliar to you, but you might enjoy the challenge of working on a speech from Shakespeare, for example.

- Classical Greek and Roman plays, although ancient, will be found in modern translations and are a very useful source for monologues in particular.

- If you have a specific interest in contemporary drama, you might decide to look only at plays and playwrights from the last ten years or so.

## The subject matters

When making your final selection, bear in mind that if you can relate to the subject matter and the characters, you are more likely to engage with the work enthusiastically. The story of the play and the way it is told should be something that interests you and, in the case of a duologue, your partner. If the answers to the following two questions are not positive, you probably have not got the right sort of material for you:

- What is the play about and am I interested in it?

- What type (or genre) of play is it and do I like that sort of play?

## Age, gender, appearance and accent

| How old should my character be? | Playing a character up to five years younger or older than yourself will help to maintain the credibility of your acting, particularly if the play is realistic or naturalistic. Playing a character significantly older than yourself presents a challenge but can be successful depending on the play. For example, Chekhov's *A Cherry Orchard* is usually played in a naturalistic style, and an 18-year-old cast in the role of a 70-year-old servant is unlikely to be convincing, whereas such an age discrepancy in a Brecht play can be effective in emphasising a more non-naturalistic style of acting. |
|---|---|

**Examiner's tip**

Remember that if a play is well known or famous, it may have been used many times for examination purposes so it is worth considering less familiar material. For example, rather than selecting a speech from Shakespeare's *Hamlet*, you might consider a play from the same period that is not as well known, such as Middleton and Rowley's *The Changeling*.

**Tip**

If you prefer to act characters who are deeply affected by something and demand an emotional range, you may be guided towards naturalistic drama, e.g. Chekhov, Ibsen, Strindberg. If you enjoy physical theatre, you could look at plays by, for example, Berkoff, Gogol, Jarry and Godber. If you are good at comedy, your choices range from the subtleties of Ayckbourn to the broad strokes of Dario Fo.

| | |
|---|---|
| Do I need to have the physical characteristics of the character? | You need to consider your own physical appearance, and the extent to which it can be altered to match the physical qualities of the character that you're thinking about playing.<br><br>You may be able to alter the size and shape of your nose using prosthetics, for example. However, if you are physically short and the script makes continual reference to how tall your character is, such a role may put you at an unnecessary disadvantage. See the descriptions of Helena and Hermia in Shakespeare's *A Midsummer Night's Dream*, for example; to cast a shorter actor in the role of Helena would play against the text. |
| If I am female, can I play a male role, or if I am male, can I play a female role? | There is no easy answer to this question. There have been many successful productions where all of the male characters are played by females and vice-versa. However, you would need to be absolutely certain that you have a justifiable reason for casting yourself in a male role if you are female, or in a female role if you are male.<br><br>For example, Godber's *Bouncers* is deliberately written to emphasise cross-gender. It is doubtful whether Chekhov envisaged three men playing the title characters in *The Three Sisters*, yet there have been productions of the play with men in the title role, just as there are examples of women playing male characters such as Shakespeare's Hamlet and Brecht's Arturo Ui. If you attempt this, you should play the character in your own gender rather than trying to impersonate the opposite sex. |
| Do I need to speak with the same accent as the character? | It is vitally important to consider how the character sounds. For example, if you choose the role of Blanche in Tennessee Williams' *A Streetcar Named Desire*, you should at least suggest a Southern American accent. |

## Length

### The monologue

In the examination you are required to perform a monologue lasting **no more than** two minutes. Once you start working on the piece and add pauses, changes of pace and any stage business, the length will alter, so it is impossible to be exact at the selection stage; the safest average to aim for at this point in the process will be about 90 seconds.

Above all though, the extract must both make sense and be interesting in its own right when you take it out of context. For this reason, you may need to make some subtle alterations to the original in order for it to work as a monologue.

By flicking through any play, you can easily spot a potential monologue by the way it appears on the page: it will be a substantial paragraph or block of text assigned to a single character. You are looking for a speech that is somewhere between 25 and 35 lines long or approximately 300 to 400 words in length. The three examples given on pages 93, 101 and 105 will give you a good idea as to the right sort of length.

You can use extracts from different parts of a play to create a monologue, but it is advisable to restrict this to no more than three sizeable speeches. Equally you can take a longer speech and by careful editing adjust it to fit the time limit of the examination. It is a challenge to construct a monologue from different short speeches by cutting out the lines spoken by other characters as this can upset the rhythm of the original, but it can be done.

**The duologue**

In the examination you are required to perform a duologue lasting **no more than** five minutes. The time is shared equally between you and your partner, but it is best to think of it as two performers being on stage for more or less the whole five minutes together.

With a duologue you are looking for a section of between three and four A5 pages of script where only two character names are alternating with each other throughout. Stitching sections of dialogue together from different parts of the play is an option, but the selection of text will need to be carefully considered.

When you are looking for suitable duologue material, consider the following:

• whether there is a balance between the two characters so that one is not doing more talking or required to be more active on stage than the other

• where the sequence begins and ends so that in performance it can work in its own right

• whether both you and your partner are equally comfortable with the roles that the piece has to offer.

## Summary

Before moving on to the next stage, you should have done the following so far:

• decided to work on your own (on a monologue) or decided to work with a partner (on a duologue)

• read and explored a number of different plays and selected an appropriate monologue or duologue

• discussed and agreed with your teacher that your choice of material is right for you (and your partner in the case of a duologue)

• written yourself a timetabled plan for the forthcoming weeks.

The following pages take you through the process of preparing your role. See page 116 for details of how to complete your written performance concept.

## The acting process

There is no right nor wrong way to go about approaching a role, but there are stages of work that you need to go through as an actor in order to develop your character. Five broad stages of development are outlined below that will be relevant whether you are performing a monologue or duologue.

## Reading and analysing the text

As an actor, you have to be able to analyse the text to find out all you can about your character. Although you are only performing an extract in the examination, you have to read the whole play in order to come to as complete an understanding of the character you are playing as possible. To help with this, ask yourself questions and answer them in the first person as though you are the character. For example, instead of saying about Olivia in Shakespeare's *Twelfth Night* 'She is in mourning because her brother has recently died', phrase it as: 'I am in mourning because my brother has recently died.'

### Taking it further

The following books provide more detailed approaches to acting a role:
*The Actor and the Target* by Declan Donnellan (Nick Hern Books, 2005)
*An Actor Prepares* by Constantin Stanislavski (Methuen, 1980)
*Being an Actor* by Simon Callow (Vintage, 2004)
*Year of the King* by Anthony Sher (Nick Hern Books, 2004)

See pages 51 and 154 for more on **given circumstances**.

### Activity 1

Read through your chosen plays and ask yourself the following questions:

a) Who am I?

b) What do I look like?

c) How do I behave?

d) How do I think?

e) What do I sound like?

f) What happens to me in the play?

g) How do I react to other characters in the play?

h) How do other characters react to me?

i) What motivates me?

j) What feelings do I experience and show in the play?

k) How do I react to events?

l) What attitudes do I have?

Such questions will help you start to build up the 'given circumstances': the story, the events, historical detail related to the time the play is set, the things that your character says about himself or herself or other characters say about him or her, information from the stage directions, and so on.

## Researching the context

The advice on research on page 7 and different contexts on pages 53–56 will also be useful here.

In order to take on the life of a character in a play, you need to know as much as possible about the world in which they live. This will vary considerably depending upon the type of play you have chosen, but there are likely to be some essentials that you need to find out about the character however imaginary or real they are.

You are required to demonstrate your understanding of the historical, social, cultural and political contexts of the play as part of your overall preparation process and interpretation of the play. The results of your research will form part of the **written performance concept** (see page 116), but just as importantly, they will inform and underpin your performance of the role. This may be in a look, an attitude, a movement, the sub-text behind something you say, the way that you say something, or any number of different ways.

| Historical context | When is the play set? What do you need to know about this period of history in order for you to understand the play? Even if the play is contemporary, there may be certain events that have been in the news that might have some influence on the play. |
|---|---|
| Social context | To what sort of society do the people in the play belong? This could be to do with their social class (e.g. working class, middle class, aristocrats) or the nature of their work (e.g. professional, manual, clerical) or the type of social grouping they are in (e.g. member of a street gang, teachers in a secondary school, managers of a company). Social contexts change over time, so this will also relate back to historical context. |
| Cultural context | 'Culture' is more difficult to define but relates to something that distinguishes one group of people from another. This could be to do with race, for example, in that there are differences between American culture and French culture (in their music, art, films and food, as well as language). It could also refer to religious beliefs: playing a Jewish character would mean understanding different kinds of cultural influences from a Catholic character for instance. |
| Political context | This is to do with beliefs and ideas and often helps to provide some understanding of the way a character behaves or what they say. At a basic level, it can refer to the way a character is trying to influence another and is often related to power and control. |

## Experimentation

While a structured approach helps in developing a role, much of what you find out about how to act a character can happen by chance. In order for this to happen, you need to experiment and play around with the text. The process of creating and interpreting a character from a play is like a journey of discovery. You will learn new things about yourself as well as about the character.

### Activity 2

Try these different ways of experimenting with your text to see if you can find different meanings and to explore different ways of playing it:

a) reading the text at different speeds

b) trying out different voices and accents

c) walking in different ways as you speak the lines

d) speaking the text against different types of musical background

e) acting out the text while another person speaks the lines

f) acting out the speech in a confined space, then in a large open space

g) wearing different clothes (especially hats and shoes) each time you act out the speech

h) putting the character in different situations from those in the text (e.g. eating a meal, riding a bicycle, playing cards)

i) trying out the scene using different props and furniture.

## Building the character

See also page 6 on imagination and research.

You need to build the character from the inside (the psychological), as well as from the outside (the physical), to get a sense of exactly who the person is. In most plays there is an 'on stage' life and an 'off stage' life; you need to use your imagination to suggest what the character's life outside of the text is like.

### Activity 3

To help deepen your understanding of the character, try writing a short biography of the character, or writing some diary entries or letters as though they are written by the character.

Very few actors are able to pick up a script and produce a fully formed character on first reading. Each rehearsal will involve trying out a different move, thought, expression or way of saying something, so that layer by layer the character is built up. Set yourself a target for each rehearsal of the character: if you want to explore what motivates the character in the speech, set a target of playing the speech with a particular motive in mind. Then reflect on how you felt playing it that way and whether it has thrown any light on your understanding of the character. Write down your findings and decide whether this will be a building block in the development of your character. Gradually you will find that you have a range of ideas that you feel work for the character.

### Annotating the text

To accompany your written performance concept, you can submit an annotated version of the text, showing the decisions you have made about your performance. You may have several copies of the script on which you have written ideas that have occurred to you while rehearsing. Nearer the exam, you can prepare a copy of the text to go with your written performance concept that shows your analysis of the text. Your annotations plus the written performance concept should not exceed 500 words. See pages 99 and 116.

The annotated text can contain the following:

- a sketch of the stage space showing the position of any furniture

- the *mise-en-scène* (staging instructions)

- notes about the meaning of certain words or phrases

- reminders to yourself about how a line is spoken

- references to movement and gesture

- notes on sub-text or inner thoughts

- decisions you have made about the character's objective(s) in the scene.

## Preparing for the performance

Before the exam, you will have put in many hours of preparation: you will know your lines perfectly, you will have rehearsed the moves, worked with the props, lived in the costume and inhabited the environment of the character to such an extent that you can perform the role like clockwork. But this brings us to a paradox about acting: you need to know your role almost by rote, but the last thing you want a performance to be is mechanical. You have to be able to perform your role as though it is the first time for each and every performance.

**Key term**

mise-en-scène

**Tip**

You need to develop a warm-up routine for yourself that will enable you to be physically and mentally prepared (see pages 13 and 15). It is essential that all of your energy is focused and concentrated on the performance.

# Approaches to performing a monologue

As you will already be aware, the choice of monologue open to you is enormous, and the initial challenge will be to select one that suits your own interests and acting skills. What follows are three examples of monologues from plays of a variety of period and genre. The first example, from *Educating Rita*, takes you through each stage of the process; the second, from *The Government Inspector*, looks in more detail at some of the techniques you might use to develop your role; and the third, from *The Taming of the Shrew*, gives questions as prompts to help you apply the process to your own role.

See pages 109–115 for approaches to performing a duologue.

## *Educating Rita*

The first monologue example is from *Educating Rita* by Willy Russell. The play was first performed in 1980, and has become relatively well known with popular audience appeal.

### Selection

As there are only two characters, it is relatively straightforward to map out Rita's character through the play. The play's familiarity and the fact that Julie Walters' interpretation of the role is captured on film, would present you with the challenge of ensuring that you were able to make the role your own.

- **Age**: having left school at 16 and worked as a hairdresser, at age 26 Rita now decides to return to education. It should be a comfortable age to play for anyone around ten years younger or older than the character.

- **Gender**: the play is written naturalistically and Rita is intended to be played by a female performer. The sexual tension throughout the play between Rita and her older male teacher, Frank, is an essential ingredient to the mood and atmosphere; casting Rita and Frank against gender would seriously alter this relationship and the style of the play.

- **Appearance**: how Rita looks is a matter of interpretation as there is no direct or detailed description of her in the script. *The Sunday Times* reviewer (John Peters) describes the way Julie Walters looked in the original production as someone 'clad in shabby-glamorous clothes and sleek high boots (striding) gawkily about like a nervous, sexy flamingo (who) graduates to boilersuits and plimsolls.'

- **Accent**: Rita is a woman from Liverpool with a pronounced Liverpudlian accent. The playwright, Willy Russell, is from Merseyside and he has captured the sound and rhythm of a working-class character from the world that he knows. Productions of the play have been moved to different locations including Wales and France, so with some justification and minor alterations to specific references to Liverpool, it is possible to relocate Rita to a different place. Nearly 30 years ago when the play was written, it was not so commonplace to hear regional accents on the radio and television as it is today. Speaking with a regional accent like cockney or scouse, more or less defined an individual as being from a working-class background and not very well educated. Rita speaks with an accent throughout the play, but as she becomes more educated her vocabulary changes and the rough edges of her accent become more rounded.

From these notes, you can see, therefore, that unless you are female and were prepared to act a part that requires you to speak in a regional accent, then the role of Rita in *Educating Rita* would not be for you.

*Educating Rita* is about an uneducated 26-year-old working-class woman from Liverpool who decides to do an Open University degree course in English Literature. The play is set in the book-lined study of her tutor, Frank, and depicts Rita's journey from relative literary ignorance to becoming an educated woman. In the process, she also educates Frank, who has never taught anyone like Rita, and a special bond develops between them. The play is a two-hander, but became well known through the film version, starring Julie Walters (who originally created the role on stage) and Michael Caine, which was 'opened out' to include a range of other characters that are mentioned in the play but never seen.

- **Length**: before reading the play in detail, a quick skim through the script of *Educating Rita* finds eight sizeable 'chunks' of speech that might be suitable monologues. Rita does have a number of longer speeches, so the play is worth exploring further for possible monologue material.

Look at the example below to see how two speeches from Act 1 Scene 2 have been edited to create a monologue that can be performed in its own right. This monologue is 341 words.

Rita is responding to Frank's question, 'What sort of a school *did* you go to?' but beginning with Rita's answer 'Just normal' does not provide a very definite start. Adding 'It was' provides a stronger lead into the speech.

This indicates a cut line – Frank's 'Not allowed by whom?' Two speeches have been added together to make this into a monologue, so the performer has to find a way of acting the missing line from Frank to make it work.

**RITA:** [It was] Just normal; like all the other schools by us; borin', ripped-up books, glass everywhere, knives and fights an' sadists – an' that was just the staff room. No, they tried their best I suppose, always tellin' us we stood much more of a chance if we studied and worked hard. But studyin' was just for the geeks an' the wimps, wasn't it? See, if I'd started takin' school seriously then I would have had to become different from my mates; an' that's not allowed.

[...]

By y' mates, y' family, by everyone. So y' never admit that school could be anythin' other than useless an' irrelevant. An' what you've really got to be into are things like music an' clothes and gettin' pissed an' coppin' off an' all that kind of stuff. Not that I didn't go along with it because I did. But at the same time, there was always somethin' tappin' away in my head, tryin' to tell me I might have got it all wrong. But I'd just put the music back on or buy another dress an' stop worryin'. 'Cos there's always something that can make y' forget. An' so y' keep on goin', tellin' y'self that life is great – there's always another club to go to, a new feller to be chasin', a laugh an' a joke with the girls. Till one day, you just stop an' own up to yourself. Y' say, 'Is this it? Is this the absolute maximum that I can expect from this livin' lark?' An' that's the really big moment that is. Because that is when you've got to decide whether it's gonna be another change of dress or a change in yourself. And it's really tempting to go out an' get that other dress. Because that way it's easy; y' know that you won't be upsettin' anyone or hurtin' anyone – apart from y'self! An' sometimes it's easier to do that, to take the pain y'self instead of hurtin' those around y'; those who don't want you to change.

This works as a monologue because Rita is telling a story about what her life at school was like, but at the same time revealing something about her own thoughts and feelings. On first reading, this monologue is less than two minutes long, but there are opportunities for pauses for thought and for audience reaction, so overall it is likely to be about right for the examination.

# Research: reading and analysing the play

Having found a monologue that is suitable for you, the next stage is to read the whole play and begin gathering as much information as you can about the character from the text.

## Given circumstances

*Educating Rita* is a play with only two characters, so the focus of the story is on what happens to each of them and between them. As an actor playing Rita, you would need to map out the character's journey by writing your own version of her story and putting the monologue in context, describing what happens to her before and after that scene.

**Building up a life for Rita:**

1. I'm aged 26, nearly 27.

2. I'm married to Denny. We've been trying for a baby for over two years. My husband wants a child, but I don't.

3. I'm a hairdresser, but I hate the job and I'm not particularly good at it.

4. My real name is Susan White, but I call myself Rita after Rita Mae Brown who wrote my favourite book, *Rubyfruit Jungle*.

5. I'm from a working-class family and I live in Liverpool. I speak with a Scouse accent and I swear too much.

6. I went to a 'rubbish' secondary school and didn't learn much. I didn't want to be different from me mates.

> The chosen monologue gives an account of what her school life meant to her.

7. I want to better myself so I've decided to study on this Open University course.

> The monologue gives some of her ideas about what 'change' means for her.

8. My tutor's this mad piss artist called Frank. I think he'd like to get into bed wi' me, but I'm not having it because I want him to teach me about books an' that.

9. I had this amazin' time at the Summer School in London and met all sorts of interestin' people.

10. I've jacked in the hairdressing job and I'm working in a Bistro.

11. Denny and me are finished because we just want different things out of life.

12. Now I'm more confident with this university lark and I know lots of the 'proper students', I've gone back to being called Susan. Frank still calls me Rita though.

13. Frank used to think I was barely literate, but I didn't let him give up on me. He's been a great teacher, and thanks to him, I did well in me exams.

14. I know what clothes to wear, what wine to buy, what plays to see, what papers and books to read.

15. Frank says I'm 'an irresistible thing' and thinks it a 'terrible pity' that I'm not prepared to rape him in the middle of a production of *The Seagull*.

16. Frank says I'm 'funny, delightful and charming'.

These are just a few given circumstances about Rita; it would take you several readings of the play to pick up the kind of detail you'd need to fully understand the character. Rita's life is depicted over a period of at least a year and the play gives you 'snapshots' of her life in each scene. As in most plays, the character also has a life before the play begins and a life after the play. The important thing is that the evidence from the text informs your decisions about how you are going to portray the character and helps you create an imaginary life for him or her.

## Research

Exploring the given circumstances of the character is the start of your research, but you are likely to find references and ideas in the text that will require you to research beyond the play itself. For example, just from the given circumstances about Rita described above, you might need to find answers to the following questions.

1. Who is Rita Mae Brown and what is her novel *Rubyfruit Jungle* about? What is it about the novel that might have attracted Rita?

2. Where is Liverpool? What sort of place is it? What is it famous for? What is it like living there? What are people from Liverpool like?

3. What is a 'scouse' accent? What does it sound like?

4. What is the Open University? How is it possible for someone like Rita who has no qualifications to study for a degree course?

5. What is the significance of going to a production of *The Seagull*? Who wrote the play and what is it about?

Your research into the answers to such questions is another important part of gaining as detailed an understanding of your character as possible.

### Historical context

*Educating Rita* was first performed in 1980 and it is set at the time it was written. Although revised in 2002 to remove some of the references that Willy Russell felt had made the play dated, it is still influenced by what things were like for someone like Rita in the late 1970s or early 1980s in Britain. If you were playing Rita, you might want to update the play slightly, but you would still need to consider the history of the character. Rita would have been born in the mid-1950s and have gone to secondary school during the late 1960s; if you decided to set the play later, you would have to justify your decision and recognise how this might change the historical context for the character.

### Research facts for 1979–1980 might include:

- May 4 1979: The Conservative Party wins the General Election and Margaret Thatcher becomes Britain's first woman Prime Minister.

- 1978–1979: This period in Britain became known as the 'Winter of Discontent' after a series of strikes almost brought the country to its knees. There were piles of rubbish uncollected in the streets and stories of the dead being left unburied.

- During the 1980s, Liverpool City Council was controlled by the Labour Party and its militant Deputy Leader, Derek Hatton, was at loggerheads with the Conservative Thatcher Government over budget cuts.

- The Toxteth Riots of July 1981 were an indication of the level of social unrest in Liverpool at the time.

- Between 1979 and 1983, unemployment in Britain reached an all-time high. On Merseyside alone there were around 100,000 unemployed.

- Number one records in the charts in the 1980s included The Pretenders *Brass in Pocket*; Kenny Rogers *Coward Of The County*; Johnny Logan *What's Another Year*; and Abba *The Winner Takes It All*. This might give you some idea as to the type of music Rita might have been listening to at the time.

### Tip

The internet is a valuable research tool, but use it with caution because it is not always entirely accurate. The important thing is not to copy or print whole pages of information from the internet and just insert them into your research folder. You must read and extract the relevant information and make it your own. You can turn it into your own words, use quotes or highlight important passages and sentences. You should only include information that has helped you to gain more understanding about the play or the character, and that you have annotated or quoted from. Never cut and paste information from the internet (or anywhere else) and try to pass it off as your own: this is plagiarism and you will be found out and risk being disqualified from the examination. There is nothing wrong with using other people's material in your research, just as long as you acknowledge and reference your sources.

Two useful websites for historical information are: http://news.bbc.co.uk/onthisday and www.bl.uk/chronology.

## Social context

Rita is from a working-class background and she sees getting an education as a way to better herself. In 1979–1980 less than five per cent of people between the ages of 18 and 25 went to university, compared with today's government target that by 2010 around 50 per cent will have gained a higher education experience. Social class is a central theme of the play in that education is seen as a means to move from one class to another. Near the end of the play Rita declares:

> I'm educated, I've got what you have an' y' don't like it because you'd rather see me as the peasant I once was; you're like the rest of them – you like to keep your natives thick, because that way they still look charming and delightful. I don't need you. I know what clothes to wear, what wine to buy, what plays to see, what papers and books to read.

## Cultural context

Having been a thriving seaport on the banks of the River Mersey, Liverpool has a history of embracing people from different cultures and countries, all contributing to the city's distinctive character. The area has a dialect of its own known as Scouse and anyone from the region is instantly recognisable by their accent. When The Beatles hit the international stage in the 1960s, Liverpool became associated with a whole genre of popular music known as the Mersey Sound. At the same time, a generation of Liverpool poets emerged that included Roger McGough, Brian Pattern and Adrian Henri who performed their work live and gave poetry a huge popular appeal. Liverpool is also known for its comedians such as Ken Dodd, Jimmy Tarbuck and Stan Boardman, and the particular kind of wit associated with Scousers was made popular by the writer Carla Lane in her BBC comedy series *The Liver Birds* and *Bread*.

According to Rita:

> Me; an' the people I come from – people I work with, live with, grew up with – us, we've got no culture.

Rita thinks that by 'culture' Frank is referring to her working-class roots, but for her it's like this:

> I don't see any culture; I just see everyone pissed or stoned, tryin' to find their way from one empty day to the next. There's more culture in a pot of yoghurt. Y' daren't say somethin' like that round our way though, because they're proud; an' they'll tell you we have got culture, doin' the pub quiz, goin' the club, singin' karaoke.

Culture is associated with someone having 'good taste' which in itself is a difficult concept because it can often be associated with snobbery. One of the issues of 'taste' that is explored in the play is to do with literature and what makes something intellectually worthwhile and stimulating compared with something that is often disparagingly referred to as pulp fiction. Frank's first task is to get Rita to appreciate *Howards End* by E.M. Forster when she is used to reading what might be called 'trashy fiction' rather than literature.

**Political context**

Rita says that she is not interested in politics, but of course politics affects all of our lives in some way or other. For example, the Labour Government developed the idea of a 'University of the Air' that became the Open University in 1971; this enabled people like Rita to have a chance to return to education and gain a degree. One of the policies of the Thatcher Government during the 1980s was to encourage more home ownership by enabling people to buy their own council houses. This was also a period during which personal economic gain seemed to be valued more highly than social and community policies. Willy Russell takes a swipe at the effects of this political philosophy in the following speech he has written for Rita in the revised 2002 version of the text.

> …what's stupid is that *now*….now that most of them have got some kind of a house an' there is food an' money around, they're better off but, honest, they know they've got nothin' as well – because the meanin's all gone; so there's nothin' to believe in. It's like there's this sort of disease but no one mentions it; everyone behaves as though it's normal, y' know, inevitable, that there's vandalism an' violence an' houses burnt out and wrecked by the people they were built for. But this disease, it just keeps on bein' hidden; because everyone's caught up in the 'Got-To-Have' game, all runnin' round like headless chickens chasin' the latest got-to-have tellies an' got-to-have cars, got-to-have haircuts an' got-to-have phones an' all the other got-to-have garbage that leaves y' wonderin' why you've still got nothin' – even when you've got it.

## Activity 4

To help you build up a picture of the historical, social, cultural and political background to your character, create a 'contextual poster'. From the images, newspaper headlines, quotes and articles you have collected surrounding the background to your chosen play, select items that you feel are the most relevant. Arrange them on a sheet of A2 or A3 paper to create a collage.

**Primary research**

The kind of research outlined above is all based around secondary sources such as reference books, newspapers, gallery and museum visits and the internet. Primary research is about finding out things first hand. It is not always possible to do this because of cost, legal or time constraints, but where it is possible, primary research is an invaluable tool for an actor.

For *Educating Rita*, possible avenues of primary research might be:

- visiting Liverpool to soak up the atmosphere of the place
- going to a hairdressing salon in a working-class area of a city to observe behaviour and listen to conversations
- interviewing someone who has taken an Open University course
- speaking to someone with a native Liverpool accent, asking them to read some of the lines of dialogue and recording it.

**Tip**

Observational research is something that you can carry out in the street or on public transport, or using film and television programmes. There may be something about the way a person walks, the gestures they use or what clothes they wear that you find useful in suggesting movement for your character. However, you must make sure you are subtle about the way you observe people, so that they are unaware of you doing so. It is not a good idea to try and copy another actor's performance of a character; in fact if you were playing Rita, you might do well not to watch Julie Walters' portrayal of her on film at all.

# Annotating the text

You may provide an annotated text that shows the decisions you have made and why, and this can include a sketch of the stage space. The diagram below is an example of what a sketch of the stage space for *Educating Rita* might look like. It is described as: 'A book-lined tutorial room on the first floor of a Victorian-built university in the north of England.'

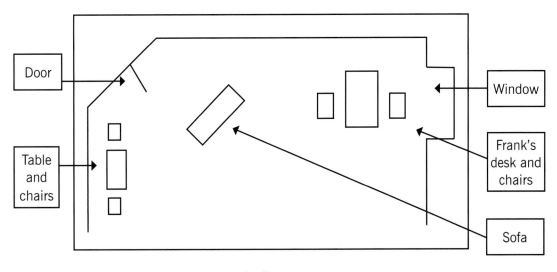

**Audience**

Below is an example of the sorts of notes an actor playing Rita might add to their text to record their decisions. This is just one approach and you may choose to record much of this information in your written performance concept (see page 116).

| | | |
|---|---|---|
| *1 – by us: dialect for 'near to where we live'.<br><br>*3 – Pause after 'sadists'. Work on comic timing before saying next line.<br><br>*5 – Extend vowel sound on 'Nooo' and through this speech put bag down on the sofa and take coat off putting it over the back of the sofa. | RITA: [It was] Just normal; like all the other schools **by us** (*1); **borin'** (*2), ripped-up books, glass everywhere, knives and fights an' **sadists** (*3) – an' that was just the staff **room** (*4). **No** (*5), they tried their best I suppose, always tellin' us we stood much more of a chance if we studied and worked hard. But studyin' was just for the geeks an' the wimps, **wasn't it?** (*6) See, if I'd started takin' school seriously then I would have had to become different from my mates; an' that's not allowed. | Rita's been talking about public schools (Harrow and Eton). She is describing her secondary school to Frank.<br><br>*2 – borin': stress word and roll 'r' to emphasise Scouse accent. Slight pause while she remembers what was borin' about it and comes up with the list.<br><br>*4 – Look at Frank to judge his reaction. Aim to get a laugh on this line.<br><br>*6 – Rhetorical question. Follow straight into 'See', but pause after it to allow mind time to conjure up the next thoughts. |

*7 – tried leaving a pause here as though Frank was speaking but it interrupts the flow. Found it worked much better by cutting this line and going straight into 'So y' never admit'.

*9 – Really good line to emphasise Rita's roots: 'coppin' off' is Scouse for getting off with a bloke.

*10 – This felt like natural moment to light the cigarette which by now I've got out of the packet.

*11 – Tap side of temple with hand holding the cigarette.

*13 – Through this section put cigarette packet and lighter back into bag.

*15 – Take a drag on cigarette.

*18 – Word 'really' stands out with Scouse accent, so emphasise it here.

*19 – Important sub-text here for Rita. She is particularly thinking about her husband, Denny. He wants to have a baby and she doesn't. She knows she is hurting him by going to her classes.

---

[Frank's line.]
[**By y' mates, y' family, by everyone**.] (*7)

So y' never admit that school could be anythin' other than useless an' **irrelevant**. (*8) An' what you've really got to be into are things like music an' clothes and **gettin' pissed an' coppin' off** (*9) an' all that kind of **stuff**. (*10) Not that I didn't go along with it because I did. But at the same time, there was always somethin' **tappin' away in my head**, (*11) tryin' to tell me I might have got it all wrong. But I'd just put the **music back on** (*12) or buy another dress an' stop worryin'. 'Cos there's always something that can make y' forget. An' so y' keep on goin', tellin' y'self that life **is great** (*13) – there's always another club to go to, a new feller to be chasin', a laugh an' a joke with the girls. **Till one day** (*14), you just stop an' own up to yourself. Y' say, **'Is this it?** (*15) Is this the absolute maximum that I can expect from this livin' lark?' An' that's the really big **moment that** is. (*16) Because that is when you've got to decide whether it's gonna be another change of dress or a **change in yourself** (*17). And it's **really** (*18) tempting to go out an' get that other dress. Because that way it's easy; y' know that you won't be upsettin' anyone or **hurtin' anyone** (*19) – apart from y'self! An' sometimes it's easier to do that, to take the **pain y'self** (*20) instead of hurtin' those around y'; those who don't want you to **change** (*21).

---

*8 – Before she gets a bit serious, felt she needed some business here to help slow down the thought process. In Scene 1 Rita smokes and Frank says he doesn't mind: the smoking helps her relax and settle down in Frank's company. She doesn't offer Frank one because he says he's given up.

*12 – Works well taking a puff of cigarette here and blowing out smoke.

*14 – Slow down here and make sure I am facing where I imagine Frank is now sitting, behind his desk.

*16 – Slight pause here while I think about 'the big moment.' A drag on the cigarette and a slight move away from Frank.

*17 – For me the climax of the speech because this is Rita's overriding objective in the play: to change from being an uneducated hairdresser to an educated woman with more choice out of life.

*20 – Moment of self-determination: decided not going to take the pain: inevitably going to hurt others.

*21 – By this point want to stub cigarette out in ashtray on Frank's desk.

## *The Government Inspector*

This second monologue example comes from *The Government Inspector* by Nikolai Gogol. In the play, the corrupt officials of a remote Russian town, led by the Governor, have fooled themselves into believing that Khlestakov is an important government official. Khlestakov is, in fact, a penniless government clerk from St Petersburg, who was about to leave his hotel without paying the bill. Realising that he has been mistaken for somebody else, Khlestakov takes full advantage of the situation.

In this monologue from Act 1 Scene 3, Khlestakov makes up all sorts of stories about his life back in St Petersburg. The Governor, his wife, his daughter, five other officials and townspeople are listening in awe to what Khlestakov has to say. Khlestakov drinks more and more champagne until he nearly falls over and is taken off to bed. (The extract is 376 words.)

> KHLESTAKOV: Even my letters come addressed 'Your Excellency.' Yes, once I was put in charge of the whole department. It was very weird. Our boss had gone off. Vanished. Nobody knew where. And then of course there were the same old arguments – who's going to take over? Some of the generals wanted the job and they tried it, one after another. But they hadn't got it, they hadn't got it – here. *(He taps his head.)* Say what you like about the men at the top, but oh, when you get up there … it's not so simple. No! They found out. Yes. And so they asked me. They sent urgent messages every minute. The streets were thronging with messengers. Can you imagine a street? Right. Now imagine it filled with thirty-five thousand messengers. And I come out on my balcony and I say, 'What can I do for you, my friends?' And thirty-five thousand messengers shout with a single voice, 'Your Excellency, Ivan Khlestakov, go and take charge of the Department!' It was a bit embarrassing, I was still in my dressing-gown – which is embroidered with golden foxes – so I went and changed and when I was ready I found ministers of state and princes and elders of the church kneeling in silent prayer at the foot of my marble staircase which is worth … And I looked at them and I said, 'Gentlemen, what do I want with power?' And they set up such a piteous whimpering sound, ah, it would crack your heart. And I thought – I thought of the Czar, and how he'd feel if I refused. So I said, 'Get up off your knees – I accept. But gentlemen, but, I – I – I have eyes in my head. So you'd better watch out and if any of you try to…' And you know I marched through that department like some great elephant, like an enormous elephant. And everything and everyone in that building trembled, trembled, trembled.

*(They all are now trembling like mad.* KHLESTAKOV *is very worked up, his speech more violent, but still clear.)*

> No, I don't fool about! I flogged them with my tongue! I even put the fear of God into the state council. That's it! That's how I am! Nobody stops me! I told them, 'I know everything! I see everything! I know you! And you! And you!'

*(He staggers and nearly falls.)*

**Nikolai Vasilievich Gogol** was born in the Ukraine in 1809. He died in 1852, his mind unbalanced, as a result of his refusal to eat. He started writing for periodicals when working as a minor government official in St Petersburg at the age of 20. His writing career as a novelist and dramatist flourished after he met the famous Russian writer Alexander Pushkin in 1831. In fact, Pushkin suggested the plot of *The Government Inspector*, because he himself had been mistaken for a government official. *The Government Inspector* was first performed in 1836 in the presence of Tsar Nicholas and was an instant success. However, Gogol was sensitive to the criticism of those in authority who considered the play to be subversive and he left Russia to travel Europe for much of the rest of his life.

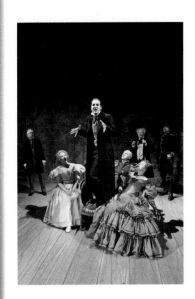

## Selection

- **Age**: Gogol describes Khlestakov as 'a young man of about twenty-three', but the role has been played by actors in their thirties and could be played by someone several years younger.

- **Gender**: traditionally the role is written to be played by a male and there are two scenes in which Khlestakov first tries to seduce the Governor's daughter, Maria, and then his wife, Anna. However, the style of the play, which has been described as a satirical comedy, might lend itself to an interesting interpretation of the role if played by a female performer.

- **Appearance**: Gogol describes Khlestakov as 'slender, rather silly and gormless – one of those people whom office colleagues call skivers. He speaks and behaves without any consideration for anything or anybody. He's quite incapable of giving his whole attention to any single idea. His speech is convulsive and words jerk out quite unexpectedly. The more simple and ingenuous the actor in this part can be, the better. He dresses fashionably.'

- **Accent**: no particular accent is specified but as a man from the City of St Petersburg, he must be distinguished from the local people. Khlestakov is more likely to have an educated or more posh accent than the country bumpkins who mistake him for a government official.

- **Length**: the speech is about two minutes at the line 'trembled, trembled, trembled,' and it could end there. However, the additional lines provide a safety net if the playing speed of the previous section comes in under time, and it has slightly more impact as a climax.

## Research

This is an example of a play set in a particular period. The Russia of Gogol's time was a country ruled by the Tsar, and the structure of Russian society was very much like that of the rest of 19th-century Europe. It is important for an actor approaching a period role to find out as much as possible about the way people lived at the time a play is set.

### Activity 5

Answer the following questions for the play you have chosen for Section A:

a) What was it like to live when and where the play is set?

b) How was society structured and where would your character fit into it?c) What sort of clothes would your character have worn?

d) What would other people have thought of the type of character you are playing during their lifetime?

## Rehearsing the role

The early stages of the work on your role will involve experimentation to unlock as many answers and ideas about your character as possible. The following approaches could apply to any role: the important thing is that you reflect and make notes on the effect of each exercise as you complete it. There is not always a rational or logical reason why one thing works and another does not. The more accidentally a thought, gesture or way of saying something occurs, the more likely it is to be the most appropriate one.

## Activity 6

**Finding the pulse of the text.** For this exercise you will need a metronome. The aim is to help you sense how fast or slow to take the speech. Set the metronome at a fairly slow speed (around 60 beats per minute) and speak the speech against this pulse. You may need to repeat this several times and go through the speech six or seven lines or sentences at a time.

a) Which lines felt right being spoken at this sort of pace? Underline the lines that worked.

b) Where did you feel you had to stop and wait before you spoke the next word or line? Mark the places in the text where you feel there is a need to pause.

Try again with the metronome ten beats faster and continue to repeat the exercise in ten beat steps until you reach 120 beats per minute, unless you have already found that none of the speech works at the faster speeds.

c) Which lines work at a slower pace and which at the faster pace? It may help to use a scoring system giving a line a low number if it is slow and a higher number if it is faster.

d) What does this exercise tell you about any changes of pace and rhythm? Mark the text with words like, 'faster', 'slower', 'wait a beat (or several beats)', 'accelerate up through this bit', 'slow down through this section'.

## Activity 7

**Fitting actions to the words.** This activity is about trying to find the right kind of movement for a speech, and exploring how the use of gesture and the handling of props can be integrated into the characterisation and arise naturally out of the dialogue.

You will need a piece of fruit to peel. It helps if you have someone to observe you and take notes or film yourself doing the exercise. The purpose of the exercise is to carry out a fairly normal activity like peeling an apple (with a knife) and eating it whilst speaking through your speech. If you haven't learnt the speech yet, pin it up in front of you on large sheets of paper.

a) On which lines did you have to stop the action to concentrate on what you were saying? Highlight in the text moments where it was difficult to speak and do a movement at the same time. (This will suggest that this is a moment where the focus needs to be on what is being said, rather than what is being done.)

b) During which parts of the speech was it easiest to peel the fruit and speak at the same time? Highlight these moments in the text.

It won't always be obvious what props and actions there are in the text, and you will need to try out a range of different possibilities. It could be an item of clothing for instance, like a tie or a scarf, which you may find the character fiddles with or uses in a certain way at various points in the speech. Introduce the props as early as possible. In the Khlestakov example an actor will need to work with the champagne glass, and find the right moments to take a drink from it or to refill the glass when it is empty.

## Building the character

There is no simple way of building a character, but you can think of it rather like an oil painting where you, as the artist, are creating a portrait of your character by adding different layers of meaning. Here are some sample exercises that you can use.

**Parallel improvisation** can be used for most monologues. It involves using a parallel or similar situation to one in the text and improvising around the scene to get a sense of what it feels like to be the character in the scene, before having to learn the dialogue.

- **Organisation**: work with a group of people who are going to represent the other characters in the scene. If you were playing Khlestakov, the group would be the town officials who are going to believe everything you tell them. The important thing is that they react enthusiastically to your stories.

- **Situation**: Khlestakov is telling one of his exaggerated accounts of life in St Petersburg. The 'listeners' must believe and accept what the person playing Khlestakov is saying and reply with positive statements like: 'Oh, really, what were they like?', 'How exciting!', 'Tell me more.' The improvisation should then build from here, so that Khlestakov can say almost anything he likes.

### Activity 8

Try creating a parallel improvisation for your text. Then return to the monologue and apply what you have learned.

(a) Act out the monologue capturing the same sense of spontaneity you experienced in the improvisation and as though you were responding to the reactions of others.

(b) Ask someone else to act out your speech and put yourself in the role of someone reacting to it.

**Hot-seating** is an invaluable way of getting to know your character and to start to think the way your character might think. Prepare suitable questions that you want other people to ask you and that you are then going to answer in role. These are some sample questions that could be asked of Khlestakov:

- What are your friends like?

- Would you say that you are a responsible person?

- Why have you let the townspeople think that you are a Government Inspector?

- What is your job in the office like?

- Why do you imagine that you could be the boss of your department?

**Writing in role** is another way of getting to know and understand your character. Again you can adapt the circumstances to suit a role in any play.

### Activity 9

Imagine that you are Khlestakov and that you have arrived back in St Petersburg. Write a letter to a friend telling them all about the events that happened in the small town and about the people you met there.

---

**Tip**

Get feedback from the people who have been asking the questions as to what impressions they have gleaned about your character, and whether or not your answers were consistent. It is also useful to record your hot-seating exercise on video or DVD so that you can analyse it at a later stage.

---

**Key term**

writing in role

---

## *The Taming of the Shrew*

The third monologue example is from *The Taming of the Shrew* by William Shakespeare, which was first performed in about 1593. The 'shrew' of the title is Katharina, the oldest daughter of Baptista Minola, a wealthy gentleman of Padua in Italy. Katharina has a reputation for being aggressive and strong-willed, and no man wants to marry her. Petruchio, a gentleman from the country, is in search of a wife and he takes up the challenge of wooing, marrying and 'taming' Katharina.

This monologue comes from the end of the play at a wedding feast for the three married couples in the play. Petruchio and the other two husbands make a bet that will be won by the husband with the most obedient wife. No one believes for one moment that Petruchio has any chance of winning, but Katharina proves them all wrong with this final speech in which she advises all wives to obey their husbands in everything.

This speech is written in blank verse (see page 36), which means that the rhythm and metre of the language have an important part to play in how the speech is performed. It is 364 words.

## Approaches to the work

From the previous two examples, you should have developed a good understanding of ways of approaching a monologue. Rather than providing a third full example, questions are given here as a means of guiding you through the process of working on your monologue. You can use these questions to help you find solutions and analyse the monologue of your choice.

**Practical questions**

- How old is this character?
- What age can you play the character at?
- Is the role gender specific?
- If you are going to play against gender, what is your justification for this?
- What does the character look like?
- How do you resemble the character physically? How does the character move/ sit/stand/gesture?
- What will you have to do to alter your appearance to suit the character?
- What does the character sound like? Does the role require an accent?
- Is the monologue the right length?
- Have you chosen the right line to start the speech with and the right place to finish it?

**Reading and analysing the play**

- What is the play about? (themes and ideas)
- What kind of play is it? (genre, form and style)
- How is the play written? (language and structure)
- What have other critics, writers, actors, directors said about the play? (critical and professional reaction)
- What is your character's journey through the play? (contextual mapping)

KATHARINA:     Fie, fie! unknit that threatening unkind brow,
And dart not scornful glances from those eyes,
To wound thy lord, thy king, thy governor:
It blots thy beauty as frosts do bite the meads,
Confounds thy fame as whirlwinds shake fair buds,
And in no sense is meet or amiable.
A woman moved is like a fountain troubled,
Muddy, ill-seeming, thick, bereft of beauty;
And while it is so, none so dry or thirsty
Will deign to sip or touch one drop of it.
Thy husband is thy lord, thy life, thy keeper,
Thy head, thy sovereign; one that cares for thee,
And for thy maintenance commits his body
To painful labour both by sea and land,
To watch the night in storms, the day in cold,
Whilst thou liest warm at home, secure and safe;
And craves no other tribute at thy hands
But love, fair looks and true obedience;
Too little payment for so great a debt.
Such duty as the subject owes the prince
Even such a woman oweth to her husband;
And when she is froward, peevish, sullen, sour,
And not obedient to his honest will,
What is she but a foul contending rebel
And graceless traitor to her loving lord?
I am ashamed that women are so simple
To offer war where they should kneel for peace;
Or seek for rule, supremacy and sway,
When they are bound to serve, love and obey.
Why are our bodies soft and weak and smooth,
Unapt to toil and trouble in the world,
But that our soft conditions and our hearts
Should well agree with our external parts?
Come, come, you froward and unable worms!
My mind hath been as big as one of yours,
My heart as great, my reason haply more,
To bandy word for word and frown for frown;
But now I see our lances are but straws,
Our strength as weak, our weakness past compare,
That seeming to be most which we indeed least are.
Then vail your stomachs, for it is no boot,
And place your hands below your husband's foot:
In token of which duty, if he please,
My hand is ready; may it do him ease.

**Researching the context**

- What are the possible historical, social, cultural and political influences on the play in terms of **where**, **when** and **how** it was written?

- What are the possible historical, social, cultural and political influences on the play in terms of the **time(s)** it is set or **when** you intend to set it?

- What are the possible historical, social, cultural and political influences on the play in terms of the **place(s)** it is set or **where** you intend to set it?

- How would you describe the historical, social, cultural and political world of the play?

- What kind of background information do you need in order to understand and familiarise yourself with the historical, social, cultural and political world of the play and of your character?

In the example of *The Taming of the Shrew*, understanding the way in which the status and role of women in society has changed historically, socially, culturally and politically is key to any interpretation of the play. This is what the playwright George Bernard Shaw, an influential supporter of the emancipation of women, had to say about this speech in 1897:

> ... the last scene is altogether disgusting to modern sensibility. No man with any decency of feeling can sit it out without feeling extremely ashamed of the lord-of-creation moral implied in the wager and the speech put into the woman's own mouth.

Germaine Greer, the author of one of the first major books on the feminist movement (*The Female Eunuch*) writing in 1970, has a different perspective:

> Kate is a woman striving for her own existence in a world where she is a ... decoy to be bid for against her sister's higher market value, so she opts out by becoming unmanageable... [S]he has the uncommon good fortune to find Petruchio, who is man enough to know what he wants and how to get it. He wants her spirit and her energy because he wants a wife worth keeping.

What these quotes demonstrate is that there are at least two equally valid interpretations of the play. For the audience of Shakespeare's day, the reaction may have been different again, and the theatrical problem that has to be solved is how you would want this speech to come across to a contemporary audience. Katharina's speech can be played in any number of ways, as long as the interpretation is justified.

**Rehearsing the role**

What are you saying, how and why?

- Write and/or improvise the speech in your own words: how does this compare to the original? Repeat the exercise until you get as close to the writer's words as possible.

- Annotate the script, underlining difficult and unusual words. What do they mean?

- Experiment with different ways of speaking the lines. What is the effect of pausing in different places, speaking different parts at varying speeds, or altering the tempo (speed and pace) and the rhythm (emphasis and pause)?

- Experiment with different sounds. What happens if you change the tone (hard/soft), the pitch (high/low) or the volume (loud/quiet) of your voice?

Why are you saying it and who are you saying it to?

- What is the motivation behind the words? (objective)

- What is your character thinking when you say a particular word, line or phrase? (thought and reason)

- Do you really mean what you say or is there something else you are trying to say? (sub-text)

- What kind of speech is it? For example, a description, an explanation, a response to something someone else has said, a soliloquy, an argument?

- What does the speech reveal about your character?

- Who else is on stage with you? Is the speech directed at them?

- How are other characters reacting to you and to what you are saying?

- What reaction or response are you intending to get from anyone else on stage and/or the audience?

Where are you?

As an actor, you have to imagine that you are in the world of the character. According to Stanislavski, 'Every movement you make on stage, every word you speak, is the result of the right life of your imagination.' For example, an actor playing Katharina in *The Taming of the Shrew* would have to imagine that she was speaking at a wedding banquet in a room surrounded by guests that include her father, her sister and her husband. One of the best ways to create the environment for the character in your head, is to gather together some visual research material, so that you get a sense of place, scale, colour and shape. For the examination performance, you will be using the basic requirements for the scene, but in your imagination you need to be able to visualise things such as where the door is or where the horizon is.

What are you doing and how are you moving?

- The actions for the character need to arise almost naturally or spontaneously from the text. What are your muscles doing at various points in the play? When do you sit/stand/gesture/remain still?

- Annotate the script, marking the moves and actions against the appropriate words and phrases.

- Experiment with different ways of walking, posturing and positioning. What is the effect of standing in different ways? What is the effect of placing your weight on different parts of the body?

- Experiment with different forms of non-verbal communication. What happens if you cross your legs or uncross them? What happens if you scratch your face? What happens if you have your arms folded or unfolded?

Why are you doing this or that?

- What is the motivation behind a particular action? (objective)

- Does a particular action refer to some inner meaning in the text? (sub-text)

- What kind of movement is it? For example, why are you standing, sitting, leaning, lying down, holding on to something, smiling, grimacing?

- What do your actions tell you and the audience about your character?

**Practitioner note**

According to Stanislavski, every action a character makes is the result of some inner action or thought. For example, a character may be nervous in the presence of another character, and might show this in the way that he or she fiddles with a glove.

# Approaches to performing a duologue

For a duologue, apart from the fact that there are two of you performing a scene from one play, the processes involved in approaching and developing a role are identical to those of an actor working on a monologue and the assessment criteria are the same (see page 85). You should, therefore, refer to the questions and procedures outlined in the previous section on monologues as they are equally applicable to the ways in which you can work on your character in a duologue.

## The difference with a duologue

The fundamental difference you will find in working on a duologue is that you and your partner will have to come to a shared and agreed understanding and interpretation of the play as a whole. In other words, you must agree on what Stanislavski calls the 'super-objective' ('the essential idea, the core, which provided the impetus for the writing of a play') and 'the through line of action' ('that inner line of effort that guides the actors from the beginning to the end of the play') so that there is a consistency of approach. If you and your partner work in isolation from each other and do not discuss your ideas and the results of your individual research, it is likely that your performance will give the impression of you being in two different productions of the same scene.

> **Key terms**
>
> super-objective
> through line of action

## Making the work your own

It is important that in your supporting notes and in your written performance concept you convey your individual contribution to the research and rehearsal process. Outlining the ideas and information that you have brought to the partnership and how these have been altered through your discussions and in rehearsal, will provide essential evidence regarding your personal involvement in the final decisions. It may also be the case that you have made suggestions about your partner's characterisation, and that you have mutually benefited from the collaborative process. Your individual commentary on your own character should take precedence over writing about the other character, except where it has impacted on the way that you are playing your role.

## Interaction

The added dimension that exists between two characters is that of interaction: one character will react to the other and the behaviour of one will affect the other. An action (physical and/or spoken) by Character A will provoke a reaction by Character B (and vice-versa), even if that response is inaction.

Proxemics (see page 61) can say a lot about the relationship between two individuals on stage at any one point. Having one character standing and the other sitting, for example, can say something about their status. Characters standing close to one another will suggest a more intimate relationship than those standing at opposite ends of a room. The way in which characters react and respond to each other, and are positioned in relation to one another on stage, will communicate another layer of meaning which you will have to consider in your approach to staging the scene.

## *The Importance of Being Earnest*

The following example uses *The Importance of Being Earnest* by Oscar Wilde (1895) to provide an illustration of a way of working on a duologue extract. The strategies used here to explore and explain the process will be transferable to your own choice of duologue. The extract is given on pages 113–115.

### Context

The plot revolves around the unusual circumstances surrounding the name and birth of Jack Worthing. As a baby, Jack's governess, Miss Prism, mistakenly deposited him in a handbag that she left in the cloakroom at Victoria Station, so Jack has grown up not knowing his real parents. Jack's best friend is Algernon Moncrieff who has a cousin called Gwendolen with whom Jack Worthing is in love. The problem is that Jack is known as Jack in the country and as Ernest in town, and since Gwendolen only knows Jack in town, she thinks his name is Ernest.

Jack Worthing has a niece in the country called Cecily whom Algernon goes to meet in the guise of being Jack's brother, Ernest, and he falls in love with her. Gwendolen has travelled to the country too, and as a result of the confusion arising from both Jack and Algernon using the name Ernest, she thinks that Cecily is a rival in love. This extract is the scene in which Cecily and Gwendolen first meet and fall out over the misunderstanding that they are each betrothed to the same man.

### Length

Judging the length of a duologue is more difficult than a monologue, because it is difficult to judge the response times between the characters from just reading the text on the page. This extract is around 1,100 words and has a playing time of around five minutes.

### The ending

Read the last four speeches of the extract. What do you think about the way the extract ends? How could it be made to work to fit one or more of the following descriptions: definite, inconclusive, abrupt, funny, climactic, anti-climactic?

How will your duologe end? What might you have to do to make the ending work effectively? You could use any combination of these types of ending to finish your duologue. Remember that there is nothing wrong with leaving the audience wanting more by ending the extract with a sense of anticipation as to what might happen or be said next.

### Editing the text

This extract is followed by the entrance of the butler and servants who are bringing in afternoon tea. This is a well-known scene which exemplifies the genre of *comedy of manners*. Cecily proceeds to get her own back on Gwendolen by putting sugar in her tea when she does not want any and giving her cake when she asks for bread and butter.

If you wanted to include this in your duologue, you would have to consider the following:

- starting the scene later

- making a few minor cuts

- getting the tea things to the table

- dealing with the butler's (Merriman) lines

- timing how long it takes to pour the tea, add the sugar and cut the cake.

This is all part of the process of finding an appropriate starting point and finishing point for your duologue that fits within the time limit of five minutes. Experiment with different opening and closing lines, running the scene with a stopwatch.

### Age, gender and appearance

A duologue has to suit two people; each of you has to be right for one or other of the two roles. If, as in this example, the two roles are both female or both male, it might be that at the start of the process you can each see yourselves playing either role. In this case, it is a good idea to keep swapping around before making a final decision about who to cast in which role.

With Cecily and Gwendolen there are obvious character differences, but they are quite close in age. Gwendolen gives a clue to Cecily's age and appearance when she says: 'I cannot help expressing a wish you were – well, just a little older than you seem to be – and not quite so very alluring in appearance… I wish that you were fully forty-two, and more than usually plain for your age.' They are both young women from fairly wealthy backgrounds, which is a pointer to the way they might dress.

### Questions for you to consider

- What is the age difference (if any) between the two characters?

- How does their age difference or similarity affect their relationship?

- Is there a difference in status between the characters?

- How do social class, wealth and position affect the relationship?

- When looking at the other character, how does your character perceive him or her?

- What do you think the other character thinks of your character?

- How does each character's perception of the other compare with the reality?

- How does your character behave towards the other character?

- How does the other character behave towards your character?

- How do you feel about the other character?

- How does the other character feel about you?

The response to these questions is something you should explore throughout the exploration and development process. It could well change as you discover more about each of the characters. Part of the excitement of working with a partner is that when they do or say something differently in a rehearsal, it may throw you, and you will want to respond differently. In the early stages of rehearsals, it is important that you keep trying things out and discovering what effect changing behaviour and actions have on the portrayal of the roles.

### Historical, social, cultural and political contexts

It is important that you are aware of what sort of influences the various contexts in the play have on the characters and how this can inform your performance. The social and historical backgrounds of the characters will, to some extent, dictate how they behave. If the situation were recast as a scene in *EastEnders*, for example, it is highly unlikely that the characters would behave as civilly or talk in the language they do.

*The Importance of Being Earnest* is an historical record of the manners and behaviour of the upper classes in late Victorian England. Oscar Wilde is holding up a mirror to the very society that was watching the play and getting them to laugh at themselves. Everything about the play is artificial and it aims to please an audience with its cleverness. The female characters in the play have very strong personalities, but they exist at a time when women in society did not have the vote and were considered to be second-class citizens.

### Speaking the words

> See page 12 for more on voice and speech organs.

Transforming words from the page into spoken dialogue is central to your work as an actor. It seems an obvious point to make, but if an audience cannot hear what you are saying on stage, all the work that you do on understanding and interpreting the text will be wasted. The danger with a duologue is that you get so used to performing it to another person that you forget that the conversation has to project out to the audience.

### Taking it further

Going through the text, highlighting the sounds of words and practising them will improve your pronunciation and enunciation. Work out which are the **lip vowels** (e.g. ow), **tongue vowels** (e.g. ay), **voiced consonants** (e.g. very), **unvoiced plosives** (e.g. person), **voiced plosives** (e.g. dead).

This extract requires highly refined and precise speaking because the characters are upper class and have been taught to speak with clear enunciation. Working with a partner gives you the advantage that someone else is listening to your speech, and you should encourage each other to help you to improve your speaking. Constantly ask yourselves the following questions:

- Are you pronouncing each word correctly?

- Is the emphasis in that word on the right syllable?

- Can the ends of words be heard?

- Are you speaking clearly?

- Will you be heard at the back of the performing space?

### Speaking dialogue

Since a duologue is usually a dialogue between two characters, there is the added dimension of changes in speech patterns and rhythms between the two speakers. It is just as important for one character to be listening to what the other is saying, as it is for each to come in on cue with the next line.

### Activity 10

This exercise will help develop your listening and response skills. Using a beach ball, Character A throws it to Character B once they have spoken their line. Character B starts to speak once they have caught the ball. Continue to throw the ball between the two of you to build up the rhythm of the speeches. You can alter the distance between the two of you, which will alter the pace of lines. If you catch the ball too early and you are not ready to respond, this will suggest that there should be a longer pause between the lines.

## Notes and questions to consider when approaching a text

**Making an entrance.** Getting the entrance right can be tricky. Here, Cecily is already on stage and Gwendolen enters; you could experiment with where Cecily is when the lights come up in relation to Gwendolen's entry point. Gwendolen could already be moving towards Cecily as the lights slowly come up, or the actors could start in a frozen position and go into action with the lights coming up suddenly. Your choice of entrance is dependent on what you want to communicate to the audience in the first ten seconds of the scene. The tone you set at the start of the scene will carry through into the mood of the whole piece.

How do the characters in your scene meet? The presentation of your duologue is the audience's first encounter with the characters, but where are the characters in their relationship to each other? In this example, it is the first time they have met, but in your play they could be at a very different stage in their relationship.

How sincere are the characters in what they are saying to each other? Are the characters saying one thing and thinking another?

*Garden at the Manor House. A flight of grey stone steps leads up to the house. The garden, an old-fashioned one, full of roses. Time of year, July. Basket chairs, and a table covered with books, are set under a large yew-tree.*

CECILY     *(advancing to meet her)*: Pray let me introduce myself to you. My name is Cecily Cardew.

GWENDOLEN:     Cecily Cardew? *(moving to her and shaking hands)* What a very sweet name! Something tells me that we are going to be great friends. I like you already more than I can say. My first impressions of people are never wrong.

CECILY:     How nice of you to like me so much after we have known each other such a comparatively short time. Pray sit down.

GWENDOLEN     *(still standing up)*: I may call you Cecily, may I not?

CECILY:     With pleasure!

GWENDOLEN:     And you will always call me Gwendolen, won't you?

CECILY:     If you wish.

GWENDOLEN:     Then that is all quite settled, is it not?

CECILY:     I hope so.

*A pause. They both sit down together.*

GWENDOLEN:     Perhaps this might be a favourable opportunity for my mentioning who I am. My father is Lord Bracknell. You have never heard of papa, I suppose?

CECILY:     I don't think so.

**Where are we?** Being able to imagine **where** your characters are is essential, and in a duologue you and your partner have to have a shared vision of the location. For this exercise you will have little stage set, so in your joint imaginations you have to build up a 'mind map' of where things are on stage. How big is the garden? What types of trees, shrubs and flowers are planted? What can you smell in the garden? You could visit a country house, for example, and take photographs of the grounds to help you build up a picture.

**First encounters.** This rather formal introduction also has a comic element as Gwendolen suggests that their handshake is the start of a long lasting friendship.

What does the way they speak to each other and behave tell you about the characters?

Try speaking the lines with a different thought about the other character in mind as you say them. For example, think: 'I really like you.' 'I'm jealous of you.' 'I don't trust you.' 'You're too good to be true.' 'I think you are honest.' 'I like what you're wearing.' 'You're full of yourself, aren't you?' 'You scare me.'

**113**

GWENDOLEN: Outside the family circle, papa, I am glad to say, is entirely unknown. I think that is quite as it should be. The home seems to me to be the proper sphere for the man. And certainly once a man begins to neglect his domestic duties he becomes painfully effeminate, does he not? And I don't like that. It makes men so very attractive. Cecily, mamma, whose views on education are remarkably strict, has brought me up to be extremely short-sighted; it is part of her system; so do you mind my looking at you through my glasses?

CECILY: Oh! not at all, Gwendolen. I am very fond of being looked at.

GWENDOLEN: (after examining CECILY carefully through a lorgnette): You are here on a short visit, I suppose.

CECILY: Oh no! I live here.

GWENDOLEN: (severely): Really? Your mother, no doubt, or some female relative of advanced years, resides here also?

CECILY: Oh no! I have no mother, nor, in fact, any relations.

GWENDOLEN: Indeed?

CECILY: My dear guardian, with the assistance of Miss Prism, has the arduous task of looking after me.

GWENDOLEN: Your guardian?

CECILY: Yes, I am Mr. Worthing's ward.

GWENDOLEN: Oh! It is strange he never mentioned to me that he had a ward. How secretive of him! He grows more interesting hourly. I am not sure, however, that the news inspires me with feelings of unmixed delight. *(Rising and going to her.)* I am very fond of you, Cecily; I have liked you ever since I met you! But I am bound to state that now that I know that you are Mr. Worthing's ward, I cannot help expressing a wish you were – well, just a little older than you seem to be – and not quite so very alluring in appearance. In fact, if I may speak candidly –

CECILY: Pray do! I think that whenever one has anything unpleasant to say, one should always be quite candid.

GWENDOLEN: Well, to speak with perfect candour, Cecily, I wish that you were fully forty-two, and more than usually plain for your age. Ernest has a strong upright nature. He is the very soul of truth and honour. Disloyalty would be as impossible to him as deception. But even men of the noblest possible moral character are extremely susceptible to the influence of the physical charms of others. Modern, no less than Ancient History, supplies us with many most painful examples of what I refer to. If it were not so, indeed, History would be quite unreadable.

CECILY: I beg your pardon, Gwendolen, did you say Ernest?

GWENDOLEN: Yes.

CECILY: Oh, but it is not Mr. Ernest Worthing who is my guardian. It is his brother – his elder brother.

---

**Handling the props.**
Gwendolen is using a particular type of glasses (a lorgnette), which will be unfamiliar to most people. Working with any objects early on will enable you to work out how, when and where to use them.

**Finding the meaning of the text.** You need to understand what every word means so that you know what your character is intending to say. Some words or sentences may have several meanings depending upon how they are interpreted; you and your partner must decide what the lines mean within the context or within your understanding and concept of your characters and their circumstances.

**Finding the meaning behind the words.** People do not always say what they mean and subconsciously a character can be saying something because they want a certain response from the other person. Your analysis of the dialogue has to include a judgement about the purpose behind what is being said. Look out for what are called 'vocables', sounds such as 'Oh..', 'Ah…', 'Er…'. Behind them usually lies a thought, or an emotion or a change of mind about what to say next.

| | |
|---|---|
| GWENDOLEN | *(sitting down again)*: Ernest never mentioned to me that he had a brother. |
| CECILY: | I am sorry to say they have not been on good terms for a long time. |
| GWENDOLEN: | Ah! that accounts for it. And now that I think of it I have never heard any man mention his brother. The subject seems distasteful to most men. Cecily, you have lifted a load from my mind. I was growing almost anxious. It would have been terrible if any cloud had come across a friendship like ours, would it not? Of course you are quite, quite sure that it is not Mr. Ernest Worthing who is your guardian? |
| CECILY: | Quite sure. *(A pause.)* In fact, I am going to be his. |
| GWENDOLEN | *(inquiringly)*: I beg your pardon? |
| CECILY | *(rather shy and confidingly)*: Dearest Gwendolen, there is no reason why I should make a secret of it to you. Our little county newspaper is sure to chronicle the fact next week. Mr. Ernest Worthing and I are engaged to be married. |
| GWENDOLEN | *(quite politely, rising)*: My darling Cecily, I think there must be some slight error. Mr. Ernest Worthing is engaged to me. The announcement will appear in the "Morning Post" on Saturday at the latest. |
| CECILY | *(very politely, rising)*: I am afraid you must be under some misconception. Ernest proposed to me exactly ten minutes ago. *(Shows diary.)* |
| GWENDOLEN | *(examines diary through her lorgnette carefully)*: It is certainly very curious, for he asked me to be his wife yesterday afternoon at 5.30. If you would care to verify the incident, pray do so. *(Produces diary of her own.)* I never travel without my diary. One should always have something sensational to read in the train. I am so sorry, dear Cecily, if it is any disappointment to you, but I am afraid I have the prior claim. |
| CECILY: | It would distress me more than I can tell you, dear Gwendolen, if it caused you any mental or physical anguish, but I feel bound to point out that since Ernest proposed to you he clearly has changed his mind. |
| GWENDOLEN | *(meditatively)*: If the poor fellow has been entrapped into any foolish promise I shall consider it my duty to rescue him at once, and with a firm hand. |
| CECILY | *(thoughtfully and sadly)*: Whatever unfortunate entanglement my dear boy may have got into, I will never reproach him with it after we are married. |
| GWENDOLEN: | Do you allude to me, Miss Cardew, as an entanglement? You are presumptuous. On an occasion of this kind it becomes more than a moral duty to speak one's mind. It becomes a pleasure. |
| CECILY: | Do you suggest, Miss Fairfax, that I entrapped Ernest into an engagement? How dare you? This is no time for wearing the shallow mask of manners. When I see a spade I call it a spade. |
| GWENDOLEN | *(satirically)*: I am glad to say that I have never seen a spade. It is obvious that our social spheres have been widely different. |

**Acting style.** Working out the most appropriate way of performing a piece is, to some extent, determined by the genre of the play and the way in which it is written. Style is a difficult concept to quantify; the style needs to communicate the 'feel and form' of a text in the most effective way.

**Suiting the acting style to the text.** Ironically, the more knowingly the dialogue is delivered, the less effectively it works on stage. As an actor, you have to believe what Gwendolen and Cecily say and the way they say it, however artificial and ridiculous they might sound. There is a difference between 'playing a scene for laughs' and allowing the laughs to arise naturally from the dialogue. In this instance, as in the case of most playwrights, you have to trust in the writing and allow the comedy to arise from the situation and from your skills as an actor in playing the role and delivering the lines.

**Changing points of view.** To help with character development, try swapping roles from time to time to see your own character from the other character's point of view. In this example, Gwendolen is trying to prove to Cecily that she was proposed to first; swapping the roles would give you a sense of how Cecily feels to be told this.

**Pushing the button.** Arguments between two characters are a common feature because they provide dramatic interest. In this extract, Cecily's use of the phrase 'unfortunate entanglement' hits a nerve and sets Gwendolen off, ending with her pronouncement in the final line. Look for similar moments in your choice of extract.

## Written performance concept

At least two weeks **before** the date of the performance examination, you are required to write a written performance concept, which carries 25 per cent of the marks for Section A. You will write it under supervised conditions, although you will be able to use the notes you have made during the preparation process. Your teacher will send your concept to the visiting examiner so that when they come to watch your performance, they will already have a summary account of your research, rehearsal process and the justification for your interpretation of the role.

The written performance concept requires you to show your response to the play you have chosen in the following **three** ways:

- how well you have researched and understood the relevance and importance of the social, historical, cultural and political contexts of the play

- the way in which you have prepared for the role

- a justified argument for your interpretation of the role.

If you have kept carefully prepared notes and highlighted the most important aspects of your journey towards creating the character, you should find this task relatively straightforward. You can only be successful in this part of the examination if you have carried out the research and preparation steps that have been highlighted in the previous examples.

Remember that you can also submit an annotated text for your monologue or duologue. Your annotations on this text do count towards the 500 words for the written design concept so you will need to balance your words carefully across two elements. You may wish to incorporate your annotated text into your written performance concept.

### Writing a concept

The maximum word limit for the concept is 500 words so you will need to organise your notes carefully and pare your ideas down to the essence of what you need to say. The writing frame below is a guide to help you practise writing your concept but you do not have to follow this exact structure – it is given here as a suggestion.

| Written performance concept for (*name of character*) in (*title of the play*) by (*name of the playwright*) | | |
|---|---|---|
| Social, historical, cultural and political contexts | From your notes, you should highlight the factors which, in your opinion, have the most impact on your interpretation of the play. | Allow 300–350 words for this aspect of the concept. |
| Preparation process | Here you should draw on your complete set of notes for the preparation process and present those 'revelatory' moments from your rehearsal process to demonstrate how they have informed your performance of the role. | Allow 75–100 words for this aspect of the concept. |
| Interpretation | This is a brief account of what has led you to play the role in the way that you have decided to do so. What evidence, information and thought processes have informed the decisions you have made in coming up with your particular interpretation? | Allow 75–100 words for this aspect of the concept. |

# BEING A DESIGNER IN UNIT 2 SECTION A

If you choose to be a designer rather than a performer, it will be because you already have a strong interest in the visual and aural elements of theatre. For costume, lighting, mask, makeup and set and props, you will have a background in art and design, and for sound design a background in music or music technology. For lighting and sound you will also be interested in physics from the point of view of knowing about the physical properties of light and sound and how they are created technically.

In addition, it is important that you have access to a teacher who has some specialist knowledge and expertise in your chosen design skill and who can give you appropriate advice and guidance. Your school or college will also have to have the resources and an appropriate level of equipment available to you to meet the requirements of the examination. This is particularly the case in terms of lighting and sound (see pages 129–133).

In the professional theatre, it is very rare that a designer works in isolation from other members of a creative team, because the directing and design of a production is a collaborative process: all of the design elements in a production have to interact and relate to one another. Section B of Unit 2 provides you with this realistic experience of working with a director and providing design ideas that are realised for a full staged performance. The purpose of Section A is to test your individual skill as a designer in one particular specialism.

## What are the requirements?

As a designer you have to offer one design skill in support of performer(s). This means you have to demonstrate your skill in the performance of the monologue or duologue, or in another extract from the play being performed. Bear in mind that a duologue is likely to give you more scope to demonstrate your skill than a monologue, and that if you decide to demonstrate your skill in another part of the play, you will have to enlist performer(s) to learn and perform this extract for you. Once you have decided which skill you are going to offer, you need to work with the performer(s) to ensure that you find a play which not only meets their needs but is also suitable for you to work on.

You are required to plan your design for the whole play. You will demonstrate a short section in performance, but you will also present to the examiner a demonstration of up to ten minutes about the design process and your ideas for the play. The examiner will have been sent your written design concept in advance and will expect on the day of the examination to see your portfolio, a justification of your final design decisions and other design documentation specific to your chosen design skill. These elements are covered in more detail on pages 120–133.

Your use of materials and equipment and your realisation of design are assessed against Assessment objective 1: Demonstrate the application of performance and/or production skills through the realisation of drama and theatre. Your written design concept and design documentation are assessed against Assessment objective 3: Interpret plays from different periods and genres.

## Assessment requirements

There are four areas on which you will be assessed, each of which has a maximum of ten marks. The table below shows what you would have to do to achieve the **top mark band** for each area

| AO1 Use of materials and equipment | There is outstanding use and manipulation of materials and equipment, techniques and applications. |
|---|---|
| AO1 Realisation of design | Designs are realised and executed with an outstanding level of technical skill and take absolute account of the physical demands of the production. |
| AO3 Written design concept | There is an an outstanding design concept taking an excellent account of the style, genre and overall demands of the production. |
| AO3 Design documentation | The documentation shows an outstanding response to the chosen play in relation to its social, historical, cultural and political context. There is a comprehensive design plan for the complete play and a highly detailed rationale of the final design as seen in performance. |

## Organisation

One of the real challenges for you in Unit 2 is managing your time and the resources available to you, because you are likely to be working on both Section A and Section B simultaneously. You can offer the same or different design skills for both sections of the unit, but you will be working on two different productions. However, if you have a real flair and enthusiasm for working on the non-performance aspects of a production, offering design skills can be really rewarding.

Whether you offer design skills for both sections or just Section A, if the two sections are examined on the same day it is advisable to more or less complete the work for Section A at least two weeks earlier than Section B and to put the work 'on hold' until a few days before the examination. It will be easier for you to work on an individual basis on your Section A work and to fit it around the group demands of the Section B work.

## Individual design skills

The following section is devoted to each of the six design skills options available to you for the examination. It is worth looking at each section, because in a production all of the design components work together, and it is important to understand the role of each designer. Once you have decided which design skill to offer, you will need to refer to more specialist reference books and manuals.

# Written design concept

Whichever design skill you choose, you need to complete a written design concept of no more than 500 words. Your written design concept should show your response to the play you have designed for in the following ways:

- your ability to articulate the nature of your design concept for the play

- an account of the style and genre of the play

- a recognition of the design requirements (or production demands) of the play.

The concept enables you to provide a concise account of your overriding idea for the design of the play in terms of its setting, costumes, lighting, masks, sound or makeup. It will also provide the examiner with a sense of how well you have understood and can explain the design requirements of the play. The written design concept has to be completed at least two weeks **before** the date of the examination, so you have to be at a stage where you can write in detail about what has led you to make your final design decisions.

This aspect carries 25 per cent of the marks of Unit 2, Section A, but there is a lot of crossover with the work you will have carried out during the design process and you will draw on all your other research and documentation. You will have kept a sketchbook and carefully prepared notes, which you can use as the basis for your written design concept. While you can use all of the notes and drawings you have made during the preparation process, the actual writing of the concept has to take place while you are being supervised by a teacher or invigilator.

## Writing a concept

The table below is a guide to help you practise writing your own design concept. The structure and words for each element are suggestions only and do not have to be adhered to strictly, as long as you remain within the overall 500 word limit.

| Written design concept for the set/costume/lighting/sound/masks/makeup design for (*title of the play*) by (*name of the playwright*) | | |
| --- | --- | --- |
| Nature of the design concept | This should outline how the play has stimulated your thinking and the direction that your design ideas have taken. For the visual skills, what has inspired the 'look' you have come up with for the play; and for the sound, what have you focused on in the text to 'compose' your sound tape? | Allow 300–350 words for this aspect of the concept. |
| Style and genre of the play | Here you will be writing about how you have interpreted the genre of the play and how this has influenced the design process. The style of the play itself may have inspired your particular way of working on it, or you may have adopted a style of presentation which you can argue is a valid way of interpreting the play. | Allow 75–100 words for this aspect of the concept. |
| Demands of the production | This is where you must show that you have understood all of the practical demands and requirements of the play, and considered how you are going to deal with them. | Allow 75–100 words for this aspect of the concept. |

## Costume design

The role of a costume designer is to visualise how the characters look in terms of their dress. A background in fashion and textiles is useful, but a costume designer has to be able to analyse a play's characters and design clothes with reference to personality characteristics, social position and period. For contemporary plays, it is possible to use 'off-the-peg' and shop-bought clothes, but the designer's role in this instance is to select clothes that fit in with an overall design concept for the play, and that are suitable for the characters. Clothes say a lot about who a person is, they communicate significant meaning about a character on stage and they can affect the way in which an actor can or cannot interpret a role.

## Points for consideration

- **Play analysis:** your exploration of the play will be very similar to that of a performer, mining the text for clues about their character, and you should refer to this process on pages 90–92. The difference is that you have to go through the process for all of the characters in the play. The costume requirements for the play will derive primarily from the kinds of clothes you imagine each character wearing. Look out for obvious references to costume requirements in the dialogue and in the stage directions. For example: 'Enter Malvolio, cross-gartered and wearing yellow stockings' (*Twelfth Night*, Act 3 Scene 4); 'Olivia: Give me my veil. Come, throw it o'er my face.' (Act 1 Scene 5).

- **Costume research:** your best sources of research for period costumes are portraits and social paintings in galleries or art books, or visiting costume collections in specialist museums. For contemporary costumes, magazines, photographs, clothing catalogues and films will provide you with useful resource ideas.

- **Visual research:** the natural world has given many a designer an idea for a fabric design or for the shape and texture of a garment. Patterns in nature found on leaves and plants and the look of some of nature's more curious wildlife, can be a source of inspiration.

## Examination requirements

### 1. A portfolio of research and sketches showing the development of ideas

This is a folder consisting of:

- appropriate research material that you have carefully selected and used to inform your design ideas. You should ensure that you focus on the social, historical, cultural and political contexts of the play and illustrate how these have influenced the design.

- a sketch book with samples of materials, fabrics and initial drawings of your costume designs.

You will be assessed on the quality of this design documentation and its contents will help you in writing your written design concept.

## 2. A justification for the final design decisions

This comes from your notes on the play and your analysis of the characters which will provide the evidence for your final design decisions. You need to show how you have arrived at your overall concept for the production and how this has informed the final designs for the costumes. This aspect of the work will also contribute to the assessment of the quality of your design documentation and you may want to refer to it in your written design concept.

## 3. The final designs for all of the characters in the production (minimum of three different designs)

These will be used in your presentation to the examiner, so it is a good idea to work on a large scale by illustrating your costume designs for each character on A2 sheets of paper or card. The images for each costume can be presented in any appropriate medium such as drawings, paintings, collages or as digitally produced images, so long as they give the actors, the director and the costume makers as realistic an idea of what the final costumes will look like as possible. You should think about attaching samples of fabric and material to the presentation boards to indicate what you see the costumes being made from, and provide notes about the construction methods you are suggesting should be used.

Note that you have to present the designs for all of the characters in the play and that you must show that you can demonstrate the design of at least three different costumes, although only one needs to be shown in performance for Section A. Given the limited time available to you, it is advisable to work on a play that has no more than nine and no fewer than two characters, with at least one character having a costume change in the case of the lower limit. The complexity of the design will impact on time and on costs. If you choose a play that requires elaborate costumes, they will inevitably take you longer to design and to make than costumes that are simpler in design. Getting a balance between inventive and creative design on the one hand (form) and the practicalities of the design on the other (function), is one of the central challenges you face as a designer.

This part of your presentation will demonstrate how effectively you are able to use materials and equipment.

## 4. A costume plot or list of costumes/accessories worn by each actor, indicating any changes

This is the most straightforward part of the whole process and requires you to complete a simple table or list, which maps out the costume requirements for each character in the play. This forms part of the overall quality of the design documentation and without it, you are unlikely to achieve the higher marks.

This is an example of a costume plot for *Educating Rita*:

| Roles | Rita | Frank |
|-------|------|-------|
| Act 1 Scene 1 | Pink blouse, low-cut blouse<br>Short floral patterned dress<br>High-heeled shoes (red) with straps<br>Red coat<br>Shoulder bag (fake leather) | Brown leather jacket<br>White shirt<br>Green patterned tie<br>Brown trousers<br>Brown suede shoes |
| Act 1 Scene 2 | White blouse with neat pattern<br>Cream lightweight cardigan<br>Pleated beige skirt<br>Light coloured raincoat<br>Flat brown shoes | Same as previous scene |
| Act 1 Scene 3 | Work overall from the hairdresser's<br>Plain T-shirt underneath<br>Black leggings<br>Trainers | Faded brown jumper<br>Harris Tweed jacket<br>Open-necked twill shirt<br>Black trousers<br>Black shoes |

### 5. Supervise the construction, buying, dyeing, altering, hiring and/or finding of the designed costumes and carry out one of the tasks yourself

This is where you have to turn your designs into the real thing. The assessment criteria ask you to show how well you are able to construct, make and demonstrate the finished costumes, so you need to demonstrate at least one of the tasks listed above. You are allowed to ask for help from other people in making the costumes, but you must clearly show where and when you have asked others to do things and where you have done them yourself. Communicating clear instructions to a costume maker is a skill in itself, but you must show that you can buy, dye, alter or acquire if you do not make.

### 6. Written design concept

See page 119 for information regarding the writing of the design concept.

### 7. A demonstration of the costumes

In the ten minutes available to you on the day of the examination, you have to present the examiner with your design documentation, your design ideas and the finished costumes, at least one of which must also be seen in performance.

You can finish the demonstration by highlighting aspects of each costume you have designed and saying why you have dressed the character in the way you have. Use the opportunity to sell yourself and the work that you have put into designing, making and demonstrating the costumes.

# Set and props design

The role of a set designer is to create the visual environment for a play; he or she is responsible for designing the imaginative world of the play by shaping the three-dimensional space in which a production takes place through the use of structures, colour, materials and textures. You will already have some skills in being able to work in three dimensions and be able to draw plans. The set designer's role is to suggest location, mood and atmosphere as the text and the director's interpretation requires. Props design (properties) is included because there may be a particular object or piece of furniture that is an integral part of the design. As the set designer, it is part of your role to ensure that every visual element that appears on stage has been thought through and relates to the design concept as a whole.

## Points to consider

It is important that you understand the features, layout, possibilities and limitations of the space for which you are designing. One key decision at the outset is deciding what the relationship between the audience and the performers is like. To some extent, this will depend on the type of theatre you are working in, but if you are designing for a flexible space, you can choose to design the set for any one of the following types of staging:

- end-on (with or without proscenium)

- traverse

- arena

- in-the-round

- promenade.

See pages 147–152 for more on these types of staging.

The type of staging will dictate the kind of structures you can use to create your set, but whichever type you choose, remember that the flooring material and its design can be as significant as anything else you put on stage.

## Examination requirements

### 1. A portfolio of research and sketches showing the development of ideas

The starting point for your set design is reading the text as many times as possible and then noting down responses to the following questions:

- Where is the play set? (This means geographically, i.e. what country, universe, etc., as well as more specifically, i.e. in a room, in a forest, etc.)

- When is the play set? (This might be the historical context in which the playwright intended it to be set or the one in which a director has decided to set it. For example, a production of Shakespeare's *Macbeth* could be set in ancient Scotland, or in Jacobean times or in a more contemporary period.)

- What do the stage directions (if there are any) require?

- Are there any striking visual references in the play? (These could be in the characters' lines.)

- What are the practical requirements of the text? (Does it need to have doors, walls, windows, carpets, chairs, etc.?)

- What visual reference material can I use as a starting point? (This can include architectural images, paintings, interior design catalogues and magazines.)

- What sort of materials should I put on stage? (Remember that it is not always necessary to use the 'real' thing, but there is a difference between using two-dimensional techniques, e.g. painting bricks, and three-dimensional techniques, e.g. brick mouldings.)

- What size of budget am I working with? (You have got to take into account the fact that the set for the performed extract has to be built and demonstrated under stage conditions, so you must make sure that the resources are available to you and that the design is affordable.)

- What size space am I designing for? (You will need accurate scale drawings of the theatre space that show the relationship between the stage and the audience so that you can work out 'sight-lines'.)

- What style am I working in on this production? (This is a difficult question, but you need to consider things like: how realistic has the design got to be? How abstract can the design be? How fluid will the scene changes (if any) need to be? What kind of 'look' does the set need to have?)

## 2. A justification for the final design decisions

This is a summary of your notes on the play from which you will draw your conclusions and ideas, and which will provide the evidence for your final design decisions. You need to show how you have arrived at your overall concept for the production and how this has informed the final design(s) for the set and props. This aspect of the work will contribute to the assessment of the quality of your design documentation and you may want to refer to it in your written design concept.

## 3. A scale ground plan and scale drawing of any designed properties

These are vital tools in providing instructions for the production crew when constructing and setting up the set. If you have access to a Computer Aided Design (CAD) programme, you will be able to work in three dimensions and use this information to produce a ground plan. The ground plan(s) can form part of your presentation to the examiner, so you should work on A1 or A2 sheets of paper or card and mount the plans for display purposes. The ground plan and any working drawings of stage props that are going to be made, will be assessed as part of the quality of your design documentation.

## 4. A scale model of the final design to be realised in the performance space

You are required to make your own scale model. From your drawings and sketches, you will have to put together a set model that will give a fairly good representation of how the stage will look when the set is constructed. The model should indicate what materials you want used and provide all the information about colour and positioning of different parts of the scenery. You should work on a scale of no less than 1:25. The model is your way of communicating your design intentions to the director and to the entire cast and crew of the production. As part of your presentation to the examiner, you will need to talk through the model and explain how the set works during performance. This part of your presentation will demonstrate how effectively you are able to use materials and equipment and how well you are able to realise the design.

## 5. Supervision of the construction, painting, hiring and/or finding of scenic elements to meet the requirements of the design

You may well find yourself carrying out some or all of these tasks, but it is acceptable to call on the skills and expertise of carpenters, painters and scenic builders if you require them and they are available. The most important thing is that you keep records of the instructions you give to other people, so that you can demonstrate your input into the construction and making process. The key message is to keep the design simple but effective, because you will probably not have the time and resources to build a complex set. You will need to build one aspect of the set to demonstrate how you can get from the model stage to the building stage.

## 6. The written design concept

See page 119 for information on the writing of the design concept.

## 7. Demonstration of your set design

You have ten minutes to demonstrate to the examiner how you have approached the role of set designer for your selected play. You should treat the presentation as though it were a performance: make sure you rehearse it and time it, and that you have the confidence to sell your ideas. You should plan to:

- outline your inspiration for the design, your understanding of the play and how you have researched the social, cultural, historical and political contexts of the play. You might consider taking digital images of pages from your research portfolio and using PowerPoint to explain the process you have gone through

- present your ground plan, working drawings and developmental sketches

- demonstrate the set model – again, this could include a previously recorded demonstration that you play back using a digital projector

- show the set for the chosen extract to the examiner in a performance context.

Above all, you must show that you have a grasp of the practicalities of set design and can produce a set design that is both artistically satisfying and one that works in practice.

## Masks and makeup design

These two skills are discussed together here, since they are both to do with altering, enhancing or highlighting an actor's appearance; however, you must remember that in Section A you have to choose between being **either** a mask designer **or** a makeup designer.

- **Makeup designer**: it is a makeup designer's responsibility to use facial and body makeup, wigs and hairpieces and possibly prosthetics (the addition of false pieces of skin) to give an actor an added dimension to the portrayal of a particular role or roles. There is some overlap with masks because latex mouldings can be used to alter a performer's facial appearance (especially with special effects makeup), and makeup and additional hair will then be added to create a character makeup. Similarly, there are types of makeup, such as those used in Japanese Kabuki theatre, which are so stylised that they take on the appearance of a mask.

- **Mask designer:** masks are an ancient way of creating character based in ritual, where the function of the mask is to depersonalise the individual and enable the performer to embody a character as depicted by the mask. In ancient Greek theatre, all actors wore masks and in the Italian *commedia dell'arte*, there were masks for each of the stock comic characters. In contemporary theatre, there are companies such as *Trestle* that specialise in performances with masks. Masks are also a common feature of non-western performance traditions.

## Examination requirements

### 1. A portfolio of research and sketches showing the development of ideas

Start by reading the text as many times as possible and noting down references to how a character looks and behaves. You can refer to the questions on pages 105–108 and use much the same approach as a performer in gaining an understanding of the characters in the play.

A section of your portfolio should contain visual research material. For masks, you should carry some exploration of different types of masks and comment on their appearance. There will be aspects of their shape, size, texture, materials and style that might act as a starting point for your own ideas. For makeup, you should collect appropriate images of faces that have been made up and assess the appropriateness of the ways in which makeup has been used to emphasise different aspects of the face, and how this communicates different characteristics.

Once you have gathered ideas from the play and research material, you can progress to developmental drawings. You should make several attempts at drawing masks or makeups for each character, and select what you consider to be the most visually satisfying solutions for your design. Include an explanation as to why you have selected the ones you have for further development into the finished article.

### 2. A justification for the final design decisions

This leads on from the range of drawings and research you have done and is your opportunity to discuss the reasons for your approach and for the look you have given the masks or the makeups. You should support your design decisions with examples of lines or stage directions from the text that have triggered particular ideas.

Equally, you should refer back to research material you have used and say how it has inspired your thinking and ideas. You need to provide an overall concept for the production and illustrate how this has formed the basis for your final designs. This will also contribute to the assessment of the quality of your design documentation and you may want to refer to it in your written design concept.

### 3. A list showing the choice of materials and application methods for your makeup design or the materials and construction methods being used for your mask design

This is a straightforward list of the resources used in the final designs and could take the form of a table like the ones below:

| Makeup resource list | | |
|---|---|---|
| **No.** | **Item** | **Application method** |
| 1 | Latex prosthetic nose | Glue and glue brush |
| 2 | Black eyeliner | Eyebrow pencil and thin brush |

| Mask resource list | | |
|---|---|---|
| **No.** | **Item** | **Construction method** |
| 1 | Alginate mould | Vaseline performer's face, use breathing straws and apply to make 'negative' impression |
| 2 | Plaster cast | Pour plaster of Paris into alginate mould to create 'positive' impression of performer's face |

The accuracy and detail of your resource list will be assessed as part of the quality of your design documentation.

### 4. The final design for all of the characters in the production (minimum of three different designs)

It is a good idea to work on a large scale by illustrating your mask or makeup designs for each character on A2 or A3 sheets of paper or card, so they can form part of your presentation to the examiner. The images can be presented in any appropriate medium, such as drawings, paintings, collages or digitally produced images, so long as they give the examiner a realistic impression of what you intend the final design to look like.

- For masks, you can attach samples of materials or textures to the presentation boards to indicate what you see the masks being made from, and provide notes about the construction methods you are using.

- For makeup, you can attach samples of hair and try-outs of makeup colour and types, and provide notes about how you are going to apply the makeup and in what stages.

For both masks and makeup, it is a good idea to present the designs that you have selected as the ones that will be executed as 'staged drawings'. In most cases, the process of applying makeup or mask making consists of building up different layers of material.

- With makeup, stage one could be showing the foundation colour with cheek bones shaded in; the next drawing or image might add the jaw bones shaded in, and so on.

- With mask making, stage one could be an image of the basic mould structure, followed by a second stage showing the application of some kind of texturing (for example, gluing on rope to create eyebrows), and so on.

You have to present the design drawings for all of the characters in the play and demonstrate the complete design of at least three different masks or makeups, although only one needs to be demonstrated in performance. It is, therefore, advisable to work on a play with no more than nine and no fewer than three characters. You may find a play that has a section with special makeup or mask design requirements, while the rest of the play has none (for example, the play within a play in Shakespeare's *Hamlet*). In this instance, you could justify your mask or makeup assignment in terms of focusing on this specialist area.

You will be designing a mask or makeup for a particular performer, and it will help you in the design process if you can work with your model fairly early on. No two faces or heads are alike, and a mask or makeup that works on a head and face of one shape and size may not work so well on another.

- For makeup, it will help you in making the final design decisions to practise your makeup design on the model as many times as possible. Taking digital photographs at each stage will also help you record the process and act as a visual aid, so that you can reproduce as identical a makeup as possible for each performance.

- For masks, it will help if you build the mask around the head and face of the performer and check out how well it fits at each stage of the process. If the performer has to speak wearing the mask, it is vital that nothing covers the mouth and that you have designed the mouthpiece to act as a sort of megaphone to project the voice forward. If you intend to use a microphone because you want the actor's mouth to be covered, you will need to test the technology and work out the best place to fit the microphone inside the mask.

This part of your presentation will demonstrate how effectively you are able to use materials and equipment.

### 5. You must create at least one of the masks or makeup designs yourself but can supervise a mask maker or makeup artist creating the other two

Depending upon the complexity of the design, you can distribute your workload by calling on the help of other people. However, you must keep records of the instructions you give to other people, so that you can demonstrate your input into the construction, making and application process. If you can display photographs of the working process, these will support your demonstration.

### 6. The written design concept

See page 119 for information regarding the writing of the design concept.

### 7. A demonstration of at least one mask or makeup in performance

On the day of the examination, you have ten minutes to present your design documentation, your design ideas and the completed masks or makeups. Apply or fit the makeup or masks before the examination so that you do not have to make adjustments or wait for makeup to dry. The examiner will want to see the performer(s) wearing your designed mask(s) or makeup under stage lighting and gauge whether they work practically. In your demonstration you should highlight those aspects of each mask or makeup that you think are particularly important to your overall design concept. Above all, take the opportunity to demonstrate your confidence and passion for the work and your knowledge of mask or makeup design.

# Lighting design

The lighting designer's role is to control and engineer the way in which the audience perceives what is on stage through the careful and selective manipulation of stage lighting. It requires someone with visual skills and sensibilities (to understand how light, shade and colour play on surfaces and enhance the three-dimensional space), and technical skills (to use stage lanterns and control equipment).

In most productions, the lighting designer is responsible for lighting a set, and works closely with the set designer to use lighting to suggest location, mood and atmosphere as the text and the director's interpretation requires. The lighting designer also has to light the performers, their costumes and masks and makeup to their best advantage. In addition, a lighting designer might design and use still or moving projections within a production.

## Points for consideration

- **Directional use of lighting**: this can affect the way designed objects look on stage and can be a creative way of thinking about lantern placement. For example, a textured surface will have a different appearance if lit from above than if lit to the side.

- **Colour theory**: you will need to know about the physics and psychology of additive and subtractive colour, because using coloured lighting can affect the perceived colour of an object. For example, lighting a costume that is mostly red with green light will make it appear brown or black.

- **Behaviour of materials**: you will have to investigate the way that light behaves on different surfaces and materials, because some will absorb different levels of light, while others will reflect it.

- **Lighting research**: photographs and films from different periods (especially black and white ones) will provide you with a useful resource to examine the way subjects have been lit and what effects can be created using light.

- **Lighting as scenery**: in productions with minimal setting and plays that require short scenes in different locations, lighting is often used to suggest a location and to move quickly from one place to another. Lighting an area of the stage with a dappled effect and a hint of green can be enough to suggest a forest scene, and changing to an area of the stage lit by the projection of light coming through the bars of a window can instantly indicate a scene set in a prison cell.

In order to demonstrate your skill, you must have access to a control desk (preferably with computer controlled memory) as standard with lighting bars or a grid that will enable you to position at least 16 lanterns. It is also important that you can use at least two different kinds of lanterns, such as a fresnel and a profile spot. If you have access to a Computer Aided Design (CAD) programme or specialist lighting design software, you will be able to produce plans in three dimensions as well as a two-dimensional rigging plan. There is no maximum specification, so having access to automated lanterns and more sophisticated equipment is a bonus, as long as you are able to use it creatively and in keeping with the play you are lighting.

## Examination requirements

### 1. A portfolio of research and sketches showing the development of ideas

This will contain all of the ideas, notes, sketches and research material that you have produced while investigating the lighting possibilities and requirements of the play. It should illustrate your thinking process and explain why some items of research were rejected, while others were selected.

### 2. A justification for the final lighting design

This will be a summary statement based on the notes you have made on the play, and detailing the conclusions and ideas you have come to as evidence for your final design decisions. You need to show how you have arrived at your overall concept for the production, and how this has informed the final lighting design. Your design justification will contribute to the assessment of the quality of your design documentation and you may want to refer to it in your written design concept.

### 3. The final lighting design with grid plan and lantern schedule that shows the use of at least two different kinds of lantern and uses a minimum of 16 lanterns

The lantern schedule is an essential document that lists all the lanterns that you are using and their function and it usually has a key linked to the lighting plan. Your plans can form part of the presentation you give to the examiner, so you should work on A1 or A2 sheets of paper or card and mount the plans for display purposes. The lighting plan and schedule and any other visuals will be assessed as part of the quality of your design documentation, and will indicate how you have been able to work with the equipment.

### 4. A lighting plot or cue sheet showing at least six different lighting states

Draw up a cue sheet like the one below. You should also have a copy of the script with the lighting cue numbers marked on the actual word where each cue happens.

With some computer memory boards, it is possible to print out a chart showing the setup of each lighting cue in terms of the level of each lantern and the timings of each transition; this replaces the need to have a manual list like this one.

| Cue no. | Description of lighting setup | Lantern settings | Timings |
|---------|-------------------------------|------------------|---------|
| 1 | General warm cover to suggest early morning light coming through window. | Channel 1 @ 65% Channel 4 @ 85% etc. | Fade up from black over 10 seconds. |

### 5. You must carry out at least one of the following tasks: rigging, focusing or operating of the design, and you must supervise any that you do not do yourself

If you do delegate tasks, you must keep records of the instructions you give so that you can demonstrate how you have communicated your intentions to a rigger or operator. Unless you can physically move the lighting board into the auditorium, it is not a good idea for you to set and programme the lighting desk yourself, because what is seen from the control room is never the same as what the audience will see. Once you are happy with the lighting levels and the type and speed of transitions, you can then operate the desk yourself if you choose to do so.

### 6. The written design concept

See page 119 for information on the writing of the design concept.

### 7. Demonstration of your lighting design

In the ten minute demonstration to the examiner, you have to talk through your approach to the play and show how you have interpreted it. In the performed extract you will need to demonstrate at least one lighting change.

# Sound design

Sound in the theatre is like aural scenery. On hearing the sound of rain, wind blowing through the trees or a motorcar engine, an audience can immediately locate the action of a scene. The sound designer's role is to create the most appropriate and effective sound world for a production. Sound can be both live and pre-recorded, so you need the technical know-how to record sound and play it back through a sound reproduction system, as well as to use microphones and an amplification system to reinforce the volume and effectiveness of sounds (including the speaking and singing of performers). The sound designer works with the director in deciding what music and sound effects a play requires by 'spotting' the moments in the script when sound will be used.

## Equipment requirements

At the very least you are going to need access to:

- microphones

- a means of recording (e.g. a mini disc or digital hard disk recorder)

- a means of playback (e.g. a mini disc player or digital player)

- a means of editing (e.g. computer software that will enable you to cut and paste sound data)

- a means of mixing (e.g. an analogue or digital sound mixer that will enable you to mix sounds from different sources, add effects, and also be used to play back sound from both live and recorded sources in performance)

- a means of amplification (e.g. an amplifier that can reproduce good quality sound at a range of volumes that will suit the performing space)

- a means of sound reproduction (e.g. a set of good quality stereo speakers that will project the sound effectively in and around the auditorium).

## Points for consideration

### Diegetic or non-diegetic sound

Music and sound function on at least two levels in the production of a play:

- Music or sound effects that are used to create atmosphere, suggest a period or place or used as underscoring (e.g. a melancholy violin melody to emphasise a sad moment), and are heard by the audience but are not part of the on-stage world or the narrative of the play are known as non-diegetic sound.

- Sound or music that is part of the narrative and that the characters in the play are aware of (e.g. a character puts money into a jukebox and a record plays), is known as diegetic sound.

This is an important distinction because it can alter the way that you record the sound and the volume on playback. In the case of a jukebox, you could either play the music back through the jukebox's own speakers if it were practically possible; or you might need to imitate the effect of hearing the music from a jukebox by 'thinning out' the sound of the music in the mix and playing it back at a volume that would suggest the sound was coming from on-stage. If you wanted to use the same jukebox music non-diegetically to set the period, for example, it would require a fuller mix that was played back at a fuller volume in order for the sound to fill the auditorium.

> **Tip**
>
> Live sound design, especially for musicals, is a highly sophisticated skill and requires the use of equipment that is likely to be beyond the budget available to you for this examination. It is, therefore, recommended that you focus on recorded sound and the creation of a 'sound tape' that can be played on cue during the course of a performance.

### Sound theory and technical knowledge

You need to be familiar with terms such as: frequency, equalisation, balance, stereo field, volume and ambience. You also have to have a basic understanding of acoustics, so that you are aware of how sound behaves in the auditorium that you are working in.

On the technical side, you need to know about different types of microphone and their function, and how to operate a sound mixer and an effects unit. You should be able to operate the playback and recording equipment available to you, and be able to set up the sound system. While analogue tape and tape recorders are still available, you are more likely to be using digital equipment and computer software that will enable you to record, engineer and play back the sound. You may also have access to music samplers and a sequencer to produce your own sound effects and music, or be able to work with a music student who could help you to create original music using a computer.

## Examination requirements

### 1. Notes listing the sound requirements and ideas for the play

This is the work that you will do when 'spotting' the text. There will be obvious stage directions in the play that you should highlight and list, such as: *The cock crows* (*Hamlet*, Act 1 Scene 1). Beyond the obvious indication of sound effects, your analysis of the play should extend to:

- looking out for references to sound or music in the dialogue

- identifying places (mostly at the start of a scene or for scene changes) where music might be appropriate, and suggest possible ideas for the type of music you could use

- suggesting places where sound might enhance the atmosphere of a scene or suggest a location

- considering the style, period and type of play (or the production of it) and how this will influence the way you create and reproduce the sound score and the sort of music you might use.

### 2. A justification for the choice of effects and/or music and their use

This is a summary of your notes and ideas on the play from the perspective of the sound designer. In it, you will provide the evidence and your reasoned argument for your final choice of sound effects and music. Remember that although you only have to demonstrate one sound cue in the performance extract, you have to show your understanding and ideas for your sound score for the entire play and be able to demonstrate at least six sound cues, three of which must be original. Your justification will contribute to the assessment of the quality of your design documentation and you may want to refer to it in your written design concept.

### 3. A source sheet showing the creation of at least three original sound effects and the source of the remaining cues (e.g. CD title and number, MIDI file from the internet)

This is the completion of a simple table that shows the source and type of each sound cue. You should also include a copy of the script, with the cues for each sound effect marked up and numbered.

---

**Tip**

You may have to look for authentic recordings to suit the needs of the play. For example, if the script calls for a nightingale to be heard, it is not good enough to use any kind of birdsong. Similarly if a scene is set in New York and you use street sounds recorded in London, the odd sound like the call of a street seller or a police siren will give away the fact that you have not researched the source of your sound effect with enough attention to detail.

The table below gives an example of part of a source sheet.

| Cue no. | Description of sound cue | Source(s) | Timings |
|---|---|---|---|
| 1 | The sound of an engine starting up and a car moving off outside the house with the sound of rain against the windows | (a) live location recording of car being started up and driving off on gravel driveway [Recorded 02/12/07 outside Number 17, Parkway Road] | (a) 14 seconds |
| | | (b) live studio recording of water from shower hose splashing onto a sheet of glass | (b) 4 minutes 45 seconds |

### 4. A cue sheet showing the order, length and output level of each cue

You need to complete a cue sheet for the sound cues you are going to demonstrate. This will be linked to your copy of the marked up script, which will show where all of the sound cues occur in the play. The play may call for many more cues than you will demonstrate. You should indicate all of the cue numbers on the cue sheet, but you need only complete the 'length' and 'output' levels for the cues to be demonstrated. Where a cue is fading up microphones for a 'live' cue, there is no need to include an indication of length.

### 5. You must mix and produce the final sound tape(s) which should include at least three original cues which you have created and recorded using live and/or sampled material and three further sound cues. You can either be the sound operator yourself or delegate the responsibility to someone else whom you must supervise

You must do more than just copy existing music or sound effects recordings. In the table above you can see that the effects have been recorded live and will have to be mixed together to create the effect of them happening at the same time.

### 6. The written design concept

See page 119 for information on the writing of the design concept.

### 7. A demonstration of your sound score within the context of the performance

In the ten minute demonstration to the examiner you have to talk through your approach to the play and explain your interpretation with regard to the sound effects and music. In the performed extract you will need to demonstrate at least one sound cue.

# SECTION B

You will by now have discovered that Unit 2 is about plays in performance. In Section A you perform in, or design for, an extract from a play, while in Section B you perform in, or design for, a full production of a professionally published play by a known writer. One of the crucial differences you will experience in Section B is that of working with a **director**, who is likely to be your teacher.

## What do you do if you choose to be a performer?

You will perform in a group of no fewer than three and no more than nine in a performance lasting between 15 and 60 minutes (depending on the size of your group).
You will:

- work collaboratively with a company of actors and a creative team that will include a director and possibly one or more designers

- take part in rehearsals

- work on your role outside of rehearsals

- perform to an appropriate audience.

## What do you do if you choose to be a designer?

You will offer one or more design skills (setting and props, costume, masks, makeup, lighting, sound) in support of a group performance, and work with the director in developing the designs for the production.
You will:

- work collaboratively with a director and other members of a creative team where applicable

- work with members of a production team to ensure that the design is realised for the performance

- work with the performance company as appropriate

- fulfil your role during the preparation process and in performance

- give a presentation of up to ten minutes to the visiting examiner prior to the performance, and provide relevant design documentation

- complete in advance a written design concept.

## The production process for Section B

In Section B your teacher will be directing you and will organise meetings and rehearsals. It will be important for you to organise yourself well between rehearsals and to complete any tasks you are assigned, but specific dates will be advised by your teacher.

Once the director has chosen the play for performance, there are three basic stages:

- **Pre-production**: the director works on the text and comes up with some initial ideas. The director will provide the creative (design) team with a brief outlining the overall concept for the production, and a series of meetings will follow in which design ideas are brought to the table, discussed, modified and eventually agreed. In parallel with this process, the director will also start auditioning performers and make decisions about who to cast in which role or roles.

- **Production**: the director works with the actors in rehearsals whilst the design elements are worked on. Usually it is necessary for most design decisions to be made prior to the start of rehearsals, but there can be occasions when designs are developed as rehearsals progress. It is all a matter of timing, because everything has to be ready in time for the final stage: the performance.

- **Performance**: the play is ready to be presented to an audience.

Pages 138–141 give more details on how this process works for performers and pages 144–145 give more details for designers.

## Working with a director

Whether you are a performer or designer, you will be working with a director in Section B. There is no one defining principle for what a director does or how they should carry out their role. At one extreme, there are directors who want to dictate exactly how every role should be played. At the other extreme, some take such a back seat by allowing the actors to decide everything for themselves, that they may as well not be there at all. In reality, of course, most directors are somewhere in the middle of these two extremes, but, you will find that no two directors work in exactly the same way.

It is the director's responsibility to provide a conceptual framework for the production, and to communicate this to the company of performers and designers so that it informs everyone's work. Your teacher will send to the examiner before the examination date a written intention of their interpretation of the production with regards to style and genre. It is important that you understand this interpretation and how it relates to your role.

A play for a director is like entering a new country for the first time. He or she will be stimulated by the sounds, the smells, the events, the thoughts, the spoken words and the whole look and feel of the play. The play will fire the director's imagination and he or she will begin to see possibilities in the text and potential ways of realising the playwright's work on stage.

The role of a director is a relatively new arrival in the theatre profession. In the Ancient Greek theatre it seems that playwrights like Aeschylus and Aristophanes were responsible for overseeing the production of their own plays, but the idea of having a person who has overall responsibility for the artistic concept of a production was a late 19th-century phenomenon.

### Activity 1

Read the three quotes on the next page from famous directors. What do they tell you about directing and how a director might approach a text?

### Edward Gordon Craig (1872–1966)

'His work as interpreter of the play of the dramatist is something like this: he takes the copy of the play from the hands of the dramatist and promises faithfully to interpret it as indicated in the text … He then reads the play, and during the first reading the entire colour, tone, movement and rhythm that the work must assume comes clearly before him. As for the (stage) director, descriptions of the scenes, etc. with which the author may interlard his copy, these are not to be considered by him, for if he is master of his craft he can learn nothing from them … He then puts the play aside for some time, and in his mind's eye mixes his palette (to use a painter's expression) with the colour which the impression of the play has called up. Therefore, on sitting down a second time to read through the play, he is surrounded by an atmosphere which he proposes to test. At the end of the second reading he will find that his more definite impressions have received clear and unmistakable corroboration, and that some of his impressions which were less positive have disappeared … It is possible even now to suggest, in line and colour, some of the scenes and ideas which are filling his head, but this is more likely to be delayed until he has re-read the play at least a dozen times.'

### Nicholas Hytner, Artistic Director of the Royal National Theatre

I think it would be irresponsible of me to come to a first rehearsal without some feeling, even if it's ill-defined, of where the heart of the play might be, of what essential core of it is going to bring it alive… A play on a page can and might be analysed, examined and written about for ever. But that is a different play to the experience it will be when fully inhabited by actors. In a way a play is merely a series of instructions for a group of people who will come out onto a stage and create a whole experience. There's always a three-way conversation going on between playwright, actors and audience. Whatever you might feel is the heart of the play is going to shift when you find out what the heart is of a group of people that you've asked to be in it. You might have an idea of what a play might be and cast accordingly but frankly you can never know.

### Konstantin Stanislavski (1863–1938)

The responsibility for creating an ensemble, for its artistic integrity, the expressiveness of the over-all performance lies with the director… The joint work of the director and the actors, the search for the essential kernel of the play begins with analysis and proceeds along the line of through-going action. Later comes the determination of the through line in each role – that fundamental impetus of each part which as it derives naturally from its character, fixes its place in the general action of the play… one can only advise them (directors) not to foist anything on their actors, not to tempt them beyond the range of their capacities, but to enthuse them.

# Performing for Unit 2, Section B

As a performer in Section B you are involved in the work in the rehearsal room, and the work on your role and yourself as a performer outside the rehearsal room. You will bring with you to the rehearsal your own skills, experience and knowledge of acting, and you will apply and develop these further within the context of the play that your teacher/director has chosen to produce for the examination.

You will be using similar approaches in developing a role as in Section A. From the moment when you receive the script up until the opening performance, you are concerned with the stages outlined in the table below. Look back at the relevant pages of Section A to see what is involved in each stage.

| | |
|---|---|
| **Reading and analysis** | In Section A you read and analyse a whole play text, but prepare only a short extract for performance. You identify information about your character (including the given circumstances), develop an interpretation of your role and annotate the text with your ideas (see pages 90, 95, 105 and 111). In Section B the process is similar except that you are preparing the whole play for performance and working with a director and at least two other performers. Your reading and analysis will involve:<br><br>• getting to know the play as a whole<br>• understanding the director's interpretation of the play<br>• identifying information about your character from the text<br>• contributing to a shared understanding of the meaning of the play<br>• annotating the text with questions, thoughts and ideas that have occurred from your own analysis, from the director's analysis and from the analysis of other actors. |
| **Researching the context** | In Section A you research the historical, social, cultural and political contexts of your play and consider how these relate to the interpretation of your role (see pages 90–91, 96–98, 102, 107 and 112). Your research in Section B will be similar but may be more directed by your teacher-director and will be linked to their interpretation. You will be:<br><br>• carrying out background research tasks set by the director<br>• researching the contexts in which the play was written<br>• researching the context of your character(s)<br>• carrying out research to understand the context of the production<br>• identifying the possible historical, social, cultural and political influences on the play and on the production.<br><br>Note that you do not have to produce a written performance concept for Section B, but you do have to understand the director's concept for the play. |
| **Experimentation** | The experimentation stage for Section B is much like that for Section A, although it will involve working with more than one other performer and you will have the input of your director. Look at the exercises on pages 91, 103, 107 and 112 for examples of the kinds of activities you might use. Whatever exercises you take part in, the experimentation process in Section B is likely to involve:<br><br>• taking part in and responding to rehearsal exercises to explore the meaning of the play and to develop an understanding of your character<br>• working with other actors on different ways of staging the scene<br>• experimenting with different ways of speaking and moving. |

| Building the character | As with the experimentation stage, building your character in Section B will be very similar to the process in Section A. The activities and suggestions on pages 92, 104, 108 and 113–114 will give you ideas for building your character from the inside for Section B. This stage will include: <br><br> • work you do outside the rehearsal room in order to develop your character <br> • taking part in exercises set by the director designed to develop character <br> • bringing ideas about your character to rehearsals and trying them out with other actors (for example, trying out different accents, voices, walks, using a prop). |
|---|---|
| Preparing for performance | For Section B you are preparing a longer performance than that required for Section A. The advice on the pages that follow will therefore be most useful for this stage, which involves: <br><br> • learning the lines and the moves <br> • practising your vocal and physical techniques <br> • rehearsing the stage business to ensure everyone is working together and knows what they are doing <br> • being focused and concentrated on the work <br> • finding ways of keeping your performance spontaneous. |

## Assessment requirements: performers

Your vocal and movement skills are assessed against Assessment objective 1: Demonstrate the application of performance and/or production skills through the realisation of drama and theatre.
Your characterisation and communication are assessed against Assessment objective 3: Interpret plays from different periods and genres See page 4 for more on these.

As a performer, you will be assessed on four areas, all of which are worth a maximum of ten marks. The grid below shows what you would have to achieve to reach the **top mark band** for each of the assessment areas.

| AO1 Vocal skills | An outstanding command of vocal skills is demonstrated, including clarity and use of pause, pace, pitch, tone, inflection and projection throughout the performance. |
|---|---|
| AO1 Movement skills | Student shows an outstanding ability to embody the role(s) and the ability to use gesture, poise and stillness with control and sensitivity. |
| AO3 Characterisation | There is outstanding understanding of the role(s) and its context within the play. Characterisation is complete, consistent and fully committed to the style and context. |
| AO3 Communication | There is outstanding rapport with other members of the cast. Communication with the audience and examiner is outstanding and shows a full awareness of audience response. |

## The production process for performers

### The read through

**Tip**

Before the company of actors comes together for the first time to rehearse, you may already have had the chance to read the play for yourself. From your first reading of the play, you will have formed some initial impressions and have questions about it: you should begin the habit of keeping a rehearsal notebook and recording these thoughts and questions.

While in Section A you are likely to select the play and your role, in Section B your teacher-director will choose the play and cast the roles. Your first read through of the text is therefore likely to take place with the rest of your group and the director.

The first read through of the play by performers is the start of a long journey of discovery, but while it can be fun, it can also be tedious. Your response to the play might vary from one of excitement to one of disappointment. Whatever your first response to the play, make a note of it, and as rehearsals develop, reflect on your initial thoughts and see if you can discover the reasons behind your reaction. Remember that your viewpoint of the play at the read through is likely to be from that of the character or characters that you are playing, and it might tell you something about how your character comes across in the play and how others react to you.

**Working on the script**

Your work on the script begins at the read through, so make sure that you always have a pencil to mark the script as things occur to you, for example:

- words or phrases that trip you up or require further explanation

- words or phrases that seem to flow and you are comfortable saying

- any lines that get a reaction from the rest of the cast (e.g. laughter, disgust, confusion, wonder).

You will have at least as much work to do on your role outside of the rehearsal as you will in it. There will be times when you are not in a particular scene or section and you are not called for rehearsal, so this is an opportunity for you to do your own work on building your role. In the early stages of rehearsal, it is also helpful for you to watch what the other actors are doing and how their scenes and roles are developing. You can always learn something about approaches to acting and insights into the play just from observing others.

**The rehearsal process**

As mentioned on the page 137, the rehearsal process for Section B will be similar to the way you work on your monologue or duologue in Section A, but it will be informed by the work that is going on in the rehearsal room and by the tasks set by the director. Section B is much more collaborative, which means that everyone in the cast can find things out about the play and share their research and ideas with the whole company.

**Getting the best out of rehearsals**

The rehearsal room is a very exciting place to be, as you're working together to bring a play text to life. It can also be a frustrating place to be at times, for example if a scene just does not seem to work, if an individual actor cannot get it right and you have to repeat something over and over again, or if you have to wait around until it is your turn to rehearse your 'bit'.

- Have patience and try to remain focused.

- Use the 'waiting time' to work on your own role.

- Read your notes and keep exploring the background to the play and to your character.

- Use the corridor outside or a room nearby to run through your scenes with other people (even if it is not the actor who is playing opposite you).

- If appropriate (and if the director is open to suggestions), contribute ideas or possible solutions to the problem scene or moment.

## Tip

It is worth noting Stanislavski's advice to his actors: 'Love the art in yourself and not yourself in art.' This is a tough message, but it means that working as an ensemble on the play for performance is not about 'star quality' or 'showing off'; it is about being truthful to the play and to the integrity of your production of it. Similarly, it is true to say that, 'there are no small parts, only small actors.' In other words, every actor in the play, whether they have three or 300 lines, is equally important, and it takes as much to create a character who says very little, as it does to create one that has a lot to say for themselves.

## Tip

Stage business – any action in a production that requires choreographing and relies on timing – can take longer to rehearse and set than a dialogue scene. A fight scene, for example, has to be carefully worked out so that it communicates the intended violence, but is acted in such a way that no one actually gets hurt.

### Working for the good of the company

The more you are prepared to put into rehearsals, the more you are likely to get out of them. The director's role is not about telling you how to act and how to develop your character, but is about suggesting ways you can do things better. You will probably receive a lot more comments about what is wrong with your performance than what is right with it, and you must respond to this feedback in a positive way.

One of the most difficult things for an actor is remembering everything: the lines, the moves, the cues, handling props, as well as all of the psychological aspects to the role, such as behaviour, thinking and motivation. You may often find that just when you think you have learnt everything you need to know and do in a scene, the director wants to change something. However frustrating this can be, it is something you have to cope with: remember that the director is trying to ensure that all the pieces of the jigsaw fit together and work effectively.

### Having an objective in mind

It is quite likely that the director will have a particular objective in mind for each rehearsal and will explain to the cast what he or she hopes to achieve during a particular section. Every rehearsal is about improving your understanding of the play and your role, and practising how you, as an actor, do things and say things, but it will help if you identify something particular that you want to achieve during each rehearsal. Here are some examples:

- I want to work on the pace of the dialogue in this scene.

- I want to play the scene, trying out different objectives for the character.

- I want to rehearse the difficult bit that we keep getting wrong.

- I want to explore the comic possibilities of this scene more.

- I want to see if I can get more feeling into this scene.

### Learning lines

Learning lines thoroughly (and early) is vital. The tips below should help to make the process more manageable:

- Make sure that you understand what you are saying and why you are saying it.

- It helps to learn lines after you've sorted out the movements linked with them (blocking).

- Break the text into manageable sections, with logical dividing points.

- Read through your line/speech, cover it up with a piece of paper, look at the cue and say it out loud. If you get it wrong, go back until you get it right.

- When you're familiar with a section, record the cues and say the lines in response to them.

## The technical rehearsal

By this point in the process, you will be getting very close to the performance examination date. The staging of the play will be more or less fixed, and you will have memorised everything you need to know and do on stage. You may have been lucky enough to rehearse in the actual performance space, but quite often the technical rehearsal will be the first opportunity you have to work on the stage. The primary purpose of the technical rehearsal is to rehearse all of the technical details: for the stage crew to find out where and when scenery or props are moved, and for the lighting and sound crew to set levels and time cues.

As an actor, you have to learn to have the utmost patience at technical rehearsals. You need to be ready to run a scene from one cue to the next, and stop and go back on it as many times as is required. It is sometimes the first opportunity that you will have working with the actual props and you will need to rehearse these moments. For example, in rehearsal you may have been miming the eating of a sandwich, but when you come to eat a real sandwich and speak dialogue, it is very different. You will have to work out how big a mouthful you can take at a time, and how long it takes you to swallow before you can speak.

## The dress rehearsal

Now you are even closer to opening night. You may have more than one dress rehearsal, but it is called a dress rehearsal because it is about 'dressing up' in your costume and wearing masks, wigs and makeup, if appropriate. In every respect it should be like a performance but without the audience. The purpose of the rehearsal is to get used to the costume and to acting under performance conditions with all of the technical aspects going on around you.

## The performance

This is the moment you have been waiting for and the culmination of weeks of rehearsal and preparation. Everything is poised to happen. You feel a mixture of excitement and nervousness as the body's adrenalin kicks in, but you will have prepared yourself mentally and physically. You have warmed up so that your voice and body can perform at their peak. Your mind is focused on the words, actions and inner life of the role and your imagination is fired up to enter the world of the play. You have checked your props and know where they are, and looked at yourself in the mirror to make sure that you look right for the part. You have run through any tricky bits of business with other actors at least an hour before 'curtain up'.

Thirty minutes before the performance is due to start, you are ready for your first cue. Finally, you step out on to the stage, the lights are on you and you can feel the audience's presence. The performance has begun and in 15 to 60 minutes' time the audience will undoubtedly applaud and it will all be over.

Does any of this sound familiar? As a performer, your experience will be something like that described here and there is no reason why the experience of taking part in an examination performance should be any different. If you have done all of the preparation work described earlier and you aim to give of your best, then you cannot go far wrong. So, as they say in the best theatrical tradition, 'break a leg', but not literally, of course.

'Break a leg' probably refers to getting as many bows as possible from an appreciative audience. You have to break the leg at the knee in order to bow or curtsey. Also the 'legs' in a proscenium arch theatre are the vertical side pieces of scenery that the actors have to pass to get on stage. By having to return to the stage so many times to take a bow, an actor might 'break a leg'.

# Designing for Unit 2, Section B

All of the processes and procedures outlined in the design section for Section A (pages 117–133) will be the same for you as a designer in Section B, with the exception that you will be working to a brief set by your teacher/director and you can offer more than one design skill. Read the opening paragraphs and points for consideration for each design skill in Section A, as these introduce the key aspects and requirements for each skill.

The table below shows what the requirements are for each design skill. If you are offering more than one skill, you need to cover the elements in bold for each skill. If you are offering only one skill, you need to cover all the requirements listed for that skill.

| Lighting | <ul><li>**A portfolio of research and sketches showing the development of ideas**: this will contain all of the ideas, notes, sketches and research material that you have produced while investigating the lighting possibilities and requirements of the play. It should illustrate your thinking process and explain why some items of research were rejected while others were selected.</li><li>**A justification for the final lighting design**: this comes from your notes on the play, providing evidence for your final design decisions and how these fit with the director's interpretation.</li><li>**A demonstration of the lighting plot within the context of the performance**.</li><li>The final lighting design with grid plan and lantern schedule that shows the use of at least two different kinds of lantern and uses a minimum of 16 lanterns: see page 130.</li><li>A lighting plot or cue sheet showing at least six different lighting states: see page 130.</li><li>You must supervise the rigging, focusing and operating of the design but need only carry out one of the tasks yourself: see page 130.</li></ul> |
|---|---|
| Setting/ Props | <ul><li>**A portfolio of research and sketches showing the development of ideas**: to help you build your research material and sketches, work through the questions on pages 123–124.</li><li>**A justification for the final design decisions**: this comes from your notes on the play, providing evidence for your final design decisions and how these fit with the director's interpretation.</li><li>**The design as realised within the context of the performance**.</li><li>A scale model of the final design to be realised in the performance space: see page 124.</li><li>A scale ground plan and scale drawing of any designed properties: see page 124.</li><li>You must make your own scale model of their design and supervise the construction, painting, hiring and /or finding of scenic elements to meet the requirements of the design: see page 125.</li></ul> |
| Costume | <ul><li>**A portfolio of research and sketches showing the development of ideas**: this will consist of appropriate research material that you have carefully selected and used to inform your design ideas. Show how the social, cultural, historical and political contexts have influenced the design. It will also contain a sketch book with samples of materials, fabrics and initial drawings of your designs.</li><li>**A justification for the final design decisions**: this comes from your notes on the play and your analysis of the characters, providing evidence for your final design decisions and how these fit with the director's interpretation.</li><li>**A demonstration of the costumes within the context of the performance**.</li><li>The final designs for all of the characters in the production. There must be a minimum of three different designs. You might want to illustrate your designs on large sheets of paper or card (in any appropriate medium – drawings, paintings, collages, digital images, etc.) and attach samples of fabric and material.</li><li>A costume plot or list of costumes/accessories worn by each actor, indicating any changes: see the example on page 122.</li><li>You must supervise the construction, buying, dyeing, altering, hiring and/or finding of the designed costumes but need only carry out one of the tasks yourself: see page 122.</li></ul> |

| Masks/ Makeup | • **A portfolio of research and sketches showing the development of ideas**: see page 126.<br>• **A justification for the final design decisions**: this comes from your notes on the play and your analysis of the characters, providing evidence for your final design decisions and how these fit with the director's interpretation.<br>• **A demonstration of the masks and/or makeup within the context of the performance**.<br>• The final design for all of the characters in the production. There must be a minimum of three different designs. You might want to illustrate your designs on large sheets of paper or card (in any appropriate medium – drawings, paintings, collages, digital images, etc.) and attach samples of material or hair/makeup samples. See the advice on page 128 on working with your models from an early stage in the process.<br>• A list showing the choice of materials, application methods (for makeup) and construction methods (for a mask): see page 127 for an example.<br>• You must supervise the construction and application of materials to realise the designed masks and/or makeup but need only carry out one of the tasks yourself: see page 128. |
|---|---|
| Sound | • **Notes listing the sound requirements and ideas for the play**: see page 132.<br>• **A justification for the choice of effects and/or music and their use**: this comes from your notes on the play, providing evidence for your final design decisions and how these fit with the director's interpretation.<br>• **A demonstration of the sound score within the context of the performance**.<br>• A source sheet showing the creation of at least three original sound effects and the source of the remaining cues (e.g. CD title and number, MIDI file from the internet): see the example on page 133.<br>• A cue sheet showing the order, length and output level of each cue: this will be linked to your copy of the marked up script, which will show where all of the sound cues occur in the play. Where a cue is fading up microphones for a 'live' cue, there is no need to include an indication of length.<br>• You must fix and produce the final sound tape(s) which should include at least three original cues which you have created and recorded using live and/or sampled material and three further sound cues. You must supervise the operation of the sound but you need not operate the sound yourself. |

## Assessment requirements: designers

As a designer you will be assessed on four areas, all of which are worth a maximum of ten marks. The grid below shows what you would have to achieve to reach the **top mark band** for each of the assessment areas.

| AO1 Use of materials and equipment | There is an outstanding use and manipulation of materials and equipment, techniques and applications. |
|---|---|
| AO1 Realisation of designs | Designs are realised and executed with an outstanding level of technical skill and take absolute account of the physical demands of the production. |
| AO3 Written design concept | There is an outstanding design concept taking an excellent account of the style, genre and overall demands of the production. |
| AO3 Interpretation of director's concept | There is an outstanding interpretation of the director's concept demonstrating a complete and comprehensive understanding and appreciation of the director's production ideas. The style and practicality of the design will be completely in sympathy with the director's concept and serves to enhance the resultant production. |

## The designer/director relationship

Working with a director is not straightforward because there is no guarantee that you will be like-minded in your approach. Working with a director who thinks they know exactly what they want can be equally as problematic as working with a director who does not know what they want until they see it. The best you can do as a designer is to listen to the director's ideas and thoughts, read the script with the director's interpretation in mind and present your initial design ideas to the director in as clear a format as you can.

Prepare well for the design meeting: bring plenty of drawings and sketches, and explain your intentions. If you are offering sound, prepare different versions of cues and examples of source and music cues for the director to audition. Be prepared for rejection and negative comments about your work, but also listen out for the positive points. Make notes about what the director likes and feels will work and note any changes to be made and suggestions to follow up. Agree what changes you will make before the next meeting. Agree a time and date for the next meeting.

Once you have the director's agreement, the work to produce the designs in time for the performance will begin in earnest. It is important to keep the communication channels open between the rehearsal room and the production team. As the play is rehearsed, adjustments to the design may need to be made. Attending rehearsals regularly to observe what is going on will ensure that you are aware of changes as they occur and you can plan for them.

## The production process for designers

Once the play is in production, the director's time is divided between the rehearsal room (working with the actors) and production meetings (working with the design team). As a member of the design team, your work will concentrate on your contribution to the realisation of your designs.

There is a kind of accepted order in which the design skills happen, but this has come about through convention and practice rather than through any kind of theoretical construct about the design process. The most common order in the design process is:

set ⟶ costumes ⟶ masks and makeup ⟶ sound and lighting

### Setting and props

Set design usually comes first because the director wants the actors to know, feel and see the space in which the play is going to happen. A common working method is for the set model to be presented to the cast at an early rehearsal, and for the rehearsal room floor to be marked out with the basic shape and size of the set so that the actors have certain parameters within which to work.

While the play is rehearsing, the set is being built or items for it are sourced, modified and made ready to go into the theatre space for the final rehearsal on the set. It is helpful for the actors if any props can be supplied or made as early as possible, so that they can get used to using them in rehearsals.

### Costumes

General decisions about the play's costume requirements can be made at the start of the process, but the final decisions about style, shape and colour often have to wait until the set is finalised. Whilst it may not be possible to carry out complete costume designs until the set model is completed, ideas about style, shape and types of materials can be developed and research carried out. Once the costume designs are finalised, the actors have to be measured, material and clothing have to be sourced and the making and alteration begins. Throughout the rehearsal process, there will be costume fittings, so that adjustments can be made and the actors can see what they are going to be wearing.

### Masks and makeup

When and how the masks are constructed will depend on the extent to which they are used in the production. If it is entirely in masks, the performers will need to work with them virtually from the start of rehearsals; if they are for just a single scene in the play (for a masked ball, for example), there will be more time to make them. See page 126 for how masks and makeup can work together.

Makeup tends to be left until quite close to the dress rehearsal unless it involves a prosthesis or wigs and hairpieces are required. However simple the makeup, it is a good idea to have a few trial makeup sessions and to test it with costume and under stage lighting conditions.

### Lighting and sound

Lighting is nearly always left to last in the production process because the designer has to have something to light. The lighting designer should attend the latter stages of rehearsals to see how the play has been staged, and to work out where the lighting changes are required.

Sound can happen anywhere in the production process. The director may want a rehearsal tape to give the actors some idea of timing, so you may need to provide a 'rough mix' of some of the sound cues. However, much of the production process for the sound designer is about recording, editing and mixing the final 'show tape'. Watch as many rehearsals as possible to time and place each of the sound cues.

## The technical rehearsal(s)

This is the most important point in the production process for the set, lighting, sound and props. It can be a laborious process, but it is vitally important for the technical and design teams to ensure that everything looks right and is functioning correctly.

For the set designer, it is the last chance to make any final adjustments to the set and to ensure that if there is a scene change, it happens as intended. The stage crew and the actors will be positioning and marking where props are set and recording where, when and how they are taken on and off stage. As the designer, it is your last chance to check whether a prop looks right or not. For the lighting designer, it is when each lighting state is set and levels and timings of lighting changes are decided. For the sound designer, it is when each sound cue is identified and the sound levels and timings are set.

## The dress rehearsal(s)

This is the most important point in the production process for the costume, mask and makeup designers, because it is the first run through of the play with the actors in full costume and makeup (and with masks if appropriate) on the set under stage lighting conditions and is one of the last chances to make any adjustments.

> **Tip**
>
> The technical rehearsal is sometimes referred to as the 'cut-to-cue' rehearsal, because it is about going through the play and stopping and starting at every point where there is a cue for the set, lighting and/or sound to change.

## Written design concept

You need to complete a written design concept of no more than 500 words which will be sent to the examiner at least seven working days before the performance examination. Your written design concept should show your response to the play you have chosen in the following ways:

- your ability to articulate the nature of your design concept for the play

- an account of the style and genre of the play

- a recognition of the design requirements (or production demands) of the play.

The concept enables you to provide a concise account of your overriding idea for the design of the play in terms of its setting, costumes, lighting, masks, sound and/or makeup, and how this fits with the director's concept for the play. It will also provide the examiner with a sense of how well you have understood and can explain the design requirements of the play. The written design concept has to be completed at least two weeks before the date of the examination, so you have to be at a stage where you can write in detail about what has led you to make your final design decisions.

This aspect carries 25 per cent of the marks of Unit 2, Section B, but there is a lot of crossover with the work you will have carried out during the design process, and you will draw on all your other research and documentation. You will have kept a sketchbook and carefully prepared notes, which you can use as the basis for your written design concept. While you can use all of the notes and drawings you have made during the preparation process, the actual writing of the concept has to take place while you are being supervised by a teacher or invigilator.

### Writing a concept

The table below is a guide to help you practise writing your own design concept. The structure and number of words for each element are suggestions only and do not have to be adhered to strictly, as long as you remain within the overall 500 word limit.

| Written design concept for the set/costume/lighting/sound/masks/makeup design for (*title of the play*) by (*name of the playwright*) | | |
|---|---|---|
| **Nature of the design concept** | This should outline how the play has stimulated your thinking and the direction that your design ideas have taken. For the visual skills, what has inspired the 'look' you have come up with for the play; and for the sound, what have you focused on in the text to 'compose' your sound tape? | Allow 300–350 words for this aspect of the concept. |
| **Style and genre** | Here you will be writing about how you have interpreted the genre of the play and how this has influenced the design process. The style of the play itself may have inspired your particular way of working on it, or you may have adopted a style of presentation which you can argue is a valid way of interpreting the play. | Allow 75–100 words for this aspect of the concept. |
| **Demands of the production** | This is where you must show that you have understood all of the practical demands and requirements of the play, and considered how you are going to deal with them. | Allow 75–100 words for this aspect of the concept. |

# Reference guide

## Performance spaces

Your choice of stage form is an important factor in relating to your audience. If you are a designer, the kind of design you create has to start from this. If you are a performer, the 'actor-audience relationship' will be heavily influenced by the choice of stage form.

This section will go into more detail about the reasons why you might choose one form rather than another. This will help you to understand the historical background to the different spaces and how these have developed over time and help you think about what stage forms might be suitable for your play texts.

### The theatre of ancient Greece

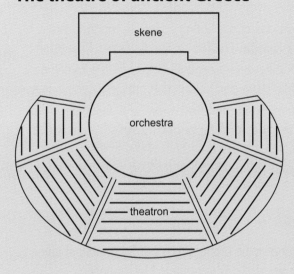

### What is it?

This theatre form offers a large performance space with the audience in a semicircle of tiered seats. Ancient Greek theatres (which flourished in the 5th century BC), and later Roman theatres, were built on this pattern. The main theatre just outside Athens could seat an audience of 15,000, which gives you some idea of the scale.

### What are the advantages?

- It works well for large performances such as musicals and rock concerts and large cast 'epic' plays.

- Large-scale effects of scenery, and more recently lighting, sound and special effects, are possible.

- The audience tends to develop a corporate identity, like a football crowd.

### What potential problems are there?

- Ancient Greek theatre doesn't suit naturalistic acting (because of the distance between actors and audience).

- Although acoustics are spectacularly good, similar modern theatres usually require sound reinforcement systems for actors.

**Key term**

epic theatre

## Thrust theatre

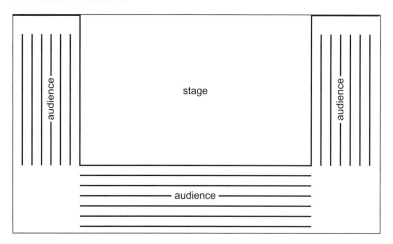

## What is it?

The audience is placed on three sides of the acting space. In modern thrust theatres, such as the Chichester Festival Theatre or The Questors Theatre in Ealing, it is often possible for actors to enter through the audience by using specially constructed entrances.

During Shakespeare's working lifetime in the Elizabethan and Jacobean periods, the thrust stage was the usual form for public theatres. There was a social and economic division between those members of the audience who stood close to the raised stage (the 'groundlings') and those who could afford to sit in the galleries.

## What are the advantages?

- The thrust theatre can stage large-scale productions, but is capable of being much more intimate as actors are partially surrounded by audience.

- It is possible to place large items of set (flats, doorways, staircases, and so on) upstage, without interfering with the audience's view of the action.

- Most types of play will work well in this form.

## What potential problems are there?

- Chairs or sofas with high backs can cause sightline problems, so the choice and positioning of furniture and the blocking of scenes, especially with large numbers of actors, need to be carefully handled.

- Actors who have to relate to the audience (for example, as a narrator, or when delivering a soliloquy or an aside) have to decide how to involve an audience, which they can't take in at a single glance without changing position or making head movements.

- Some stage business involving special effects or the misdirecting of the audience (distracting the audience from something which needs to happen unseen on stage, by getting them all to look in a different direction at the same time) can be more complex to achieve, as can surprise entrances.

- The floor tends to be a very important design feature, as the audience looks **down** on it, unlike the usual situation in a proscenium arch theatre.

- Scene changing needs to be done in full view of the audience.

## Proscenium arch

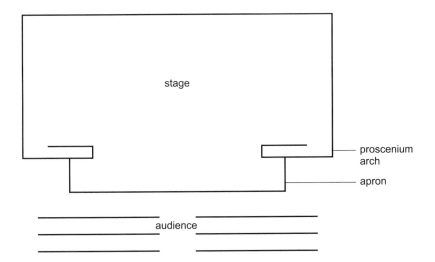

From the late 17th to the early 20th centuries, the proscenium arch became the standard form for most British theatres; most London West End theatres and older regional theatres retain this form.

## What is it?

The proscenium is actually the dividing line between the audience and the acting area; frequently an arch is built on this line to accommodate the large curtains traditionally opened and closed at the beginnings and ends of acts. It is sometimes referred to as a 'picture frame' stage and the audience is defined as having a 'single view'. Either the stage or the audience (or both) has to be raised and 'raked' (put on a slope), so that sightlines are clear. The curtain can be dropped for scene changes to take place out of the audience view, although this rarely happens in modern theatre.

**Key term**

raked

## What are the advantages?

- Audiences often feel comfortable in the proscenium arch form, as most of their experience of theatre going will probably have been to theatres of this kind. There's a clear sense of 'them' (the performers) and 'us' (the audience), which adds to this sense of comfort.

- It's easy to create realistic sets, with the 'fourth wall' removed so that the audience has the illusion of reality.

**Key term**

fourth wall

- Stage illusions and effects are usually easy to achieve, as are surprise entrances or shock revelations.

- Most types and scales of plays can be successfully presented in this form.

## What potential problems are there?

- It can be difficult to make the audience feel involved, or to take them out of their 'comfort zones' if you're presenting more challenging performances.

- Actors have more difficulty in making their performances totally naturalistic, as they have to be aware of opening out to the audience.

- Furniture needs to be placed with the audience in mind; for example, a scene with a family sitting down to dinner is often set with the down side of the table (nearest the audience) empty, so as not to interfere with audience sightlines.

- Blocking needs to combine the demands of natural behaviour with ensuring that the audience can see the characters.

# In-the-round

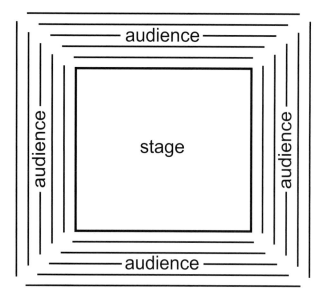

## What is it?

'In-the-round' refers to the fact that the audience completely surrounds the acting space (obviously with entrance paths for actors to come through the audience). The acting space doesn't need to be round and, in fact, it rarely is. The stage is at floor level, with the audience raised in tiers. Roman amphitheatres are examples. Relatively few theatres in Britain are built in-the-round, but many studio theatres can be easily set up in this form.

## What are the advantages?

- There is a real sense that the audience and the actors are sharing the same, intimate experience; the audience members are very aware of one another, and share a focus in their midst. Actors are usually very close to the audience, creating a dynamic sense of performance.

- The audience's imagination comes into play, as large sets are not possible for sightline reasons. A sense of an environment can be created quite simply and effectively in the audience's imagination.

- Actors can behave naturalistically, for example facing directly towards an actor with whom they are having a conversation, not having to make allowances for an audience on only one side.

- Scene changes need to take place in view of the audience and are often integrated into the production as a whole (for example, carried out by cast or stage management in costume).

## What potential problems are there?

Many of the points which apply to the thrust form also apply to the in-the-round form – but more so.

- Realistic sets – in terms of walls and doors, for example – are not possible. Designers need to focus on the choice and positioning of furniture and on the floor as a design feature.

- Actors can be very subtle, but need to ensure that their performance is shared equally by the audience all around them. They also need to be exceptionally still when not the focus of attention and should not have accidental eye contact with members of the audience. Accurate blocking is crucial.

- Unless it is possible to raise the audience, there will be sightline problems.

# Traverse

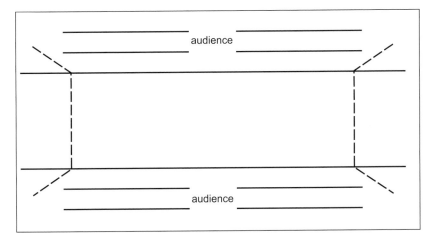

## What is it?

Sometimes referred to as 'theatre-in-the-corridor', as the acting space resembles a corridor between two blocks of audience, facing each other, this is a relatively uncommon type of stage form and few theatres have been built exclusively in this form. The Traverse Theatre in Edinburgh used to stage plays in this form, and has retained the name, even though it moved to new premises and now stages theatre in other forms.

## What are the advantages?

Some of the advantages of the in-the-round form also apply to the traverse:

- The audience is obliged to exercise its imagination, as solid and large sets are not viable – although it is possible to create walls and doorways, for example, at either end of the 'corridor' without interfering with sightlines.

- The traverse is particularly good at enabling a sense of movement and facilitating plays with swift changes of location. It can convey a sense of 'epic' action quite simply.

- It is a simple form to set up in a studio (with limited audience numbers).

- Scene changes have to be carried out in full view of the audience.

## What potential problems are there?

- The traverse is usually suitable only for a relatively small audience, although there are exceptions to this.

- The audience needs to be raked in tiers, as the performance space is on floor level, unless the acting area can be raised (like a fashion show catwalk).

- The extreme ends of the acting space can create problems for members of the audience, as sightlines may be difficult (looking sideways over the heads of other members of the audience can limit the view) and the 'Wimbledon' effect (turning the head from side to side to follow the action) can be wearing for an audience.

- During scene changes, actors from one scene usually need to exit at one end, while the cast for the new scene come on from the other.

### Promenade

### What is it?

In this form the audience and the actors share the same space, with the audience following the actors and moving to different areas inside the space. There is usually no seating, but there may be points where the audience can 'perch', or, more commonly, sit on the floor. This form of theatre is still relatively rare, but has become much more used in the last 20 years or so. Reasonable large spaces are commonly used, but small fringe theatres have also mounted successful promenade productions.

### What are the advantages?

- Promenade can be a very exciting form in which there is a real sense of community between the actors and the audience. Often the audience will be treated as part of the performance.

- It can be staged relatively simply and inexpensively.

### What potential problems are there?

- It's difficult to rehearse, because the audience is an integral part of the performance. The audience may not behave as you expect – needing to be encouraged and directed – so some rehearsals with an invited audience of the right size become necessary. They get the idea quite quickly, however, and are soon keen to catch all the action.

- Lighting can be difficult to achieve without producing glare in the audience's eyes (although it's a good way of indicating which area the action has moved to), and sound designers need to place their speakers carefully.

- Health and safety issues (trailing cables, trip hazards, etc.) need to be addressed. Audience members with disabilities need to be catered for. Shorter members of the audience may be at a disadvantage.

### Non-conventional forms

In the late 20th and 21st centuries, interest has grown in the use of unconventional stage forms. In the last few years at the Edinburgh Fringe Festival, for example, performances have taken place in: a car (audience of three driven around the city!); a public toilet; a department store; a restaurant; through the streets; a three-storey house; a car park; a quadrangle of a university Street theatre has become more common, and 'guerrilla theatre' (for example, surprising people on buses or tube trains by making them believe that a real argument is taking place in their midst) is also known as a form.

Much of this kind of theatre is known as 'site-specific': the performance arises out of the nature of a particular space and is specially devised to make use of its features; it cannot be played in the same way anywhere else. It's interesting to look around your school or college to identify areas which might be possible to perform in. There can be a variety of challenges; lighting, sound, exits and entrances, and quick changes of costume can all create problems which need imaginative solutions. The audience may have to be limited in size. On the other hand, these performances can present the audience with exciting and original experiences.

**Practitioner note**

Part of this interest in experimental theatre stems from the writings of Antonin Artaud, who wanted to take drama out of theatres and put it in other settings. He was also interested in ways of changing and disrupting conventional actor-audience relationships, in order to shake audiences out of their complacency. See page 153 for more about Artaud.

# PRACTITIONERS

## Antonin Artaud (1896–1948)

Artaud (pronounced 'arto') became influential after his death, especially when his essays were translated into English in the 1950s (they had been published in French in 1938). He was a member of the surrealist group in his youth. (This group wanted art to access dreams and other subconscious elements of human existence, which included drug taking; Artaud used both medicinal and hallucinatory drugs for much of his life and was confined to a mental hospital for some years.) Although he rarely had the opportunity to put his theories into practice (his one major production *The Cenci*, in 1935, closed after 17 performances and was not entirely successful in demonstrating his ideas), many of his theories and visions of theatre have strongly influenced more recent directors and designers.

He is the inventor of the term '**The Theatre of Cruelty**'. This has nothing to do with 'cruelty' in its usual sense. Artaud wanted an audience to have an intense, involving experience, in which their senses are pushed to an extreme limit. This could be achieved through staging plays in **unconventional settings** (anywhere except a theatre), with the **conventional actor-audience relationship completely changed**. (One of his suggestions was to have the audience on movable seats in the well of a hall, with the actors using the balconies above them to perform all around them.) Props could be vastly oversized, lighting and sound would be intense and overpowering. Conventional dialogue would be at least partially replaced by vocal noises. A **language of movement** would be developed which would communicate more directly to the audience than words. The element of **ritual** was important. Artaud believed passionately that theatre should change the lives of audiences by providing what he called '**soul therapy**' – waking up the inner life through exposing the senses to shock and spectacle.

Although it may be difficult to apply all Artaud's ideas to a conventional text, it is possible (and very exciting) to apply aspects of his ideas.

## Bertolt Brecht (1898–1956)

Brecht has had a profound influence on 20th and 21st-century theatre. He challenged the view that audiences should become entirely involved emotionally with a performance on stage. Instead he wanted to create points where the audience was encouraged to think about the situation on stage and how it might be changed. He called this effect '**Verfremdung**' (often translated as '**alienation**', but better translated as '**estrangement**' or '**distancing**'). The idea was that the audience should be able to stand back (at least for a moment) from the action and see it objectively. Brecht was motivated by strong political views, believing that theatre could be a way of encouraging audiences to come to conclusions in line with his own Marxist (Communist) views.

He called his own style of theatre '**epic**', contrasting it with what he called the 'dramatic' theatre and drew up a list of the ways in which the two kinds of theatre were different; for example, 'the audience is involved in something' (dramatic), contrasted with 'the audience is made to face something' (epic). His own plays (*Mother Courage and her Children*, *The Caucasian Chalk Circle*, *The Threepenny Opera* and *The Good Person of Szechwan* are amongst his best known works) demonstrated how his theories worked on stage.

---

**Taking it further**

The following books provide more information about Artaud and his theories.
- *Artaud for Beginners* by Gabriela Stoppelmann (Writers and Readers Publishing, 1999). Cartoon-style approach but with useful basic information.
- *The Theatre and Its Double* by Artaud, translated by Victor Corti (Calder, 1985). This can be a difficult read, but it really gives you the flavour of Artaud.
- *Antonin Artaud: The Man and His Work* by Martin Esslin (Fontana, 1976)
- *Avant Garde Theatre* by C.D. Innes (Routledge, 1993)

---

**Taking it further**

- *The Theatre of Bertolt Brecht* by John Willett (Methuen, 1977)
- *The Cambridge Companion to Brecht* edited by Peter Thomson and Glendyr Sacks (Cambridge University Press, 1994)
- *Brecht for Beginners* by Michael Thoss (Writers and Readers Publishing, 1987). Cartoon-style approach but with useful basic information.

These plays make use of a variety of methods to produce the 'Verfremdungseffekt' (the effect of distancing), including breaking up the narrative of the play with songs, direct address to the audience, placards giving titles disclosing the content of scenes, and so on. He took the idea of 'montage' (a film technique in which the editing of a series of individual shots produces an effect on the viewer) and applied it to the theatre. He believed that actors should express the 'Geste' (or 'Gestus') of a scene, finding a method of physical expression which demonstrated a social attitude. Design, lighting and sound all contributed to the overall style of production of epic theatre.

## Konstantin Stanislavski (1863–1938)

Stanislavski created a system of training actors in a methodical way. His system is still widely regarded as essential to the basic training of modern actors, and many of the terms he used have gone into the general vocabulary of actors. Although Stanislavski is strongly associated with realist theatre, some of his own productions experimented with a wider range of styles.

Stanislavski's system is designed to create a high degree of psychological involvement of the actor with the role he or she is playing. At all points, the character has an **objective** (something positive that he or she wants and actively strives to get). The play can be broken into **units** (from the character's point of view), each one with a separate **objective**. A **unit** is a section of the play; it's as long as a particular objective lasts for a character, so it may be a few lines or a few pages. There will also be a **through-objective** (an overall 'want' which motivates the character right through the play). So, for example, Romeo's **through-objective** might be 'I want to find true love'. This means that the actor/character is always actively engaged on stage, pursuing a positive desire, leading to a **through-line of action** (a clear pathway through the play). There will, of course, be **obstacles** to these objectives, which prevent their fulfilment (for example, Romeo's banishment from Verona, or the opposition of Juliet's family).

Actors used **emotion memory**, by reliving relevant moments from their past and applying them to the situation of their role in the play. (If you were playing Othello, whose jealousy leads him to murder his wife, you would make use of your own feelings of jealousy in your past.) The **magic if** (the act of imagination which enabled the actor to play the part as if real) was the key to the actor's belief in the situation. Each role had **given circumstances** (details given in the text which gave a secure grounding and which the actor's **imagination** could then expand). Late in his career, Stanislavski emphasised the importance of **physical actions** as a way of discovering a role. Essentially this meant **improvising** at an early stage, so that physical and psychological aspects of the role developed together.

Stanislavski's productions (mostly for the Moscow Art Theatre) focused on creating detailed realistic settings through set, lighting, sound, costumes and props, as well as the style of acting. The **'fourth wall'** (the idea that the audience is witnessing real life as though a wall of a room has been removed) was the standard method of presentation (note the contrast with Brecht, for example; Stanislavski's theatre creates the illusion of real life). The director's job was to create this illusion by creating a shared concept and overseeing the work of the whole production team towards this end. Stanislavski's association with the playwright Anton Chekhov resulted in outstanding productions of *The Seagull*, *Uncle Vanya*, *Three Sisters* and *The Cherry Orchard*.

---

**Tip**

Be aware of the difference between Stanislavski's 'system' and the 'method' developed from some aspects of his teaching in the United States, notably by Lee Strasberg.

---

**Taking it further**

- *Stanislavski: An Introduction* by Jean Benedetti (Methuen, 1982).
- *An Actor Prepares* by Stanislavski, translated by Elizabeth Reynolds Hapgood (Methuen, 2008).
- *Stanislavski for Beginners* by David Allen and Jeff Fallow (Writers and Readers Publishing, 1998). Cartoon-style approach but with useful basic information.

# Kneehigh Theatre

Kneehigh Theatre began in a very small way in 1980 in Cornwall. It was founded by Mike Shepherd, who still works with the group as actor and director, although in recent years Emma Rice has been its Artistic Director. It has grown into an internationally known and respected company, but has always retained its roots in Cornwall. A company is assembled specifically for each project, but there is a core of individuals who have worked consistently with the company over the years. As its name suggests, its original work was for children, and creating accessible productions for young people is still very much a feature of its work.

Kneehigh Theatre creates all its own productions as a group. Even when they take a well-known play (such as Shakespeare's *Cymbeline*), the text becomes a source to be exploited for performance. Very little of Shakespeare's original text remained in the Kneehigh production, but it was a powerful experience in the theatre which remained faithful to Shakespeare's play.

In all Kneehigh's work there is a strong emphasis on the **story** and its essential elements – the aspects of the story which appeal very strongly to the deeper parts of human nature. Fairy-tales, folk tales and myths are their natural territory. Recent productions of *Tristan and Yseult* (the medieval love story) and *The Bacchae* (classical Greek tragedy by Euripides) have shown how focusing on the power of the basics of the story works effectively in the theatre (and the 'theatre' with Kneehigh productions is often open air, such as at the Eden Project in Cornwall). The actors create strong bonds with the audience by engaging them in the action. (Before the opening of *Tristan and Yseult*, the cast (in costume) wandered through the audience, talking to them and commenting on them. The audience were given balloons, which they were encouraged to blow up and release at a point in the production.) Emma Rice believes in approaching important themes 'in a child-like way', so that strong emotions and themes can become accessible to the audience through simple means.

Trust and lack of fear is an important feature of how the company works and how they approach audiences. Emma Rice creates a rehearsal atmosphere in which actors trust each other so that they feel able to do their best work. In performance, there is a sense that the company wants to engage personally with the specific audience and to share with it. A good deal of the work is physical and there is always a strong element of comedy – although this often opens the door to contrasting powerful feelings more associated with tragedy. Kneehigh has developed the capacity to create truly populist productions, which don't compromise the nature of serious theatre; it is a theatre which explores areas of human nature and experience.

Most Kneehigh performers have multiple skills which they contribute to performances. Most play instruments (usually more than one); all sing, dance and have physical theatre skills.

It's not always easy in your own work to reproduce the methods of a company which has been developing them for over 25 years. However, their methods of devising, improvising, focusing on the elements of story, using a wide range of performance skills, audience interaction and site-specific work can all be applied to some extent in your work.

Kneehigh Theatre is offered here as just one example of many theatre companies whose work would be suitable for exploring in Unit 1 to give you ideas about the sorts of ideas that could be incorporated into your work. Other companies include Complicite, DV8 and Moscow Arts Theatre.

## Taking it further

www.kneehigh.co.uk
www.doollee.com/PlaywrightsK/
kneehigh-theatre-company.html

# Glossary of drama and theatre terms

**Action**: the events that happen in a drama or play and that an audience witnesses taking place on stage.

**Actions**: what a character does in a play. Actions may be physical or psychological but will usually impact on the plot and on other characters as well as on the individual who initiates the action.

**Acting**: acting is the art of mimicking, imitating, representing or portraying another personality or role. It is what actors do when they are performing a role to an audience or on film.

**Agit prop**: from the Russian phrase agitatsiya-propaganda, theatre which has political agitation and propaganda as its main purpose.

**Alienation effect**: a misleading translation of Brecht's expression Verfremdungseffekt which refers to the devices and acting style used in epic theatre to distance the audience from having any sense that the theatrical experience is real. See pages 21 and 153.

**Anagnorisis**: a term originally used by Aristotle to describe the way in which a character comes to recognise their true identity. Its broader meaning relates to any moment in a play when something about the characters or the situation is revealed.

**Anti-climax**: as a climax is meant to be where all things come together as a conclusion, an anti-climax is incomplete and therefore can be disappointing or unsatisfying.

**Arena staging**: a form of theatre in-the-round where the audience surrounds the stage on three or four sides. The term suggests performances on a large scale.

**Aside**: a dramatic convention in which an actor addresses the audience, while the other characters are unaware that he or she is doing so.

**Auditorium**: the area within the theatre that accommodates the audience.

**Back story**: the prior history to a character or plot before the events in the play, scene or drama being enacted.

**Blank verse**: unrhymed lines with an underlying rhythm and a standard length. See pages 36 and 105.

**Blocking**: the physical arrangement and movement of actors on the stage.

**Caricature**: an exaggerated portrayal of a character usually for comic effect. This can involve emphasising a particular vocal or physical mannerism.

**Character**: the person/persona that an actor wishes to convey. The word is often used interchangeably with 'role', but tends to have a more specific meaning to refer to an actual person. A character, for example, could play a number of roles in a play such as parent, employer and friend, as individuals do in real life. Also an actor can play a number of differing roles in a play, each of which can be different characters.

**Choreography**: in dance, the creative process of putting a series of movements together to create work. Choreographed work in drama is movement which follows a prescribed plan that has been carefully worked through and thought out. Stage fights, for example, are usually highly choreographed.

**Chorus**: a group of people working collectively using vocal and movement skills to communicate thoughts, feelings and ideas. The group may act homogeneously or be broken down into sub-groups. In the manner of a classical Greek chorus, they may narrate a story, comment on the action and express an opinion.

**Climax**: the moment when the threads of the plot or events in the play come together and are satisfactorily resolved. There is a sense in most plays or drama of a build-up in tension towards a climactic point, followed by some kind of resolution.

**Collage**: a 'patchwork' of dialogue, sounds and visual images from different contexts put together to provide an impressionistic presentation. For example, fragments of scenes from *Romeo and Juliet* could be selected and linked together and presented as a 'collage version'. The way in which the material is juxtaposed and presented can shed new meaning on the characters, their situation, the playwright's intentions and the language of the play.

**Comedy of manners**: a comedy that mocks the manners of a particular social class. See pages 110–115 on *The Importance of Being Earnest*.

**Conscience corridor** (also known as **conscience alley** or **thought tunnel**): an exercise in which two straight lines are formed and the individuals in each group face each other with a gap (corridor/alley/tunnel) of about one metre between them. A person in a role of which the whole group has prior knowledge, walks through the corridor and hears thoughts or questions from each person on either side of them as they move from one end to the other. The exercise is useful for character building and development.

**Cross-cutting**: a term which comes from film editing, this involves changing back and forth between scenes or episodes of action. The first scene runs up to a selected point and the action freezes or the lights fade out on it. Concurrently with this, the second scene starts and runs up to another 'cutting point'. The action reverts ('cuts') to a section of the first scene. The process of switching between scenes continues.

**Devising/devised work**: work that is principally developed by performers without working to a script written by a playwright in the conventional sense.

**Doubling up**: the same performer playing more than one role or part in a play. It can also be when more than one player portrays the same role.

**Dramatic irony**: the situation in which the audience knows more about events on stage than one or more of the characters.

**Dramatic tension**: a heightened sense of anticipation about what is going to happen next.

**End on staging**: a space divided in two, with the audience in one section facing the performance space in the other. The proscenium arch theatre is an example of end on staging.

**Ensemble**: performers working together as a group; the members of the cast of a production other than the protagonists or leading players.

**Enunciation**: clear pronunciation and articulation.

**Epic theatre**: a reaction to dramatic theatre which is manifest in Brecht's later work. Features of epic theatre include episodic scenes, a lack of tension, and breaking the theatrical illusion through devices such as direct audience address, use of songs, projections and narration. Elements of epic theatre can be found in earlier plays such as the use of the chorus in ancient Greek drama and short episodic scenes in Shakespeare. See page 153.

**Flashback**: a moment from a character's remembered past. Enacting a flashback can help to gain an understanding of a character's behaviour, emotions and attitude and provide some of the 'back story'.

**Form**: the shape and structure of a drama. In theatre, form is determined by the content of the drama (e.g. the way the playwright has presented the narrative) and by the way it is presented (the choices made by actors, designers and directors in interpreting the material for performance). Form is often confused with genre, with which it is closely associated. Something classified as naturalistic in terms of genre will be recognised as such by the form it takes.

**Forum theatre**: a way of working developed by Brazilian director Augusto Boal. Participants sit or stand in a large circle to observe an improvisation usually started by two of their number. The improvisation will be based on a given situation or set of circumstances agreed by the group at the outset. At any point in the proceedings, the performers can stop the action and ask the rest of the group, who are sitting around in the circle (the forum), for help or advice about what to do or say next. The improvisation may continue from the point of interruption or start again. Equally anyone from the forum can stop the action if they think what is happening is inappropriate or believe that the drama should be taken in a different direction. They can either offer advice, decide to take over from one of the performers or join in by taking on another role.

**Fourth wall**: the notion that the stage is like a room with four walls, with the audience looking in where one of the walls would be. Associated with naturalism in which there is a convention that the performers act as though the audience is not there. See page 154.

**Freeze-frame**: during an improvisation or the playing of a scene, the instruction 'freeze' is called out and the performers hold their positions at that moment: it has the effect of pressing pause on a DVD player. It is often confused with 'still image' or 'tableau', which are techniques used to set up a deliberate 'stage picture' or 'frozen image'.

**Genre**: a category or type of drama which is defined by a particular set of conventions and norms. Genres such as comedy, tragedy, musicals, melodrama and pantomime have readily identifiable features, whereas terms such as naturalism, expressionism and epic are more elusive. Difficulties arise because a genre (e.g. naturalism) can be defined by its form (e.g. naturalistic) which can be recognised by certain aesthetic elements (i.e. it has a naturalistic style).

**Gesture**: a movement of part of the body, especially a hand or the head, to express an idea or meaning.

**Gestus**: a term associated with the use of gesture. Brecht used it to refer to the attitude or stance of a character in relation to another communicated through behaviour, movement, expressions and intonation. A character's relationship to another is determined by social conditions and conventions. In other words, if two characters are separated by being rich and poor this will pre-determine the attitude of one to the other which will come across through gesture irrespective of what is being said. See pages 40 and 153.

**Given circumstances**: in Stanislavskian theory, all of the available information that an actor uses in creating a role. See pages 44, 51, 90, 95 and 154.

**Hot-seating**: a technique used to gain a deeper understanding of a character or role. An individual sits in a chair designated as the 'hot-seat'. The rest of the group asks that individual relevant questions about their feelings, thoughts, actions or circumstances. The person in the hot-seat answers the questions in role or as they think the character would answer.

**Improvisation**: performing quickly in response to something, or acting without previous planning. A distinction is made between spontaneous improvisation and prepared improvisation, the former relating to making up a role as you go along and the latter relating to working within a previously agreed structure of ideas and roles.

**Inflection**: changes in the tone and pitch of the voice when speaking.

**In-the-round staging**: a performance space in which the audience surrounds the acting space on all sides. See page 150.

**Marking the moment**: a convention used to highlight a significant point in a drama. It can be achieved through the use of techniques such as freeze-frame, spotlighting, narrated announcements, projected captions, sound effects, musical underscoring, or change of lighting state.

**Metre**: the pattern and structure of verse or poetry.

**Mise-en-scène**: the arrangement of scenery, props, actors, and so on on the stage.

**Monologue**: literally, one person speaking. It can be a genre in its own right (for example, *Shirley Valentine*), but it can also be a speech by one character in other genres. Dialogue spoken by a narrator can take the form of a monologue and a soliloquy is a particular type of monologue that involves a character speaking their inner thoughts out loud to the audience.

**Montage**: a term taken from film theory, referring to the way a dramatic sequence can be made up of a series of connected but different images edited together. It is rather like collage.

**Narrator**: a role that functions like a storyteller. A narrator can be used to describe the action, provide a commentary or give additional information. A narrator can be present on stage or be an off-stage or pre-recorded voice.

**Narration**: dialogue designed to tell the story or provide accompanying information. Narration can accompany on-stage action or be presented in its own right.

**Naturalism**: a genre that attempts to replicate nature and present events and characters on stage as though they are from real life. Not always distinguishable from realism, it attempts to hold a mirror up to nature and give the illusion of characters as actual people in real-life situations, using everyday language. As an artistic movement, naturalism originated in the late 19th century, whereas realism originated earlier in the 19th century. Naturalism is said to be less concerned with authenticity than realism.

**Objective**: an intention or aim; what a character wants to achieve.

**Off-the-text exercises**: rehearsal exercises used when the actors are not following the script.

**Pace**: the speed at which a scene, action or the whole play takes place.

**Pause**: a break in action or speech.

**Physical theatre**: a theatre form and a performance style that emphasises and exaggerates the movement and gestural qualities of performance. It is a form very close to contemporary dance and requires performers to be fit and agile. It can also extend to mask work and mime and use elements of circus skills. Companies such as DV8, Trestle and Complicite are major exponents of this type of work.

**Pitch**: the height or depth of the voice when speaking or singing.

**Plot**: the sequence of events in a play.

**Poise**: the manner in which someone carries themselves.

**Projection**: throwing the voice in performance to ensure that the audience can hear the words clearly.

**Promenade staging**: a form of staging in which the audience moves around to different areas or stages in a performance space. Medieval mystery plays performed on carts and wagons are early examples of this.

**Proscenium**: the permanent or semi-permanent wall dividing the audience from the stage. The opening in this wall frames the stage, hence the proscenium arch. See page 149.

**Proxemics**: a term borrowed from a discipline which studies the organisation of human space. When applied to the theatre, it is used to describe the way in which spatial relationships between each of the performers and between the performers and their stage environment work. See page 61.

**Raked**: describing a stage put on a slope upwards away from the audience, allowing the far end of the stage to be seen more clearly.

**Ranking**: an exercise used to explore the status of roles or character. Each performer 'ranks' their role within defined terms, such as social standing or economic prosperity, by assigning a number between one and ten. One is the lowest status and ten the highest. The exercise can be repeated at any time to determine whether the status of the roles may have altered during the course of the drama.

**Realism**: a genre that sets out to portray everyday life as faithfully as possible. It has its origins in the visual arts during the early part of the 19th century. It requires an approach to acting that depicts natural behaviour and speech and is anti-illusory in character. In practice, 'realism' and 'naturalism' are used interchangeably but the former is said to be more concerned with detail and aims to be closer to real life than naturalism.

**Rhythm**: the pattern of sounds and movements in a speech or scene.

**Role**: any part portrayed by an actor in a play. It is used less specifically than 'character' to refer to more representational figures in a drama such as Death, Devil, First Man, First Woman, or non-human representations such as War, Peace, Dog, Fidelity.

**Role-on-the-wall**: an exercise in which an outline of a figure is drawn on the wall to represent a character or role being developed or explored. Members of the group take it in turns to write facts and information about the character/role within the framework of the body. Physical details might all be written in the head area, for example, whereas things that the character likes might be written in the right leg area. Opinions and views from other people or characters can be written around the outside of the figure.

**Role-play**: the act of pretending to be someone (or something) else. Role-play is generally confined to taking on a clearly defined role such as a doctor, a bus driver or teacher without any attempt at in-depth psychological analysis or understanding. Role-play is distinguished from acting in that it is not intended for performance to an audience.

**Role reversal**: an exercise performed during an improvisation or rehearsal for a scene, in which the actors reverse the roles/characters they are portraying in order to gain a different view or understanding of their own role.

**Sculpting**: a technique used in conjunction with still-image work developed by Brazilian director Augusto Boal into Image Theatre. A group is divided into sculptors and sculptees. There are normally only one or two sculptors who create a sculpture by moving the sculptees into different positions and stances in response to a stimulus or idea.

**Soliloquy**: a speech delivered by a character to themselves rather than to another character, thereby revealing their thoughts to the audience.

**Soundscape**: an aural environment created for a scene using sounds made vocally. Each individual creates a sound appropriate for a given circumstance to accompany or introduce a scene. For example, one person makes sea sounds, while another imitates the cry of a seagull to suggest the seaside. Repeated words and phrases overlapping each other can also be used to suggest a location or might be portrayed as sounds in a character's head, as though from a nightmare or series of flashbacks.

**Spotlighting**: a technique in which an improvisation or playing of a scene is replayed, but the action is redefined by focusing attention on a selected area of the performance space. This can be done with the use of lighting or by marking the floor area so that any action that previously happened outside these confines no longer takes place.

**Stichomythia**: a term originating from ancient Greek drama to describe dialogue of alternating lines between characters, usually to build up dramatic tension. It can typically be found in a scene that involves two characters arguing with one trying to out do the other.

**Still image**: creating a picture to represent a frozen moment or to sum up what is happening in a drama. It is a useful technique to explore the effects of positioning characters in relation to one another in terms of levels and proximity and to demonstrate non-verbal communication. It is often used with sculpting and thoughts in the head.

**Storyboard**: a series of images and/or text showing the sequence of the action planned for a play.

**Style**: the aesthetic quality of a drama. Often indistinguishable from genre and form, style refers to the way the actors are performing, the visual characteristics of the setting and costumes, and the choice of particular conventions. Confusingly, a drama belonging to one genre (such as naturalism) can be presented in different styles (for example, the acting may be in a naturalistic style but the stage design can be in an abstract style).

**Sub-text**: in narrative terms, a secondary plot or storyline. In terms of acting and character analysis, it refers to the idea that there are other meanings below the surface of what is actually being said and done. See pages 38, 46–47 and 50.

**Tableau**: a variation on still image, referring to a dramatic grouping of characters. A tableau may not necessarily be a still or frozen image, as dialogue can be spoken and gestures used when it refers to the general stage picture during a sequence in a scene.

**Teacher-in-role**: a technique in which a class or group of participants in a drama accepts that the teacher or leader is going to be playing a role to which they are going to react and respond. The participants may or may not be in role.

**Techniques**: drama forms, exercises, strategies and conventions that are widely used to development understanding and explore meaning through the drama process. In a broader context, it encompasses the whole range of physical and psychological processes and exercises that an actor might use to develop their skills as a performer.

**Tempo**: speed.

**Theme**: a recurring idea or set of ideas in a play.

**Thoughts in the head** or **thought tracking**: an exercise that allows the inner thoughts of a character or role to be heard out loud. It is often used in conjunction with freeze-frame or still-image where a participant is asked to say what they are thinking at that point in time.

**Thrust staging**: a performance space that has the audience on three sides of the stage. See page 148.

**Tone**: the quality of the voice when speaking, indicating the attitude of the speaker.

**Traverse staging**: a performance space that has the audience on either side of the stage. See page 151.

**Two-hander**: a play for two characters.

**Verfremdungseffekt**: see alienation.

**Warm-up**: an exercise or game designed to warm up the body or voice in preparation for performance or to prepare participants for drama work. Warm-ups can also include icebreakers to help a group of people to work together and get to know each other, or exercises to stimulate the imagination and the creative thinking process.

**Writing in role**: an exercise that involves writing, for example, a letter, a diary or journal as though it were being written by the character or role being portrayed. It is a useful technique in character building work.

Published by:
Pearson Education Limited
Edinburgh Gate
Harlow
Essex CM20 2JE

First published 2008
10 9 8 7 6 5 4 3 2
ISBN 978-184690-240-6

Printed and bound in Great Britain by Henry Ling Limited, at the Dorset Press, Dorchester, DT1 1HD

Author team: John Davey is Head of School, Performing Arts, Kingston College, Surrey. Steve Lewis is Director for Visual and Performing Arts, City College Brighton and Hove. Ginny Spooner is a senior examiner.
The publishers are grateful to Carolyn Carnaghan for her consultancy and contribution on Unit 1.

Picture Credits
The publisher would like to thank the following for their kind permission to reproduce their photographs: Alamy Images: Chris H D Davis 81; Paul Doyle 84; Arenapal: Colin Willoughby 93; Pete Jones 8; Getty Images: Roger Viollet 50; Scoopt 64; iStockphoto: Sean Warren 133; Robbie Jack Photography: 41; Lebrecht Music and Arts Photo Library: Tristram Kenton 145; Photostage Ltd: 57, 101, 106, 114; Rex Features: Nigel R Barklie 32.
Picture Research by: Hilary Luckcock

We are grateful to the following for their permission to reproduce copyright material:
Page 8: extracts from THE ACCRINGTON PALS by Peter Whelan, Methuen; reprinted with permission of A & C Black. Pages 11, 37: extracts from THE CRUCIBLE by Arthur Miller Copyright © 1952, Arthur Miller; reproduced with permission of The Wylie Agency (UK) Limited, all rights reserved. Page 14: Cartoon 'Joy (active personal affection)' from BE BLOODY BOLD AND RESOLUTE Advice to Actors illustrated by Martin Honeysett; published by Pickpocket Books; reprinted with permission of Pickpocket Books. Page 33: extract from EQUUS by Peter Shaffer (Penguin Books 1977) Copyright © Peter Shaffer 1973; reprinted with permission of Penguin Group UK. Pages 35, 36: extracts from OUR COUNTRY'S GOOD by Timberlake Wertenbaker, published by Faber and Faber Limited Copyright © Timberlake Wertenbaker 1988, 1989, 1991, 1998 based on the novel The Playmaker by Thomas Keneally © 1987 The Serpentine Publishing Company Pty. mission of A & C Black. Pages 36, 59: extracts from THE PRAYER ROOM by Shan Khan published by Faber and Faber, 2005; reprinted with permission of Faber and Faber Limited. Pages 36, 60: extracts from A STREETCAR NAMED DESIRE by Tennessee Williams, published by Methuen Publishing; reprinted with permission of Methuen Publishing. Page 38, 42, 59: extracts from A RAISIN IN THE SUN by Lorraine Hansberry, Methuen Drama 1959; reprinted with permission of A & C Black. Pages 42, 49, 59: Extracts from THE SEAGULL by Anton Chekhov (1896) translated by Michael Frayn, Methuen 1986; reprinted with permission of A & C Black. Pages 42, 58: extracts from PYGMALION by George Bernard Shaw; reprinted with permission of The Society of Authors on behalf of the Bernard Shaw Estate. Pages 43, 46, 58: extracts from TRANSLATIONS by Brian Friel, from SELECTED PLAYS OF BRIAN FRIEL published by Faber and Faber; reprinted with permission of Faber and Faber Ltd. Page 68: 'Macbeth: who is that bloodied man?' by Joyce McMillan from The Scotsman Sat 25 August 2007 © Joyce McMillan 2007; reprinted with the kind permission of the author. Pages 94, 97, 98: extracts from EDUCATING RITA by Willy Russell, published by Methuen Drama, an imprint of A & C Black; reprinted with permission of A & C Black. Page 101: extract from THE GOVERNMENT INSPECTOR by Nikolai Gogal, trans Adrian Mitchell; reprinted with permission of A & C Black/Bloomsbury. Page 107: quote from SHAW ON SHAKESPEARE edited by Edwin Wilson, Dutton edition, 1961; reprinted with permission of Society of Authors on behalf of The Estate of Bernard Shaw. Page 107: quote from THE FEMALE EUNUCH by Germaine Greer. Page 136: extract from ON THE ART OF THE THEATRE by Edward Gordon Craig, Heinemann 1956. Page 136: extract by Nick Hytner, from PLATFORM PAPERS 3 DIRECTORS, produced by National Theatre. Page 136: extract from STANISLAVSKI'S LEGACY: A COLLECTION OF COMMENTS ON A VARIETY OF ASPECTS OF AN ACTOR'S LIFE translated by Elizabeth Reynolds Hapgood, Theatre Arts Books 1987 © 1958 , 1968 Elizabeth Reynolds Hapgood; reprinted with permission of Routledge, Inc, a division of Informa PLC.